"For several decades Jerome Murphy-O'Connor has been one of New Testament scholarship's most engaging interlocutors. Never one to mince his words or fail to engage in dialogue with those who disagree with him, Murphy-O'Connor never ceases to offer intriguing and often novel points of view. His work advances scholarship by challenging others to rethink their positions. This collection of essays is classic Murphy-O'Connor—crystal clear and thought provoking."

—Raymond F. Collins
Brown University
Author of *The Power of Images in Paul*

"The subtitle of this book could well be 'Collected Essays Old and New.' Accompanying each of his previously published articles on Galatians, Murphy-O'Connor has added a postscript, each often comparable in length to the original essay. In each postscript, with characteristic incisiveness and wit, Murphy-O'Connor considers later scholarly attempts to grapple with the questions that had engaged him in his original essays. What the reader will discover is that many of Murphy-O'Connor's original insights and explanations have stood the test of time! Fortunately, they have been collected in this handy volume."

—Maria Pascuzzi
St. Thomas University, Miami Gardens, FL
Author of *First and Second Corinthians*

Keys to Galatians

Collected Essays

Jerome Murphy-O'Connor, OP

A Michael Glazier Book

LITURGICAL PRESS
Collegeville, Minnesota

www.litpress.org

A Michael Glazier Book published by Liturgical Press

Cover design by Jodi Hendrickson. The statue *Dying Gaul* is a marble copy in the Capitoline Museum, Rome, of a bronze original commissioned from Epigonus by Attalus I of Pergamum.

1	2	3	4	5	6	7	8	9

Library of Congress Cataloging-in-Publication Data

Murphy-O'Connor, J. (Jerome), 1935–
    Keys to Galatians : collected essays / Jerome Murphy-O'Connor.
      p.   cm.
    "A Michael Glazier Book."
    Includes bibliographical references (p.   ) and indexes.
    ISBN 978-0-8146-8070-4 — ISBN 978-0-8146-8095-7 (e-book)
   1. Bible. N.T. Galatians—Criticism, interpretation, etc.   I. Title.
BS2685.52.M87   2012
227'.406—dc23
                                2012024942

Contents

Preface

My studies of individual points in the letter to the Galatians grew out of class preparation at the École Biblique, Jerusalem. If commentators had failed to reach a consensus on a particular verse, I felt that this was an opportunity to make a contribution by looking at the problem from a new angle. Occasionally I found myself confronted with a difficulty that apparently no one else had noticed. I reproduce these articles as they were printed in order to avoid gifting myself with the blessing of hindsight. In publishing, one gives hostages to fortune; mistakes are there to be deplored for eternity. In the postscript appended to each article, I draw attention to any reactions to my proposal but also to what has been said subsequently about the point at issue.

The first article, on the dating of Paul's early missionary activity, was inspired by John Knox's methodological dictum that a hint in the letters (in this case, Gal 2:5) must be given precedence over an explicit contradictory statement by Luke in Acts (chaps. 13–15). I was led to the conclusion that Paul must have evangelized Galatia *prior* to the meeting in Jerusalem (Gal 2:1-10), even though Luke places it after that meeting (Acts 15–16).

This conclusion permitted the formulation of a more satisfactory hypothesis regarding the origins of the letter to the Galatians than had yet been put forward. The Judaizers were from Antioch-on-the-Orontes, and Galatians was the first Pauline letter to be written from Ephesus.

When Paul angrily broke with Antioch in the Spring of AD 52, he had no idea that the church which had commissioned him to found communities in Galatia, Macedonia, and Achaia would consider these her daughter churches. After all, it was he who had begotten them in Christ (1 Cor 4:15). Comfortably ensconced in Ephesus in the late spring of AD 53, he would have been aware of travelers from the high country once the disappearance of the winter snows had opened the great road from India. The last thing he expected, however, was to find a deputation from Galatia on his doorstep. They informed him that Antioch had sent them teachers whose task was to make them more Jewish, as Antioch itself had become as a result of the dispute about whether Jewish converts could eat with Gentile ones (Gal 2:11-14). The Galatians had had a whole winter to listen to the intruders and knew their arguments in considerable detail, even if they could not understand them completely.

For whatever reason, Paul was not in a position to go to Galatia, as he was later to rush to Corinth (the intermediate visit) when a crisis developed there. He had to deal with the situation in writing. The problem, he quickly realized, was not just the present protection of the Galatians but the future plans of the Judaizing intruders. These latter, he could easily surmise, no doubt planned to follow his route to Philippi, Thessalonica, and Corinth once they had brought the Galatians into line with the new ethos of Antioch. Paul felt that it was imperative to disrupt their campaign against his law-free communities. If he could make them uncertain of their ground, he would give arms to the Galatians, and at the same time it would save him a lot of future trouble with his churches in Greece.

This reconstruction is much less speculative than it might at first seem, because the ostensible purpose of Galatians was not the real one. The essential theological arguments of Galatians cannot be understood without a detailed knowledge of Jewish tradition, particularly as it is reflected in the OT. As Mitchell has shown, there were no Jews in northern Galatia, and hence no "God-fearers," because there were no synagogues in the area. Therefore, even though the letter is addressed to the Galatians (Gal 1:2; 3:1), it was, in fact, directed to the Judaizers, the only ones who could appreciate the force of the argumentation when it was read aloud.

Acceptance of this risky strategy betrays Paul's confidence in his rhetorical training. I demonstrate one aspect of how he made it work in the articles on Galatians 2:2 and 2:15-16 (chaps. 4 and 6, respectively). In both cases he employs the rhetorical technique of the *consessio*. This involved writing a phrase that could be understood in two ways, in the confident belief that people hear what they want to hear. He expected his adversaries to understand it as a concession, but then he immediately negates their evident satisfaction by forcefully asserting his real position.

Another manifestation of Paul's skill in leading the Judaizers astray appears in Galatians 3:15, where he uses a common example as the starting point of a crucial argument. He says it is generally agreed that a will cannot be changed while the testator is still alive. This bothered me considerably because this example is manifestly false. Every known legal system of antiquity permits a testator to change his mind as often as he likes. I could not believe that someone as well trained as Paul could make such a simple mistake. It must have been a tactical move designed to wrong-foot the intruders. By following their instinct to condemn Paul's stupidity, they left themselves open to the riposte that well-documented legislation on adoption was what Paul really had in mind (chap. 7). An adopted son automatically became an heir (Gal 4:7).

Paul's attentiveness to the nuances of the argument of intruders is evident in his use of the names of Jerusalem. His personal preference was for the Semitic form *Iersousalēm* (Gal 4:25-26), but only in Galatians does he use the Greek form *Hierosolyma* (Gal 1:17-18; 2:1), which would have been more natural to Antiocheans. This shift intrigued me because Paul offered no explanation, and no one writing in English will shift from "London" to "Londres" without justification, for example, within a quotation in French (chap. 3). The few commentators who noticed the problem had failed to produce a satisfactory explanation.

Even though Galatians was intended to disrupt the strategy of the Antiocheans, the letter also displays concern for the Galatians. They are addressed directly in 3:1, and he appeals to their personal experience of grace in Galatians 4:13-14. The way he speaks in these latter verses, however, gives the impression that Paul made only one stop in Galatia as a sick man. I found this to be in tension with the plural of the address, "the assemblies of Galatia" (Gal 1:2). Most commentators do not notice the problem, and those who do unthinkingly assume that Paul had exactly the same illness in a series of cities and in each received the same warm welcome. This seemed to me rather improbable, and so I was forced to look for an alternative, which I found in a sophisticated use of irony that betrayed the highly trained orator (chap. 8). Paul had not wasted his time as a student of rhetoric in Tarsus. In the postscript, however, I am happy to draw attention to an alternative explanation that I had not thought of.

Paul's solicitude for the Galatians also had other dimensions. A note of impatience is clearly perceptible in his invention of the idea of "the law of Christ" (Gal 6:2). They refused the responsibility of freedom and were eager to accept the message of the Judaizers, which promised them the security of blind obedience. Paul, however, was radically antinomian and could not provide them with the set of precepts they wanted. The only "law" that he could offer them was "Christ" (chap. 9). Would the Galatians have found this intelligible? The idea of "unwritten living laws" was common in the Hellenistic world, as Philo attests in considerable detail.

In the real world one cannot avoid politics, and Paul was not exempt. If at times they worked against him, at others they could prove a benefit. What he says about his venture into Arabia (Gal 1:17) arouses curiosity by its very casualness. Why does he not tell us exactly where he preached or how long he spent there, as he does regarding his visit to Peter in Jerusalem (Gal 1:18)? A close examination of the political situation at the time provides answers to both questions (chap. 2). As a Jew he would immediately have been seen as a threat by the Nabataeans, and he escaped by the skin of his teeth. Understandably, he felt at risk when the Nabataeans were given control of Damascus by Gaius (Caligula) in late AD 37, and he had to escape by being lowered over the city wall in a basket, an ignominious experience that he expertly turns to rhetorical profit (2 Cor 11:32-33).

On the other hand, politics worked in Paul's favor at the crucial Conference in Jerusalem, where the Pillars approved Paul's law-free mission (Gal 2:9). James was party to this agreement, but in principle he should not have been. He had all the theological arguments in support of the circumcision of pagan converts to Christianity. Yet he did not use them. I could see no theological justification for this choice, but once I paid closer attention to the political background, the answer became clear (chap. 5). However high-principled one might be, there are times when reality cannot be ignored. It was not the moment to dilute Jewish identity by incorporating pagans whose attachment to Judaism was only nominal. James, however, profited by this experience, as his intervention in Antioch (Gal 2:11-14) demonstrates. There he strove to reinforce the Jewishness of converts to Christianity.

The final chapter (chap. 10) deals with Paul's Christology in Galatians. This was a problem for me because I date Galatians much earlier than most scholars. It was written in the spring of AD 53, only three years after Paul's first two letters to the Thessalonians, which were sent in the spring and summer of AD 50. The Christology of 1 and 2 Thessalonians, however, could have been written by Peter or James, or indeed anyone in the early church. It merely echoes the primitive kerygma, of which traces abound in the Pauline letters. In Galatians, on the contrary, Paul's distinctive Christology appears for the first time, notably the stress on crucifixion as the modality of Christ's death and on the union of believers with Christ and with each other.

What had prompted this sudden development on the part of a man who had been preaching Christ for the best part of twenty years? If original ideas were forced to the surface of his mind at this particular moment, it can only have been under the pressure of events. The intruders in Galatia stressed the individuality of Abraham. If Paul's reply was to carry any conviction, he had to present Christ in a similar way. Whereas before Paul had thought of Christ in the vague theological category of "Savior," he was now forced to see him as a unique human being with highly distinctive features. The embryonic insights of Galatians will flower in subsequent letters.

Obviously, this book is not a complete treatment of Galatians, but enough points have been raised to show the intense interest of this rather neglected letter. We are given illuminating hints of different facets of Paul's personality, of his openness to new ideas, and of the skill with which he put them across in a daring strategy that would have been unthinkable for one less confident in his rhetorical skills.

I conclude by warmly thanking all those who generously gave permission to republish articles for which they hold the copyright: the Ecole Biblique et Archéolgique Française (for chaps. 1, 4, 6, 7, 8, 9); the Catholic Biblical Association of America (for chap. 2); De Gruyter Publishers, Berlin (for chap. 3); Peeters Publishers, Leuven (for chap. 5); and T & T Clark, an imprint of Bloomsbury Publishing Plc. (for chap. 10).

Jerome Murphy-O'Connor, OP

Jerusalem

January 2012

Abbreviations

AB	Anchor Bible
ABD	*Anchor Bible Dictionary*
ABib	Analecta Biblica
ABRL	Anchor Bible Reference Library
AJ	Josephus, *Antiquities of the Jews*
ANF	*Ante Nicene Fathers*
ANRW	*Aufstieg und Niedergang der römischen Welt*
AYBRL	Anchor Yale Bible Reference Library
BAGD	W. Bauer, W. F. Arndt, F. W. Gingrich, and F. W. Danker, *Greek-English Lexicon of the New Testament*
BAR	*Biblical Archaeology Review*
BdeJ	*Bible de Jérusalem*
BDF	F. Blass, A. Debrunner, and R. W. Funk, *Greek Grammar of the New Testament*
BETL	Bibliotheca ephemeridum theologicarum lovaniensium
BJRL	*Bulletin of the John Rylands Library*
BNTC	Black's New Testament Commentary
CAH	*Cambridge Ancient History*
CBNT	Commentaire biblique: Nouveau Testament
CBQ	*Catholic Biblical Quarterly*
CNT	Commentaire du Nouveau Testament
DBSup	*Dictionnaire de la Bible. Supplement*

EBib	Études Bibliques
ETL	*Ephemerides Theologicae Lovanienses*
FS	Festschrift
FRLANT	Forschungen zur Religion und Literatur des Alten und Neuen Testaments
GNS	Good News Series
HNT	Handbuch zum Neuen Testament
HTKNT	Herders theologischer Kommentar zum Neuen Testament
HTR	*Harvard Theological Review*
HUCA	*Hebrew Union College Annual*
ICC	International Critical Commentary
IES	Israel Exploration Society
JBL	*Journal of Biblical Literature*
JSJ	*Journal for the Study of Judaism*
JSJSup	Journal for the Study of Judaism Supplements
JSNT	*Journal for the Study of the New Testament*
JSNTSup	Journal for the Study of the New Testament Supplements
JSOTSup	Journal for the Study of the Old Testament Supplements
JSP	*Journal for the Study of the Pseudepigrapha*
JW	Josephus, *Jewish War*
KNT	Kommentar zum Neuen Testament
KUL	Catholic University of Lublin, Poland
LCL	Loeb Classical Library
LD	*Lectio divina*
LSJ	Liddell-Scott-Jones, *Greek-English Lexicon*
m.	*Mishnah*
MeyerK	H. A. W. Meyer, Kritisch-exegetischer Kommentar über das NT
MNTC	Moffat New Testament Commentary
MT	Masoretic Text

NAB	*New American Bible*
NIBC	New International Bible Commentary
NICNT	New International Commentary on the New Testament
NIGTC	New International Greek Testament Commentary
NIV	*New International Version*
NJB	*New Jerusalem Bible*
NJBC	*New Jerome Biblical Commentary*
NovT	*Novum Testamentum*
NRSV	*New Revised Standard Version*
NTA	*New Testament Abstracts*
NTA	Neutestamentliche Abhandlungen
NTS	*New Testament Studies*
OBO	Orbis Biblicus et Orientalis
PG	Patrologia Graeca
P. Lond	Greek Papyri in the British Museum, London
PsSol	*Psalms of Solomon*
PW	Pauly-Wissowa, *Real-Encyclopädie der klassischen Altertumswissenschaft*
RB	*Revue biblique*
REG	*Revue des Études Grecques*
RSR	*Recherches de science religieuse*
RSV	*Revised Standard Version*
SBL	Society of Biblical Literature
SBLDS	Society of Biblical Literature Dissertation Series
SBLSCS	Society of Biblical Literature Septuagint and Cognate Studies
SBT	Studies in Biblical Theology
SCM	Student Christian Movement
SJLA	Studies in Judaism in Late Antiquity
SJT	*Scottish Journal of Theology*

SNTSM	Society for New Testament Studies Monograph Series
SPCK	Society for the Propagation of Christian Knowledge
SPIB	Scripta Pontificii Instituti Biblici
TSAJ	Texte und Studien zum Antiken Judentum
TU	Texte und Untersuchungen
VD	*Verbum Domini*
WBC	Word Bible Commentary
WMANT	Wissenschaftliche Monographien zum Alten und Neuen Testament
WUNT	Wissenschaftliche Untersuchungen zum Neuen Testament
ZNW	*Zeitschrift für die neutestamentliche Wissenschaft*
ZTK	*Zeitschrift für Theologie und Kirche*

Works of Philo

Abr.	*De Abrahamo*
Flacc.	*In Flaccum*
Fug.	*De Fuga*
Jos.	*De Josepho*
Leg.	*Legatio ad Gaium*
Mig.	*De Migratione Abrahami*
Quaest. in Exod.	*Quaestiones et Solutiones in Exodum*
Som.	*De Somnis*
Spec. Leg.	*De Specialibus Legibus*

I

Missions in Galatia, Macedonia, and Achaia before the Jerusalem Conference

Hypotheses concerning the dates of Paul's life and letters are legion.[1] All possible dates for every conceivable event have found their champions. Since real originality is no longer possible, the publication of three dissertations (two of them Habilitationsschriften!) within the space of five years is a phenomenon worthy of note in New Testament circles. At the very least it witnesses to the sort of malaise which develops when working hypotheses solidify into dogmas, whose effect on research is seen as stultifying. More significantly, it serves warning that the time is ripe for a reexamination of the chronological presuppositions which, consciously or unconsciously, serve as the basis for all reconstructions of Pauline theology. The purpose of this article is to participate in this process by offering a detailed evaluation of the contributions of the above-mentioned works as regards the fourteen years which, according to Galatians 2:1, separated Paul's first visit to Jerusalem as a Christian from his return to the Holy City for the Jerusalem Conference. The choice of this period was determined, not only by the need to concentrate on a limited time span but also by the fact that the three authors differ so radically.

Three Studies

The three studies to be considered are Alfred Suhl, *Paulus und seine Briefe. Ein Beitrag zur paulinischen Chronologie* (Gütersloh: Mohn,

---

[1] Originally titled "Pauline Missions before the Jerusalem Conference" and published in *RB* 89 (1982): 71–91, whose pagination appears in the text in **bold**. Material in square brackets has been added for this republication.

1975); Robert Jewett, *A Chronology of Paul's Life* (Philadelphia: Fortress, 1979); and Gerd Lüdemann, *Paulus, der Heidenapostel. Band 1. Studien zur Chronologie* (Göttingen: Vandenhoeck & Ruprecht, 1980), which was subsequently translated as *Paul, Apostle to the Gentiles: Studies in Chronology* (London: SCM, 1984). Page numbers following an author's name in the text refer to these works. When two are given in the case of Lüdemann, the second is the English version.

All agree on the methodological principles (a) that evidence from the Pauline letters must be given [**72**] priority over information derived from the Acts of the Apostles, and (b) that the latter cannot be taken at face value but must be used with extreme critical prudence. Such unity of principle is reinforced by a further characteristic which admirably exemplifies the fellowship of true research; each had access to the unpublished material of the other, and this privilege is used with the freedom and frankness that is the basis of all genuine dialogue. The resultant differences, therefore, are all the more instructive.

Suhl does not articulate his methodology as explicitly as the other two, but it is easily deduced from the layout of his book; evidence regarding Paul's movements is integrated into a framework derived essentially from Acts. Such being the case, one would expect the bulk of his study to be devoted to a systematic assessment of the value of the information provided by Luke, but this we are not given. Instead, he concentrates the greater portion of his effort on the letters, thus producing the phenomenon of an elaborate superstructure resting on very shallow foundations. He is not, of course, uncritical of Acts, but, in terms of the purpose of this article, his major contribution is to deny Luke's dating of the first missionary journey (Acts 13–14). For Suhl (pp. 44–45, 76) it actually took place between Galatians 2:10 and 11. *All* Paul's missionary activity took place after the Jerusalem Conference, which is identified with the visit in Acts 11, dated to AD 43–44 by the famine mentioned by Josephus (pp. 46–64).

Jewett's method is to focus on every detail of Acts and the epistles capable of yielding chronological information, i.e., distances which must have taken a minimum time, facts which imply a definite time of year, and events which can be dated absolutely. The result is two separate sets of data—externally ascertainable date ranges and internally ascertainable dates and time spans—which, he claims, should interlock at only one point in the life of an historical figure. "The task is to discover where the interlock occurs. And the test is whether all of the ascertainable data can successfully be placed within the resultant chronology" (p. 95).

In opposition to his predecessors, who rely principally on Acts, Lüdemann is totally faithful to Knox's principle[2] and [**73**] concentrates virtually all his attention on the exegesis of the epistles. Anything that could be considered Luke's contribution is treated with extreme skepticism, but this is balanced by a childlike faith in the objectivity of the sources used in the composition of Acts, which enables Lüdemann to equip his relative order with absolute dates.

Whereas Suhl divided Paul's life into a period of implausible idleness followed by a period of incredible activity, both Jewett and Lüdemann consider that a major portion of Paul's missionary work took place before

Lüdemann (p. 272/262)	Events	Jewett (p. 161)
33 (36)	First visit to Jerusalem	Late 37
34 (37)	Activities in Syria, Cilicia, and South Galatia	43–45
?	Mission to North Galatia	46–48
From 36 (39)	Mission in Europe	
	Philippi	48–49
	Thessalonica	49
ca. 41	Corinth	50–51
←	Conflict at Antioch	
47 (50)	Second visit to Jerusalem	October 51
	Conflict at Antioch	→

---

[2] "A fact only suggested in the letters has a status which even the most uneqivocal statement of Acts, if not otherwise supported, cannot confer. We may, with proper caution, use Acts to supplement the autobiographical data of the letters, but never to correct them" (J. Knox, *Chapters in a Life of Paul* [New York: Abingdon, 1950], 32).

the Jerusalem Conference. Despite their differing approaches, they manifest a high degree of agreement on the order in which Paul did certain things; they part company only on the date and placing of the conflict at Antioch (Gal 2:11-14).

In evaluating the arguments on which this reconstruction is based, I intend to abstract from the problem of the mission described in Acts 13–14 because none of the three authors is really interested in it. It is included by Jewett simply because there is plenty of room for it in the fourteen-year period between the two visits to Jerusalem. It is much more difficult to say why Lüdemann accepts it because the procedure contradicts his methodological principle; it is discussed only in a footnote (p. 152/180 note 2), whose unsupported affirmations parallel those formulated by Suhl (p. 45) to motivate his location of this mission after the Conference. The crucial [74] question is: do the letters furnish sufficient evidence to make it probable that Paul, in the period preceding the Conference, had undertaken the long missionary journey through Galatia, Macedonia, and Achaia, which is presented by Luke (Acts 16–18) as having followed the Conference?

Paul's First Visit to Jerusalem

In Galatians 1:18 Paul implies that this visit took place immediately after his ignominious departure from Damascus. The only passage which permits us to assign an absolute date is 2 Corinthians 11:32-33, which dates Paul's escape from Damascus to the time of King Aretas.[3] The combination is certainly justified, because the letters contain no hint that Paul ever returned to Damascus, an argument from silence that is confirmed by Acts.

All three authors accept the combination, but Suhl and Lüdemann accord it little importance; it proves only that Paul had left Damascus before Aretas died in AD 39. Suhl (pp. 314–15) asserts that the text does not necessarily mean that Aretas controlled Damascus; his troops could have been camped around the city outside. For his part Lüdemann (p. 20/31

---

[3] [For a convincing rebuttal of the objections to Nabataean control of Damascus, see J. Taylor, "The Ethnarch of King Aretas at Damascus: A Note on 2 Cor 11:32-33," *RB* 99 (1992): 719–28.]

note 10) maintains that Jewett has neither disproved Suhl's hypothesis nor proved his own view that Damascus was actually in Aretas's possession.

In fact, Jewett does both (pp. 30–33). That Lüdemann should even consider Suhl's hypothesis is indicative of bias, not only because of the totally improbable assumptions it involves (cf., Jewett, p. 31), but principally because it ignores the plain meaning of 2 Corinthians 11:32; the method of escape shows that the danger lay within the city. The text also formally affirms that the city was subject to Aretas. The only question concerns when it was possible for him to have exercised such control. Jewett (p. 32) offers two strong arguments to prove that it could not have been before AD 37: (a) the opposition of the emperor Tiberius to client kingdoms on the eastern frontier, a policy that was immediately changed by his successor, Gaius (Caligula); (b) the route of the legions under Vitellius in the punitive expedition against Aretas, which was aborted by the death of Tiberius on 16 March AD 37; had Damascus been in Nabataean hands at this point, it would have been necessary to take it before moving on Petra. Thus, the only time when Aretas could have been in control of Damascus runs from the summer of AD 37 to his death in AD 39 [75]. [I would now add that the transfer of power probably took place early in this period rather than later, because Gaius owed a debt of gratitude to the Nabataeans, who coveted the great trading crossroads city more than anything else. In AD 18–19, at great risk to their trade in northern Syria, they had supported his father, Germanicus, against the all-powerful Gnaeus Calpurnius Piso, the governor of Syria (Tacitus, *Annals*, 2.57). Thus, Paul's departure from Damascus and arrival in Jerusalem should be dated to late AD 37 or early AD 38.[4]]

The probability of this date is stronger than many accepted by Lüdemann and is founded on the same type of argument that he himself uses to date the edict of Claudius (Acts 18:2). The dogmatic casualness of his dismissal (p. 20/31 note 10) excites suspicion. One is forced to suspect that his rejection might have been motivated by the awareness that acceptance of Jewett's date for the first visit to Jerusalem would com-

---

[[4] If, as the majority assumes, "Arabia" (Gal 1:17) is to be identified with present-day Jordan, one might speculate that Paul got into trouble in Nabataean territory and only extricated himself by returning to Damascus, then in Roman hands. His position would have become perilous when the Romans transferred power to the Nabataeans. For more detail, see chap. 2 below.]

promise his own very early dating of Paul's mission in Corinth. The activities to which Lüdemann allots seven years—the plausible minimum (cf. Jewett, p. 161)—would have to be compressed into the four years between AD 37 and 41. Such a departure from his usual standards underlines the importance of the year AD 41 in Lüdemann's reconstruction.

Apart from the question of the date, Lüdemann (pp. 86–94/64–71) makes a significant, and highly original, contribution to our understanding of Paul's first visit to Jerusalem (Gal 1:18) by interpreting Galatians 2:7 as referring to an agreement made between Peter and Paul on that occasion. This verse (and the following one) has long been a problem to exegetes because of its tension with the context. In v. 7 "Peter" is the authority figure in Jerusalem and Paul is alone, whereas in v. 9 "Cephas" is but one of a triumvirate in which James is named first and Paul is accompanied by Barnabas, as in v. 1. Moreover, the language of v. 7 has a non-Pauline flavor; certainly the apostle never uses *Petros* elsewhere.

Rightly ignoring explanations which fail to take account of the evidence,[5] Lüdemann rejects the view of Barnikol, Cullmann, and Dinkler that v. 7 represents part of the minutes of the Jerusalem Conference because it is incompatible with the formulation of the verse (p. 90/68). Equally, he refuses Klein's suggestion (p. 92 note 74/120 note 78) that v. 7 reflects the situation in Jerusalem at the time of the Conference, while v. 9 was added at the time of writing of Galatians in order to recognize the change in the leadership of the Jerusalem church that had taken place in the meanwhile, because the two years [**76**] is too little time for such a change to have taken place. This argument involves too many uncontrollable assumptions to be convincing, but in any case Klein's position is untenable. How would Paul have known of the change, and if he did, would he have bothered to note it, particularly in a situation where he was desperately trying to prove his independence of Jerusalem?

The hypothesis that v. 7 refers, not to the Conference, whose conclusion is mentioned in v. 9, but to another meeting certainly explains the evidence, but regrettably Lüdemann fails to substantiate his assertion that it must be identified with that in Galatians 1:18. In my opinion, however, Lüdemann's intuition is correct; arguments can be found.

---

[5] E.g., H. D. Betz, *Galatians*, Hermeneia (Philadelphia: Fortress, 1979), 99.

The meeting with Peter (v. 7) cannot have taken place *after* the Conference. Not only would it be pointless, since Peter was party to the decision of the Conference (v. 9), but a comparison of Galatians 1:18-19 with Galatians 2:9 shows that James had superseded Peter within the Jerusalem church (a shift in the authority structure that is confirmed by Gal 2:12 and Acts) so that after the Conference Peter would not have been in a position to act alone. Hence, the meeting with Peter must have taken place *before* the Conference. Here, however, we have two possibilities. The private meeting (Gal 2:2) can be excluded immediately, both because it is not clear whether it was distinct from the Conference and because there Paul was confronted by a group, not a single individual. Thus, within the framework of the letters, we are forced to locate it during Paul's first visit to Jerusalem; there is no other known possibility.

The most important conclusion of this conclusion is that Paul was conscious of his vocation as apostle to the Gentiles fourteen years before the Jerusalem Conference. We must assume that he acted on this responsibility, and so it is probable that he undertook a missionary journey during this period. Against Suhl, it is inconceivable that he should have spent the time pointlessly in Syria and Cilicia (cf. Lüdemann, p. 23 note 14/32 note 16).

Where did Paul go? Lüdemann answers: to Galatia, because Galatians 2:7 reflects a tradition known to the Galatians. But the only argument he offers is the assertion that the use of *Petros* indicates a Greek-speaking community (pp. 93–94/69–70). This, of course, proves nothing because the Aramaic *Kephas* was currently employed at Greek-speaking Corinth (1 Cor 1:12; 3:22; 9:5; 15:5). What the form *Petros* might [77] suggest is a community without any Jewish component capable of explaining or using naturally an Aramaic term. Galatia certainly fulfills this condition[6], but the argument is still too weak to carry much weight. Again, however, this does not mean that Lüdemann is wrong, because the validity of his insight becomes clear if we ask the question that he overlooks: why does Paul mention his agreement with Peter (Gal 2:7) out of chronological sequence, referring to it in the context of his second visit to Jerusalem rather than in the context of his first visit when it actually took place?

---

[6] [On the lack of evidence for the presence of Jews in North Galatia, see S. Mitchell, *Anatolia: Land, Men, and Gods in Asia Minor* (Oxford: Clarendon, 1995), 2:31–37.]

This question can be answered only within the framework of the literary form of Galatians 1:13–2:14. The epistle to the Galatians supposes the situation of "a court of law with jury, accuser, and defendant. In the case of Galatians, the addressees are identical with the jury, with Paul being the defendant, and his opponents the accusers."[7] The letter is, in effect, the speech for the defense and, within this literary form, 1:13–2:14 occupies the place of what Quintilian terms the *narratio*. "The statement of facts (*narratio*) consists in the persuasive exposition of that which either has been done, or is supposed to have been done, or, to quote the definition of Apollodorus, is a speech instructing the audience as to the nature of the case in dispute."[8] For Quintilian, the real order of events should be followed as a general rule (*Institutio Oratoria* 4.2.87), but he disagrees with those who insist that it should always be done (4.2.83); the defendant's decision should be based on "what is most advantageous in the circumstances and nature of the case" (4.2.84).

At first sight, the transposition of v. 7 from Paul's first visit to his second visit would appear to offer no advantage. On the contrary, it would seem to be a positive disadvantage. As it stands, Galatians 2:6-9 is incoherent, and internal contradictions can do irreparable harm to any case for the defense. Unless we are willing to assume that Paul made a disastrous forensic mistake, we must suppose that he was sure that the jury (the Galatians) would recognize that v. 7 did not refer to the same meeting as v. 9 but to an earlier one. This would necessarily imply that Paul must have [78] visited the Galatians prior to the Conference, and, if he had told them something of his personal history (Gal 1:13), there is no reason why he should not have informed them of the agreement made with Peter on his first visit to Jerusalem.

By separating the *fact* of the first meeting (Gal 1:18) from its *content* (Gal 2:7) Paul gained a number of significant advantages. First, he avoided giving the impression that the missionary work done during the fourteen years that separated his two visits to Jerusalem (Gal 2:1) was carried out under the aegis of a Jerusalem commission and was able to

---

[7] Betz, *Galatians*, 24.

[8] *Institutio Oratoria* 4.2.31; trans. H. E. Butler in LCL. This hypothesis, first proposed by H. D. Betz, "The Literary Composition and Function of Paul's Letter to the Galatians," *NTS* 21 (1975): 353–79, and taken up in his *Galatians*, 14–24, was tested and found to be correct by Lüdemann (pp. 74–77/54–57)

fix in the minds of his readers the value of that meeting as an exploratory encounter. Second, by juxtaposing the two meetings, he managed to insinuate that the equality that emerged from the Conference (Gal 2:6, 9) was also true of the first meeting, where Paul certainly lacked the authority in the church that Peter enjoyed.

It is only at this point in the argument that Lüdemann's observation (p. 93/70) regarding Galatians 2:8 acquires its full force. The initial *gar* shows that the verse is intended to substantiate the previous statement (v. 7). Moreover, the use of the aorist (*enērgēsen*) indicates that the Galatians had already experienced the power of God in the ministry of Paul.

Mission in Galatia

The hint embodied in Galatians 2:7 is not the only argument that Lüdemann has in favour of a pre-Conference mission to North Galatia. The clearest (p. 94/71) is the formal assertion *hina hē alētheia tou euangeliou diameinē pros hymas* (Gal 2:5). The current translations of this phrase—"that the truth of the gospel might be preserved for you" (*RSV*); "a fin de sauvegarder pour vous la vérité de l'évangile" (*BdeJ*)— underline the valid consensus that these words were written from the time-perspective of the Conference, not from that of the composition of the letter. "Paul argues that, if he had yielded at Jerusalem, the 'truth of the gospel' would have been compromised, and the Galatians would not have received any gospel at all."[9] Obviously this interpretation is conditioned by the assumption that Paul had not preached among the Galatians prior to the Conference. Exegetes are thereby forced to give the phrase an exclusively future meaning which distorts the [79] only attested sense of *diamenē*, "to remain, to continue." If we eschew this assumption (derived from Acts and not from anything within the Pauline corpus), the verb "implies that at the time referred to the truth of the gospel . . . has already been given to those whom he refers under *hymas*." Burton tries to avoid the obvious implication of this grammatical fact by suggesting that *hymas* means "you Gentiles," evidently under the influence of the assumption we have just dismissed, but his loyalty to the text eventually forces him to acknowledge that "*diameinē pros hymas* receives its most obvious interpretation if the Galatians are supposed to have been already

---

[9] Betz, *Galatians*, 92.

in possession of the gospel at the time here referred to."[10] In this perspective, *pros* has to be translated "with," the only meaning it can possibly have in Galatians 1:18; 4:18, 20. Since there is no hint that anyone but Paul preached to the Galatians, the conclusion that he did so prior to the Conference is inescapable and, of course, this confers much greater probability on the interpretation proposed for Galatians 2:7.

At this point one might reasonably ask: if Paul had been in Galatia, why does he not say so? Would he not have been more persuasive if, instead of saying that he had not been in Jerusalem for fourteen years, he had told his readers exactly where he was? Lüdemann correctly answers (pp. 79–83/59–61) that Paul's purpose in the *narratio* was not to show where he was but to indicate where he was not. Since the point at issue was his relations with Jerusalem, the brevity demanded by the literary form[11] obliged him to mention only journeys to and from Jerusalem. Thus the statement "Then I went into the regions of Syria and Cilicia" (Gal 1:21) was intended, not as a description of his activities, but as the *terminus ad quem* of a journey from Jerusalem.

Here, once again, Lüdemann's case can be strengthened, and precisely on the basis of the rules laid down by Quintilian for the *narratio*. Had Paul told his readers exactly where he had been, he would have been *proving* his statement that he had been to Jerusalem only twice in fourteen years. In terms of the form, this would have been inappropriate because Quintilian insists that the *narratio* [**80**] should not be confused with the *probatio*.[12] Moreover, the reference to fourteen years (Gal 2:1) is easily understood as a conclusion in the sense that it is the sum total of the time that Paul was absent from Jerusalem. And this fits perfectly with Quintilian's perspective: "Whenever a conclusion gives a sufficiently clear idea of the premises, we must be content with having given a hint which

---

[10] E. de Witt Burton, *A Critical and Exegetical Commentary on the Epistle to the Galatians*, ICC (Edinburgh: Clark, 1921), 86. [The penny has finally dropped for major translations, e.g., "so that the truth of the gospel might always remain with you" (*NRSV*); "or the truth of the gospel preached to you might have been compromised" (*NJB*).]

[11] "The statement of facts . . . should be brief, lucid, and plausible" (Quintilian, *Institutio Oratoria* 4.2.31).

[12] "It will also be useful to scatter some hints of our proofs here and there, but in such a way that it is never forgotten that we are making a statement of fact and not a proof" (*Institutio Oratoria* 4.2.54).

will enable our audience to understand what we have left unsaid."[13] It is precisely because Paul had been to the Galatians that he could afford to pass over the visit in silence. The understatement would have made his presentation all the more convincing because it betrayed a confidence that carried its own persuasive power. To have given details, which, from the point of view of the Galatians, were superfluous, would have risked giving the impression of the anxiety that saps credibility.

This conclusion is confirmed by the fact that, in the period of his life of which the Galatians had no firsthand knowledge (i.e., between his conversion and his first visit to Jerusalem), Paul sketches in the details: a journey to Arabia and a three-year stay in Damascus (Gal 1:17-18).[14] The contrast between Paul's presentations of the periods preceding and following his first visit to Jerusalem would appear to imply that the Galatians knew that he had not returned to Jerusalem after having evangelized them. This inference is supported by Galatians 4:13, which reveals that the foundation of the Galatian churches was the result of an accident. Paul was on a journey *somewhere else* when illness forced him to stop in Galatia. We must, therefore, assume that, once recovered, he continued on to his original goal (Lüdemann, pp. 124–26/90–92). Thus, the Galatians knew that Paul was moving north or west when he left them. In terms of what the letters reveal of Paul's later career, it is, of course, infinitely more probable that he headed west toward [81] Macedonia. The hint is vague, but it points toward a pre-Conference mission in Greece.

Jewett's study adds nothing to Lüdemann's analysis of the data in Galatians. In his unpublished 1966 dissertation he had reached the conclusion that all possible compromises between the data of the letters and the Lucan framework of five Jerusalem journeys involved the violation of at least one ascertainable time span. This forced him to accept the

---

[13] *Institutio Oratoria* 4.2.41.

[14] Since *epeita* in Gal 1:21 and 2:1 refers to the event immediately preceding, viz., his departure from Jerusalem and his arrival in the regions of Syria and Cilicia, respectively, the obvious interpretation of *epeita* in Gal 1:18 is that it refers to Paul's *return* to Damascus. So, rightly, Lüdemann (p. 85/63); it is correctly displayed in his chart on p. 86/64, and somewhat hesitantly on that on p. 149/108, but in his final summary (p. 272/262) the three years run from Paul's conversion! Jewett (p. 52) simply assumes that the three years are counted from the conversion. On this point, then, his chart (p. 161) needs correction. Paul would have returned to Damascus in AD 34, and prior to that he had been in Arabia for an undetermined time [probably very short].

Barnikol/Knox hypothesis, which identified the Conference journey of Galatians 2:1 with that mentioned in Acts 18:22 as the conclusion of what Luke presents as the second missionary journey. Hence, he was disposed to accept Lüdemann's inferences without discussion (Jewett, p. 84), except as regards the absolute dates and the placing of the incident at Antioch (Gal 2:11-14). In my opinion, Jewett is correct in affirming that the mission in Galatia could not have begun before AD 37 (cf. above) and that the conflict at Antioch must have taken place after the Jerusalem Conference.[15]

Mission in Macedonia and Achaia

As many before him, Lüdemann maintains that Philippi, Thessalonica, and Corinth were founded during the same missionary journey (pp. 139–48/103–7). This conclusion is based on the combination of 2 Corinthians 11:9 with Philippians 4:15-18. Objections to the interpretation of one of these passages in the light of the other are without foundation (Lüdemann, p. 140/103–4). However, neither text says that the Philippians sent money to Paul in Corinth, and, in theory, 2 Corinthians 11:9 could refer to the apostle's *second* visit to Corinth (2 Cor 2:1), a possibility that Lüdemann fails to mention. This possibility, however, is easily excluded because the second ("intermediate") visit was in all probability brief and unexpected. There was time neither for support to become an issue nor for word to get to Macedonia. One might also adduce the use of the compound verb *katachrēsasthai* in 1 Corinthians 9:18b, which was intended to nuance Paul's previous categorical affirmations that he was beholden to no one (1 Cor 9:12, 15), for the implication is that he was making [82] *partial* use of his right to be supported. The accusation to which Paul replies in 2 Corinthians 11:7-11 would never have been leveled against him had he not written 1 Corinthians 9:3-28, which certainly refers to his first visit to Corinth.

---

[15] Lüdemann's (pp. 101–5/75–77) hypothesis that the conflict at Antioch must have taken place before the Conference is rooted in a radical misunderstanding of the nature of the Conference. Since discussion of this point lies outside the scope of this article, I must content myself with a reference to Jewett's (pp. 83–84) refutation, with which I am in complete agreement.

Unfortunately, Lüdemann does not discuss the relationship between this mission in Greece and the one previously mentioned in Asia Minor, but the possibility needs to be explored. Philippi was the first community founded by Paul in Macedonia (1 Thess 2:2); in thanking them for their gift, he mentions that *oudemia moi ekklēsia ekoinōnēsen eis logon doseōs kai lēmpseōs* (Phil 4:15). The necessary inference is that Paul had founded other communities capable of aiding him financially. Where were these churches? The fact that Paul's route in Macedonia and Achaia was from north to south would seem to indicate that the churches anterior to Philippi must lie further east, i.e., somewhere in Asia Minor. In light of the conclusion reached in the previous section, it is natural to think of the churches of Galatia, but perhaps others could be located between Galatia and the Aegean coast, e.g., Troas (2 Cor 11:12; cf. Acts 16:8-11).

The link between Galatians 4:13 and Philippians 4:15 is suggestive rather than probative, the former pointing west and the latter pointing east, but the hint is reinforced by information in 1 Thessalonians 2:13–4:2. This independent letter,[16] written shortly after Paul's departure from Thessalonica (1 Thess 2:17),[17] shows Timothy (3:2) to have been the apostle's partner in the founding of the churches in Macedonia. Now, according to the tradition conserved by Luke, Timothy came from Lystra and had joined Paul on the journey that brought him to Macedonia (Acts 16:1-3).[18] It would appear, therefore, that Paul had passed through Galatia on his way to Macedonia.

[83] Is it possible to date the journey during which Philippi, Thessalonica, and Corinth were founded? Lüdemann answers in the affirmative, claiming that two lines of argument from within the Pauline corpus prove

---

[16] This hypothesis has been convincingly argued by W. Schmithals, "Die Thessalonicherbriefe als Briefcompositionen," in *Zeit und Geschichte. Dankesgabe an Rudolf Bultmann zum 80. Geburtstag, im Auftrag der Alten Marburger und in Zusammenarbeit mit Hartwig Thyen*, ed. E. Dinkler (Tübingen: Mohr Siebeck, 1964), 295–315. Suhl's criticisms (pp. 96–102) of the more debatable parts of Schmithals's hypothesis have disproven the division of 1 Thessalonians into two letters.

[17] J. Hurd has argued that 1 Thess 1:8-10 shows that 1 Thessalonians must have been written a considerable time (two or three years) after the founding of the community at Thessalonica (*The Origin of 1 Corinthians* [London: SPCK, 1965], 26). His point is well taken but is valid only for the other letter, namely, 1 Thess 1:1–2:12 + 4:3–5:28.

[18] Lüdemann's criticism of this text (pp. 170–71/153–54) consists only of the dogmatic speculation that is the dominant characteristic of his treatment of Acts.

that it was before the Jerusalem Conference, and that one fact derived from Acts furnishes an absolute date.

His first argument is based on 1 Corinthians 16:1-4 (pp. 110–14, 138–39/81–83, 101–3). In this passage Paul replies to a question from the Corinthians concerning the organization of the collection for the poor which had been agreed at the Jerusalem Conference (Gal 2:10). The nature of the question is such that it would have arisen very shortly after the Corinthians had accepted the principle of the collection. Hence, we can infer that Paul did not inform them of the collection in person, because in that case he would have dealt with the organizational details on the spot. Since Paul had been in Corinth only once prior to the writing of 1 Corinthians, we can be sure that the collection had not been preached during his founding visit. Lüdemann (p. 139/102) evokes the possibility that Paul refrained from mentioning money on that occasion for purely tactical reasons but rightly rejects this speculative hypothesis. Paul must have stayed in Corinth for at least a year—the figure of eighteen months given by Acts 18:11 is eminently plausible—unless we are prepared to assume that communities jumped into being at a click of his fingers. Had he already been committed to the collection, he would certainly have mentioned it once the community had become stable. The most probable hypothesis, therefore, is that the founding of the church at Corinth took place before the Jerusalem Conference.

This conclusion is supported by a further observation. At the very earliest, the Corinthians were informed of the collection toward the end of the summer preceding the writing of 1 Corinthians, since their question reached Paul only in the late spring of the following year once roads and seas were opened again to traffic after the winter closure (cf. 1 Cor 16:6-8). Corinth, however, could not have been founded that summer, because we must allow a significant time span for the ministry of Apollos (1 Cor 3:6) who, moreover, had returned to Ephesus in time for the writing of 1 Corinthians (16:12). Given the season limitations on travel, we are forced to conclude that the community at Corinth was founded at least two or three years before the composition of 1 Corinthians. Something must have happened in the interval to explain why Paul had to write or send a messenger to request their participation [84] in the collection. The only reasonable hypothesis is that the Conference had taken place between the founding of the church at Corinth and the writing of 1 Corinthians.

Lüdemann's second argument is based on the phrase *en archē tou euangeliou hote exēlthon apo Makedonias* (Phil 4:15) which, he claims, must be interpreted as a reference to Paul's first mission in Europe (pp. 141–46/103–6). The phrase "in the early days of my preaching the gospel" does carry a comparative connotation, but Lüdemann offers no convincing argument for the point of comparison. He assumes it to be the Conference, but his evocation of the presence of Titus in Jerusalem (Gal 2:3) proves nothing, because Paul could have met Greeks anywhere in Syria or Asia Minor. Other points of comparison can be, and have been, suggested, but they remain no more than possibilities. I can see no way of raising any of them to the level of probability and, in consequence, cannot accept Philippians 4:15 as an independent argument.

Acts 18 provides the basis of Lüdemann's third argument. Both he (pp. 181–83/162–64) and Jewett (pp. 38–40) justify the common opinion that Gallio's term of office ran from 1 July 51 to 30 June 52 and agree that Paul was in Corinth during that period (Acts 18:12). However, they differ as to which journey it was. For Jewett (pp. 96–97) the arraignment before Gallio took place during Paul's founding visit, whereas for Lüdemann (p. 197/172) this event occurred during his third visit. The discrepancy derives from the different dates assigned to the edict of Claudius (Acts 18:2) which, for both authors, determines the time of Paul's arrival in Corinth to found the church.

Jewett's acceptance of AD 49 as the date of the edict is explicitly motivated by the accord between the date given by the fifth [85] century church historian Orosius for the expulsion of the Jews mentioned by Suetonius[19] and the date of the proconsulate of Gallio (p. 39). This causes him to turn a blind eye to Orosius' inaccuracy, of which an example occurs in the very text referred to; nothing in Josephus corresponds to the date given. Moreover, Orosius was a priest and certainly knew Acts. He might have worked out his date for the edict by simply subtracting eighteen months (Acts 18:11) from the date of Gallio's term of office, which may have been available in his Roman sources. The hypothesis is incapable of proof, but the mere possibility of a circular argument counsels extreme prudence in using the data supplied by Orosius.

---

[19] "Anno eiusdem nono expulsus per Claudium Urbe Iudaeos Iosephus refert. Sed me magis Suetonius movet, qui ait hoc mode: 'Claudius Iudaeos impulsore Chresto asidue tumultuantes Roma expulit'" (*Historiae adversum paganos* 7.6.15).

Lüdemann's argumentation (pp. 183–95/164–71) is much more sophisticated. Both Suetonius[20] and Dio Cassius[21] report a politically motivated action by Claudius against Jews in Rome. The former simply mentions the fact, but the latter locates it in the year AD 41. The crucial question, therefore, concerns the relationship between the two accounts: do they refer to the same event or not?

The differences are obvious. Suetonius speaks of Jews being expelled, the precise point that is denied by Dio Cassius, who, moreover, does not mention the Chrestus named by Suetonius as responsible. On the other hand, neither of these authors was an eyewitness; both use sources. We can be sure that Suetonius' account is to some extent confused, because "Chrestus" is obviously a reference to Christ, who could not have been present in the way Suetonius implies. Moreover, his formulation was probably to be understood in an exclusive sense—"He expelled from Rome the Jews constantly making disturbances at the instigation of Chrestus"—rather than in the inclusive sense ("all Jews"), which is uncritically assumed by many modern translations. In this perspective the formulation of Dio Cassius is most naturally seen as a conscious correction of Suetonius or (more probably) of his source. [86] Even if Chrestus was mentioned in the material available to Dio Cassius, it is unlikely that he would have incorporated it, because he systematically avoids any reference to Christianity. Thus, it seems more probable that both authors are alluding to the same event of AD 41, whose historical kernel would appear to be the following (Lüdemann, p. 188/166): As the result of a tumult in a Roman synagogue concerning Christ, Claudius expelled the agitators and withdrew from that community the right of assembly.

Such an action in the first year of the reign of Claudius might appear implausible in light of his letters restoring to the Jews of Alexandria the privileges they had lost under Gaius (Caligula)[22] and extending those

---

[20] "Iudaeos impulsore Chresto assidue tumultuantes Roma expulit" (*Claudius* 25).

[21] "As for the Jews, who again increased so greatly by reason of their multitude it would have been hard without raising a tumult to bar them from the city, he did not drive them out, but ordered them, while continuing their traditional mode of life, not to hold meetings" (*Roman History* 40.6.6; trans. E. C. Cary in LCL).

[22] Josephus, *AJ* 19.281–85.

privileges to other Jews throughout the empire.[23] However, this latter document contains a veiled warning whose importance has been overlooked, "I charge them to use my kindness to them with moderation" (*AJ* 19.290), a warning that is made very explicit in a letter to Alexandria dated 10 November 41:

> I explicitly order the Jews not to agitate for more privileges than they formerly possessed . . . and not to bring in or admit Jews who come down the river from Syria or Egypt, a proceeding which will compel me to conceive serious suspicions; otherwise I will by all means take vengeance on them as fomenters of what is a general plague infecting the whole world.[24]

From the outset of his reign Claudius evidently was prepared to react vigorously against anything that could be interpreted as a threat to public order. In AD 41 had certain Jews at Rome been seen as agitators, the emperor would certainly have moved against them in the way suggested by Suetonius and Dio Cassius. This year, therefore, enjoys greater probability as the date of the edict of Claudius than the alternative of AD 49 based on the sole affirmation of Orosius.[[25]]

Lüdemann then goes on to argue that, since Acts 18:2 gives the impression that Aquila and Priscilla had arrived only shortly before Paul, his arrival in Corinth must be dated to very soon after AD 41 (p. 195/171). Must we then suppose that Paul remained in Corinth until Gallio took up office there in the summer of AD 51? [**87**] To put it mildly, a stay of almost ten years would seem somewhat excessive. In order to avoid this conclusion, Lüdemann (pp. 174–80/157–62) simply modifies Hurd's development[26] of Rigaux's hypothesis that Acts 18:1-17 is made up of a number of different traditions.[27] He discerns two nuggets of traditional material: (1) In vv. 1-11 Paul lives with Aquila and Priscilla, recently arrived from Italy, while teaching first in the synagogue and then in the

---

[23] Josephus, *AJ* 19.287–91.

[24] *P. Lond.* 1912; trans. C. K. Barrett, *The New Testament Background: Selected Documents*, rev. ed. (New York: Harper & Row, 1987), 49, lines 88–97.

[25] [For a more detailed statement of the argument, see my *Saint Paul's Corinth: Texts and Archeology*, 3rd ed. (Collegeville, MN: Liturgical Press, 2002), 152–58.]

[26] *The Origins of 1 Corinthians*, 30–31.

[27] *Saint Paul: Les épitres aux Thessaloniciens*, EBib (Paris: Gabalda, 1956), 32 note 1.

house of Titius Justus (p. 180/161). This visit, which lasted eighteen months (v. 11), is dated by the edict of Claudius. (2) In vv. 12-17 Paul encounters Gallio, and this visit is dated by the latter's term of office. In other words, the various traditions conserved and combined by Luke do not all relate to the same period of Paul's life.

It is difficult to evaluate Lüdemann's discussion of Acts 18 because it cannot be considered a serious literary analysis. All we are offered is an incomplete series of observations developed by means of one-sided dogmatic assertions. Mere possibility is regularly confused with probability. What he says may be correct, but he certainly has not proved it. Thus, we have to do with nothing more than a working hypothesis whose implications merit examination.

Lüdemann's claim that Paul arrived in Corinth around AD 41 *might* appear to be justified if Acts 18:2 said that Aquila and Priscilla had recently arrived *from Rome*, but of course it does not. It presents them as having come *from Italy*, and it is both unreasonable and unnecessary to assume that those expelled from Rome immediately took to the boats. It is more natural to assume that those expelled took up residence somewhere outside Rome in order to see how things would develop. It must be remembered that Suetonius speaks only of expulsion from the city, not of exile. Thus, if we accept Acts 18:2 at face value, all that can be said is that they came to Corinth within two or three years of the enactment of the edict.

A tighter specification of the time can only be made in function of the journey that Paul has made just previously, because distances and stops can be approximately quantified. It is at this point that the calculations developed by Jewett prove their value, and it is a major flaw in Lüdemann's methodology that he refuses to take such concrete factors seriously. [88] The overland journey from Jerusalem through Galatia and Macedonia would have taken a minimum of two years, but a more reasonable estimate would be close to four years (Jewett, pp. 59–61), a figure that I would extend by a year to allow for the impossibility of winter travel in certain areas. Thus, since Paul probably left Jerusalem at the end of AD 37 (see above), he could have arrived in Corinth sometime during AD 42, but only if we consider the first missionary journey (Acts 13–14) a total fiction, which Lüdemann is not prepared to do (p. 272/262). Jewett (p. 161) estimates two years for this mission. At the earliest, therefore, Paul could have reached Corinth in AD 44, a date that fits reasonably well with Acts 18:2.

A stay in Corinth of eighteen months (Acts 18:11) is perfectly plausible, both in terms of the time required to found and stabilize an active-minded community and with respect to the seasonal limitations on travel. Paul would certainly have traveled from Thessalonica (1 Thess 3:1) before the onset of winter, and a stay of eighteen months would have permitted him to set out for Jerusalem (Acts 18:18-22) in the spring, i.e., if Paul arrived in Corinth in October AD 44, he would have taken ship in April AD 46. Thus, the Conference in Jerusalem would have taken place in late 46 or early 47, which is, in fact, the date that Lüdemann assigns to the Conference (p. 272/262). Paul could certainly have returned to Ephesus (Acts 19:1; 1 Cor 16:8) within a year, or slightly longer, if he spent some time in Galatia organizing the collection. In any case, he would have been sufficiently well established at Ephesus to permit a visit to Corinth during the proconsulate of Gallio in AD 51–52.

At first sight this reconstruction would seem to validate Lüdemann's hypothesis of two visits in Acts 18, because it appears to integrate all the available data. In reality, however, this is only an illusion. Lüdemann's chronology is nothing more than a lofty edifice of speculation floating in midair; he has committed himself to a chimera.

If we accept the data of the letters, the Jerusalem Conference cannot be dated as early as AD 47, a date, moreover, which Lüdemann never condescends to justify in detail. Since Paul probably left Jerusalem in late AD 37 (2 Cor 11:31-32; Gal 1:17-18) and was absent fourteen years (Gal 2:1), the Conference cannot be dated earlier than AD 51. Such being the case, there would not have been [89] sufficient time for Paul to have made the overland trip to Ephesus, do all that is implied in 1 Corinthians 5:9 and 16:10, and still make a trip to Corinth in Gallio's year of office. If the date of the Conference is fixed in AD 51 or 52, Paul's contact with Gallio must have taken place *before* the Conference. This renders unnecessary Lüdemann's hypothesis that Acts 18:1-17 combines traditions relating to two distinct visits of Paul to Corinth, because he had certainly been there only once prior to his settling in Ephesus after the Conference.[28]

---

[28] It will now be evident that Lüdemann's obsession with the year AD 41 has led him to abandon any reasonable methodology. He dismisses the dating provided by the mention of Aretas in 2 Cor 11:31 simply because it does not fit, and for the same reason he hedges regarding the date of the mission to North Galatia (p. 272/262). His awareness

If acceptance of Lüdemann's hypothesis involves an impossible time compression, its rejection produces an equally difficult situation, because it would appear to force us (against Acts 18:11) to postulate that Paul was in Corinth from AD 44 to 51. Were this in fact the case, it becomes impossible to explain the sort of problems that Paul had to face in 1 Corinthians. Hence, we need to look at the value of the information provided by Luke in Acts 18 rather more critically than either Lüdemann or Jewett has done.

Since dates established on the basis of the letters have methodological priority over those derived from Acts, Luke must be in error in one of the chronological elements that he provides. We have seen that eighteen months is a plausible figure for Paul's founding visit to Corinth. It is equally clear that the date of Gallio and the virtually direct journey to Jerusalem (Acts 18:18-22), which for both Lüdemann and Jewett comes from one of Luke's sources, are compatible with the Conference date derived from the letters. The weak point, therefore, must be the dating of Paul's arrival in Corinth by reference to Aquila and Priscilla and the edict of Claudius. It is on this, therefore, that attention must be focused.

In my opinion, Lüdemann has convincingly established that the edict must be dated to AD 41. Methodologically there can be no question of refusing this date, as Jewett does, simply because of the difficulties it causes. What must be questioned is the relation between the edict and the advent of Aquila and Priscilla in Corinth. Luke's assertion that there was a direct causal relationship is confirmed [90] by no other source. Moreover, such a connection is not necessitated by the nature of the event. What we can infer from admittedly inadequate sources regarding the reality of what Claudius did in Rome contradicts the idea of a general exodus of Jews from Italy. I would suggest that Luke alone is responsible for the introduction of the edict of Claudius at this point. It provided a link to world history which at the same time seemed to explain how Jews, who had been living in Rome, came to be artisans in Corinth. The probability of this hypothesis is enhanced by the fact that Luke made precisely the same type of error when he introduced the census of Quirinius as the explanation of the presence of Mary and Joseph in Bethlehem (Luke 2:2). Lüdemann manifests such skepticism concerning Luke's refer-

---

of the unreasonable time compression that his chronology imposed induced him to reject the internal logic of Paul's movements.

ences to world history (pp. 26–31/8–11) that it is disconcerting to find that he accepts Acts 18:2 at face value. Evidently he had formulated his chronological hypothesis before adequately criticizing *all* the available data that had to be integrated.

If Paul came to Corinth after Aquila and Priscilla, whose arrival in reality had nothing to do with the edict of Claudius, then our only means of dating Paul's founding visit to Corinth is the overlap with the proconsulate of Gallio. We have no way of knowing exactly when he arrived. Here we part company with Jewett, who argues, "Since the latest Paul could have met Priscilla and Aquila was March 51, and the earliest Paul could have arrived in Corinth to appear before Gallio at the end of an eighteen month ministry was January 51, it follows that Paul's arrival in Corinth fell somewhere in this three month period" (p. 97). Such precision is unjustifiable. We do not know when Aquila and Priscilla arrived, and we cannot say with precision when during Paul's stay he encountered Gallio, since the manner in which Luke juxtaposes traditions is no guarantee of the real order of events.

To sum up. There are sufficient indications in Paul's letters to show that prior to the Jerusalem Conference of AD 51 he had evangelized Galatia, Macedonia, and Achaia. The evidence that all these churches were founded during the same journey is less strong, but there are hints that should not be ignored and that must take precedence over mere speculation. In fact, there is a striking parallel between the order of Paul's stops on a single journey as derived from the letters and the stations on his second missionary journey according to Acts 15–18:

Stops	Acts	Letters
Jerusalem	15:4	Gal 1:18
Antioch	15:30	
Syria and Cilicia	15:41	Gal 1:21
Derbe and Lystra	16:1	
Phrygia and Galatia	16:6	Gal 2:5
Troas	16:8	
Neapolis	16:11	
Philippi	16:12	1 Thess 2:2

continued next page

Stops	Acts	Letters
Thessalonica	17:1	Phil 4:16
Beroea	17:10	
Athens	17:15	1 Thess 3:1
Corinth	18:1	
Jerusalem	18:22	Gal 2:1

Such close correspondence forces us to conclude that Luke transposed this pre-Conference journey to the post-Conference period. This shift provides an important clue to his intention in writing Acts, but its significance can be evaluated only in the context of that work which is impossible here. As regards dating, all that can be said is that the journey occurred during the latter part of the period AD 37–51, probably between AD 45 and 51.

Postscript

I returned to the chronological problem of this article in writing my *Paul: A Critical Life* (Oxford: Clarendon Press, 1996) and found it possible to postulate a more detailed account of the different stages of Paul's journey through Galatia to Macedonia and Achaia (pp. 26–28), which I reproduce here:

> The starting point is Paul's arrival in Corinth in the spring of AD 50, i.e., eighteen months before his departure from Corinth in September AD 51. Given the objection to traveling in winter, he must have spent at least the winter of AD 49–50 in Macedonia. This is the bare minimum, but it is very probable that he stayed longer. The quality of the communities he established in Thessalonica [1 Thess 1:6-8] and Philippi [Phil 1:5] betrays protracted careful formation which could hardly be accomplished in a six-month period. The eighteen months Paul spent in Corinth (Acts 18:11) and the two years and three months in Ephesus (Acts 19:8-10) are illustrative of the time span required. Hence, I think it highly probable that he spent at least two winters in Galatia, which would mean that he arrived in Philippi sometime in the late summer or early autumn of AD 48.

The journey from Galatia to the coast would have taken Paul most of the summer of AD 48. Where exactly he was in Galatia and the details of the route he took are not certain. Here it is necessary only to note Jewett's estimate (p. 60) of the distance at 771 km. (463 miles), which would not be sensibly different, whichever route is chosen, and the time required as six weeks. This is an average of eighteen km. (eleven miles) per day, which is low in terms of the general daily figure[29] but may realistically reflect the maximum feasible in the brutal heat of the Anatolian summer.

Paul must have left Galatia in the late spring of AD 48, after the snows had melted, having certainly spent the winter of AD 47–48 holed up with one of his communities.[30] A ministry of six months, however, is probably too short. The impression given by Galatians 4:13 is that Paul's illness must have been rather serious, and so time must be allowed for convalescence. Jewett (p. 59) assigns a year to Paul's stay among the Galatians. But this hypothesis involves obvious difficulties. Paul must have arrived in Galatia at the latest by late September, when it begins to snow on the plateau of Anatolia. His sickness and recovery probably occupied most of the first winter. The following summer he made converts and established churches. By then, however, it would have been too late to undertake a journey to the west.[31] Hence, we must postulate that he spent two winters in Galatia, namely, AD 46–48. Not all this time would have been active ministry, owing to his illness and the difficulty, if not the impossibility, of even local travel in winter; the brevity of his ministry by comparison with his stay is confirmed by the fact that the communities in Galatia subsequently proved not as well grounded in the faith as those in Thessalonica and Philippi.

---

[29] The Bordeaux Pilgrim lists twelve "cities" and "inns" for the 258 Roman miles between Nicomedia and Ancyria, which is an average of twenty-one Roman miles (thirty kms/eighteen miles) per day.

[30] Jewett (p. 137 note 49) appositely quotes Sir William Ramsay: "All travel across the mountains [of Anatolia] was avoided between the latter part of November and the latter part of March; and ordinary travellers, not forced by official duties, but free to choose their own time would avoid the crossing [of the plateau] between October (an extremely wet month on the plateau) and May." After a battle against the Galatians near the river Halys in autumn, the Roman general C. Manlius Vulso had to go all the way back to Ephesus on the coast to find suitable winter quarters for his troops (Livy, *History of Rome* 38.27).

[31] If he did set out, he must have wintered somewhere en route to the Dardanelles, which leaves my relative chronology intact.

Jewett calculates the journey from Antioch to Galatia to be 1069 km. (641 miles) and estimates the travel time to be forty-three days. This is an average of twenty-five km. (fifteen miles) per day, which is feasible, particularly since Paul would have been starting after a winter's rest.[32] In addition, Jewett (p. 59) postulates stops of varying duration, namely, ten weeks in Syria-Cilicia-Derbe; eight weeks in Lystra-Iconium; and four weeks in Antioch in Pisidia. The arbitrary character of these latter figures is evident, but it is undeniable that Paul would have spent time in each of these places.

If we add Jewett's figures for the segment Antioch-Galatia, which he does not do, a problem immediately becomes apparent. The total is twenty-eight weeks. The earliest that Paul could have left Antioch is the latter part of April, because he would not want to face the Cilician Gates, the narrow pass through the Taurus Mountains behind Tarsus, until well into May. Twenty-eight weeks from mid-April, however, brings us to the middle of November, which is far too late for travelers to be abroad in Anatolia. Paul must have been settled in Galatia by mid-September at the latest. While the travel time cannot be reduced, and might probably be extended, it is perfectly feasible to reduce Jewett's rest/ministry time by two months, because Paul had no responsibility for the churches in the cities mentioned. He participated in their evangelization, but only in a subordinate position. The minimum time, therefore, for the journey from Antioch to Galatia is the summer of AD 46. It is not impossible, however, that it took a year longer.

The results of this analysis and calculations can be tabulated as follows:

Antioch	Winter 45–46
Departure from Antioch	April 46
Journey to Galatia	April–September 46
Ministry in Galatia	September 46–May 48
Journey to Macedonia	Summer 48
Ministry in Macedonia	September 48–April 50
Journey to Corinth	April 50

continued next page

[32] A section of the route that Paul would have taken is documented by the Bordeaux Pilgrim. The segment Antioch–Tarsus–Faustinopolis is 202 Roman miles and took nine days, an average of twenty-two Roman miles (thirty-two kms/twenty miles) per day.

Ministry in Corinth	April 50–September 51
Journey to Jerusalem	September 51
Conference in Jerusalem	October 51

These dates, it should be remembered, are the rock-bottom minimum and are substantially identical with those proposed by Jewett (p. 100). Under no circumstances can fewer than five to six years be allowed for the journey into Europe which ended with the Jerusalem Conference. It goes without saying, however, that Paul may have traveled more slowly and labored longer in any one place than my calculations allow. In which case, the nine hidden years (AD 37–46), about which we know only that he spent time in Syria and Cilicia (Gal 1:21; Acts 11:25), could be significantly reduced.

It will be clear that this reconstruction was developed by working backward from the date of Paul's founding visit to Corinth. The absolute date of this visit is provided by his encounter with the proconsul Gallio. According to D. Slingerland, however, this event cannot bear the weight imposed upon it.[33] In response I wrote:[34]

Dixon Slingerland has argued that Acts 18:12 prove no more than that Paul arrived in Corinth sometime between AD 47 and 54. Challenges to received orthodoxy are always welcome, and a number of the points made by Slingerland are well taken, notably his exposure of the unwarranted character of certain assumptions which have led to blatant illogicality in some assessments of what little data we have. His basic criticism of the current consensus, however, is simply that it is not certain! He gives the impression that he alone is aware of the amount of conjecture involved in the attempt to establish an absolute date in Paul's career, and considers the pointing out of such conjecture sufficient to make his case. He idealistically makes certitude the test, whereas the question that realists ask of any reconstruction concerns its relative probability: is this hypothesis more probable than any alternative? From this perspective one can do much better than Slingerland imagines.

[33] "Acts 18:1-18, the Gallio Inscription and Absolute Pauline Chronology," *JBL* 110 (1991): 439–49. Page numbers within the text refer to this article.

[34] Originally published as "Paul and Gallio," *JBL* 112 (1993): 315–17.

He overstates his case by referring to Paul's appearance before Gallio as a "trial" which leads to the public humiliation of the Jewish community (p. 441). He is led to do so by his concern to make the episode appear typical of what he considers to be Luke's *Tendenz* and thus of no historical value. In fact, there is no trial, because Gallio denies that he has jurisdiction and returns the matter to the appropriate authority in Roman law, namely, the Jewish community.

In his desire to heighten the element of doubt Slingerland exaggerates the incertitude regarding the length of Gallio's term of office; "there is no way to ascertain whether his position lasted one or two years" (p. 446). It is true that we cannot be absolutely sure, but one can answer with a significant degree of probability because of a piece of evidence which Slingerland did not check.[35] Seneca reports concerning his brother, "When, in Achaia, he [Gallio] began to feel feverish, he immediately took ship, claiming that it was not a malady of the body but of the place."[36] First, this positively excludes the two-year option because it is certain that Gallio did not finish his term of office, whether it was one or two years. Second, the natural interpretation of Seneca's sardonic reference to a "malady of the place" is that Gallio was antipathetic to Achaia and used the excuse of a minor illness to leave. This type of instinctive aversion normally results from a first impression. It does not usually begin late, although it may intensify with the passage of time. The impression of a fussy hypochondriac given by Seneca is confirmed by Pliny.[37] We can go a step further by invoking a factor which Slingerland does not take into account. The closing of the seas to winter travel meant that after September Gallio could not have returned to Rome except by ordering a military ship to sea and risking serious danger, a proceeding alien to his personality. In consequence, it is probable that Gallio stayed only a summer in Achaia. Whatever the year, Paul could have met Gallio in Corinth only between 1 July[38] and mid-September.

---

[35] He dismisses as speculative the view of Ogg that Gallio's health would not have permitted him to spend two years in Achaia (p. 446 note 28).

[36] *Letters* 104.1.

[37] *Natural History* 31.62.

[38] The ruling of Tiberius in AD 15 that provincial officeholders should leave Rome by 1 June (Dio Cassius, *Roman History* 57.14.5) implies that they took up their posts a month later. That time was allowed for travel is confirmed by the AD 42 legislation of Claudius, who moved the departure date back to 1 April only because officials tarried in

In addition to ignoring the seasonal limitations on travel, so appropriately emphasized by R. Jewett,[39] Slingerland also ignores the duration of the battle season (April to October) and the fact that the symbolic value of acclamations would diminish in proportion to their frequency.[40] When a serious effort is made to correlate the six acclamations in question (the twenty-second to the twenty-seventh) with the time spans available in AD 51 and 52, it becomes clear that it is most probable that the twenty-sixth acclamation (mentioned in the letter of Claudius to Delphi) took place after the first major military action in the battle season of AD 52.[41] Thus, even though we do not have the unrealistic standard of proof which Slingerland expects, we can say with a high degree of security that the letter of Claudius was written between April AD 52 at the earliest and 1 August AD 52 (by which date Claudius had been acclaimed Imperator for the twenty-seventh time) at the latest.

Further, because of the limitations on travel, the information to which the letter responded must have reached the emperor either sometime during the late summer of AD 51 or by the first boats coming from Greece in the spring of AD 52. Claudius' special predilection for Achaia[42] makes it improbable that he delayed in responding to a report on the plight of Delphi.

Slingerland would reply that there is no legitimate absolute criterion that would decide between the two dates which, moreover, he would consider unduly limited because he recognizes that Gallio could have been appointed as early as AD 50 (p. 446). Reflection, however, suggests that the report was brought to Rome by Gallio in September AD 51. Gallio's decision to leave his post without authorization was certain to incur the displeasure of Claudius, and

---

Rome (Dio Cassius, *Roman History* 60.11.3). This was too early for sea travel, and the following year he was forced to change the date to 15 April (Dio Cassius, *Roman History* 60.17.3). There is no evidence of any modification of the date of assumption of office. The problem is not "unresolvable," as Slingerland claims (p. 445 note 22), apparently in order to justify his acceptance of 1 May.

[39] *A Chronology of Paul's Life* (Philadelphia: Fortress, 1977), 56–57.

[40] On the necessary connection between the *salutatio imperatoria* and military victory, see Dio Cassius, *Roman History* 43.44.4–5; 46.38.1; 52.41.3–4, and the article "Imperator" in *PW* 9:1147–50, or *The Oxford Classical Dictionary*, 3rd ed. (1996), 750.

[41] For details, see my *Saint Paul's Corinth*, 162–64.

[42] "In commending Achaia to the senators he [Claudius] declared that it was a province dear to him through the association of kindred studies" (Suetonius, *Claudius* 42).

it would have been in his interest both to redeem himself and to distract the emperor by informing the latter of a subject close to his heart. This line of argument makes it most unlikely that Gallio's truncated term of office was the summer of AD 50. What reason could he have had to withhold the report for a year? Slingerland will, of course, dismiss such reasoning as mere conjecture. In fact, it represents an effort to resist the intellectual paralysis to which his approach leads by attempting to find reasonable grounds for discriminating between the various possibilities all of which he considers equally valid.

Slingerland is on much more solid ground in arguing that Acts 18:1-18 provides no basis for determining either a *terminus a quo* or a *terminus ad quem* for Paul's eighteen-month stay in Corinth (pp. 442–43). There is, however, another approach which Slingerland ignores. On the basis of Galatians 1:18; 2:1; and 2 Corinthians 11:32-33, it has been argued with a high degree of probability that Paul's second visit to Jerusalem coming from Corinth took place in the fall of AD 51 (see above).[43] If this is correct, Paul would have left Corinth roughly about the same time as Gallio. In consequence, his arrival there must be dated in the early spring of AD 50.

The English version of Lüdemann's chronological study concludes with a postscript in which he deals with the responses to its thesis published up to 1982 (pp. 289–93). With his usual laconic clarity he summarizes them as follows:

> I am glad to report that the major thesis of the book, that is, a Pauline mission in Greece before the conference, has been confirmed by Murphy-O'Connor. His many brilliant insights make it easy to overlook the tone of some of his remarks against my book (p. 291) [whose] main thesis has been rejected in the reviews by Hübner, Lindemann, Trocmé, and Wedderburn. Reviewers such as Aletti, Gnilka, Farmer, Penna and Stanley have expressed approval, ranging from enthusiastic endorsement (Stanley) to cautious acceptance (Gnilka). Others, such as Rese and Murphy-O'Connor, have remained undecided (Rese), or while approving of parts of the book, have developed their own solution (Murphy-O'Connor) (p. 293).

---

[43] See, in particular, Jewett, *Chronology*, 30–33 (with the corrections of C. Saulnier, "Hérode Antipas et Jean le Baptiste. Quelques remarques sur les confusions chronologiques de Flavius Josèphe," *RB* 91 [1984]: 371–75).

One wishes, however, that he had gone beyond mere description and responded in some detail to the criticisms that have been leveled against some elements of his study. For example, he claims that the majority, while approving his methodological principle of giving priority to data from the letters, have nonetheless found problems with his treatment of Acts. Unfortunately, in response he does no more than reaffirm his belief that the historical value of the sources used by Luke is self-evident. Equally, while accepting his dating of the edict of Claudius to AD 41, I questioned whether there was really a causal connection between that event and the arrival of Prisca and Aquila in Corinth, which is used to date Paul's founding visit. In response, Lüdemann simply says that Luke affirms such a connection in Acts 18:2 and refuses to deal with my arguments that a mission in Corinth as early as AD 41 is not at all probable.

Lüdemann's suggestion that Galatians 2:7-8 referred to Paul's first encounter with Peter in Jerusalem (Gal 1:18) was refused by Bradley H. McLean,[44] but on grounds that do not take into account my strengthening of Lüdemann's arguments in the above article. Having exposed the weaknesses of the hypothesis that these verses represent an official document emanating from the Jerusalem Conference, W. O. Walker explains these verses as a post-Pauline interpolation.[45] His arguments are the points which we have seen have caused difficulties for generations of exegetes. They have force for him because he is predisposed to find interpolations everywhere in the Pauline letters and presumes that he knows what Paul ought and ought not to have said.[46] More important, even a *prima facie* case for an interpolation demands a convincing reason why the interpolation should have been inserted. In this instance Walker does not even attempt to provide one.

Lüdemann's hypothesis regarding Galatians 2:7-8 has been taken a step further by A. Schmidt, who claims to be able to reconstruct the actual words of the agreement, namely, "Paul is entrusted with the gospel as

---

[44] "Galatians 2:7-9 and the Recognition of Paul's Apostolic Status at the Jerusalem Conference: A Critique of G. Luedemann's Solution," *NTS* 37 (1991): 67–76.

[45] "Galatians 2:7b-8 as a Non-Pauline Interpolation," *CBQ* 65 (2003): 568–87; "Galatians 2:8 and the Question of Paul's Apostleship," *JBL* 124 (2004): 323–27.

[46] See his *Interpolations in the Pauline Letters*, JSNTSup 213 (London: Sheffield Academic Press, 2001), whose methodological approach I have criticized in my *Keys to First Corinthians* (Oxford: Oxford University Press, 2009), 269–72.

it is directed to those who are not circumcised, just as Peter is entrusted with the gospel to those who are circumcised."[47] Without, however, committing himself, Martyn considers it a real possibility that "the issue of the meeting was quite specifically whether they would come to share a perception already reached by himself and Peter when he visited the latter in Jerusalem a number of years earlier."[48] More specifically, "All in all, it seems best to find at the core of vv. 7-8 the central motifs, and even some of the actual terms, of a formulation arrived at by Peter and Paul prior to the conference. Verse 9, then, reflects the adoption of that earlier formula by all participants in the conference itself."[49] Martyn appears not to have noticed that the only time that Peter and Paul had met previously was on the occasion of the latter's first visit to Jerusalem (Gal 1:18).

Légasse recognises the problems of Galatians 2:7-9, and in particular the non-Pauline expressions, but he is only prepared to admit that "Paul est ici influencé par des formules proncées in la circonstance qu'il evoque [i.e. the Conference]."[50] Lémonon, for his part, is prepared to follow Lüdemann and myself:

> En effet, Pierre, et lui seul, est en parallèle avec Paul, et *idontes* suppose le recours à un document circulant dans les communauté de langue grecque, connu ausi des gens de Jérusaelm et antérieur à l'Assemblée. Lorsqu'il fait mention de sa première montée, Paul ne dirait rien de cet accord afin que les Galates ne pense pas que son travail missionnaire se serait déroulé sous la protection de celui-ci. Ainsi, dès les premiers contacts avec Jérusalem, l'Évangile de Paul aurait été reconnu ; l'insertion soulignerait le caractère insupportable du retrait de Céphas à Antioche. Cette perspective est plus plausible que l'idée d'un extrait d'un accord rédigé lors de l'Assemblée, mais on demeure dans le domainte de la reconstitution.[51]

Lüdemann's brilliant insights have not fared well in his own country, even though the problems of Paul's early life have been the subject of

---

[47] A. Schmidt, "Das *Missionsdekret* in Galater 2:7-8 als Vereinbarung vom ersten Besuch Pauli in Jerusalem," *NTS* 39 (1992): 149–52.

[48] J. L. Martyn, *Galatians*, AB (New York: Doubleday, 1997), 201.

[49] *Galatians*, 212.

[50] S. Légasse, *L'épître de Paul aux Galates*, LD Comm. 9 (Paris: Cerf, 2000), 141, quoting Betz *in loc.*

[51] J.-P. Lémonon, *L'épitre aux Galates*, CBNT 9 (Paris: Cerf, 2008), 90, 95.

a number of intensive studies. The first in date is Rainer Riesner's *Die Frühzeit des Apostles Paulus. Studien zur Chronologie, Missionsstrategie und Theologie* (WUNT 71; Tübingen: Mohr Siebeck, 1994), which appeared in English as *Paul's Early Period* (Grand Rapids, MI: Eerdmans, 1997), followed by Martin Hengel and Anna Maria Schwemer's *Paul between Damascus and Antioch: The Unknown Years* (Louisville: Westminster Knox, 1997), which spawned a greatly expanded German edition a year later, *Paulus zwischen Damaskus und Antiochien. Die Unbekannten Jahre des Apostles* (WUNT 108; Tübingen: Mohr Siebeck, 1998), and finally Ruth Schäfer's *Paulus bis zum Apostelkonzil. Ein Beitrag zur Einleitung in den Galaterbrief, zur Geschichte der Jesusbewegung und zur Pauluschronologie* (WUNT 2.179; Tübingen: Mohr Siebeck, 2004).

Despite the inevitable differences in detail, these three books share a fundamental methodological option, which is never either clearly stated or adequately justified, namely, that Luke was an accurate historian whose observations are to be preferred to those of Paul. Such confidence in Luke's ability goes hand in hand with a firm refusal to take seriously anything in the letters that might appear to contradict Luke. Criticism of Acts is cavalierly dismissed by Hengel, who no doubt influenced the other two, as the ill-informed ravings of the incompetents who today masquerade as New Testament scholars.[52] Thus, the basic concern of these three studies is to save the veracity of Luke at all costs. To this end a possibility that cannot be excluded acquires the status of a demonstrated probability!

In the above article I showed that 2 Corinthians 11:32-33 provides a key element in the chronology of Paul's early life, namely, the date of his first visit to Jerusalem. Paul's own version of his escape from Damascus differs radically from that provided by Luke in Acts 9:23-25. How the tension is resolved is a perfect test case for the methodologies of Riesner, Hengel and Schwemer, and Schäfer.

Riesner refuses to give any chronological value to 2 Corinthians 11:32-33, because he cannot reconcile it with the very early date he assigns to Paul's conversion. Without ever asking how the authors could possibly have known, he takes at face value the statements of Irenaeus, the *Ascension of Isaiah*, and the *Apocryphon of James* that the risen Jesus

---

[52] *Paulus zwischen Damaskus und Antiochien*, viii–ix, 30, 193–94.

spent eighteen months, 545 days, and 550 days, respectively, with his disciples before ascending into heaven. Since Paul was the last to see Jesus (1 Cor 15:9), his conversion must be dated within a year and a half of the crucifixion, i.e., in AD 31 or 32. Knowing that he cannot simply set 2 Corinthians 11:32-33 aside, Riesner then feels free to harmonize it with Acts 9:23-25. Sought by the Jews in Damascus, Paul fled into the neighboring Nabataean Quarter, but its "consul" was bribed by the Jews to deny him security.[53]

Hengel and Schwemer at least recognize that Paul's account of the escape from Damascus is to be preferred to Luke's, where Jewish hostility is a familiar topos. Nonetheless, out of the blue, we are offered the possibility of Jewish involvement, and a harmonization identical with that of Riesner and designed to save Luke. "Nicht auszuschliessen ist dabei, dass Paulus *und* Apg Recht haben, nämlich dass die jüdische Gemeindebehörde *und* der nabatäische 'Konsul'. . . zusammenarbeiten."[54] Neither they nor Riesner deign to explain why the Jews would have sought help from the Nabataeans, when the obvious thing would have been to go to the Roman authorities (cf. Acts 18:12-13), who in their view still controlled the city, and have Paul declared a *persona non grata*.

The date of the evangelization of the Galatians is another touchstone. The evidence of the letters is unambiguous. The Jerusalem Conference took place in AD 51, fourteen years after Paul's first visit (Gal 2:1), and at that stage the Galatians had already been converted (Gal 2:5). This is flatly contradicted by Luke, who places Paul's founding visit to Galatia after the Conference (Acts 15–18). Here, the treatment of Hengel and Schwemer must take pride of place. Just because Galatians 2:5 contradicts their completely unfounded assumptions, any stringent grammatical interpretation is contemptuously dismissed as "completely perverse, absurd." Their only counterargument is blatant bluster, "Denn dadurch werden nicht nur die klaren Reihenfolge der Ausssagen Gal 1 und 2, sondern auch grosse zusammenhängende Textkomplexe bei Lukas heillos durcheinander gebracht."[55] In point of fact, there is plenty of time in the "fourteen years" of Galatians 2:1 for a mission to Galatia, and to move one block of material (Acts 16–18) and place it between

---

[53] *Frühzeit*, 76–79.

[54] *Paulus zwischen Damaskus und Antiochien*, 213, their emphasis.

[55] *Paulus zwischen Damaskus und Antiochien*, 396.

Acts 14 and 15 yields a perfectly coherent picture of Paul's activity as an apostle of Antioch.

Schäfer must be mentioned apart from her German colleagues. While they attempt to respect some of the evidence, she either ignores it completely or interprets it in a most unusual fashion, as will be clear from her reconstruction of the key events. Paul and Barnabas brought financial support to Jerusalem in AD 40 in response to the prophecy of famine (Acts 11:27-30) and used the opportunity to win the approval of the Pillars for their law-free gospel (Gal 2:1-10). Shortly after their return to Antioch, Peter arrived to experience life in a mixed community. Urged by James' people, he refused to eat with Gentiles, but Paul's vigorous protests forced him to change his mind and the Jerusalemites retired vanquished (Gal 2:11-14). Some years later, Antioch sent Paul and Barnabas to Cyprus and the province of Galatia (Acts 13–14). On their return to Antioch they found that some questioned the validity of a law-free mission, which necessitated another trip to Jerusalem for a meeting at which the "Apostolic Decree" was enacted (Acts 15).[56] Manifestly, Schäfer accepts neither Paul nor Acts regarding the number of Paul's visits to Jerusalem.

English and French commentators on Galatians do not seem to have the same axe to grind regarding Acts as their German counterparts. Nonetheless, Martyn is opposed to a pre-Conference mission to Galatia. His version of Galatians 2:5, "so that the truth of the gospel might remain, coming eventually to you," is presented as a translation,[57] but it is, in fact, a loose paraphrase; "coming eventually" corresponds to nothing in the Greek. It merely serves to articulate Martyn's conviction that linguistics alone cannot decide whether *pros hymas* means "with you" or "for you." The latter, he insists, is the more common meaning,[58] but he concedes that it must mean "with you" in Galatians 4:18, 24, and goes even further by pointing out that other compounds of the verb *menō* (*katamenō* and

---

[56] *Paulus bis zum Apostelkonzil*, 492–94.

[57] *Galatians*, 187. P. Esler simply ignores the implications of Gal 2:5 but redeems himself by agreeing that Pessinus was the focus of Paul's ministry in North Galatia (*Galatians*, NT Readings [London: Routledge, 1998], 34).

[58] Presumably this is why it is adopted without discussion by B. Witherington, *Grace in Galatia: A Commentary on Paul's Letter to the Galatians* (Grand Rapids, MI: Eerdmans, 1998), 138.

epimenō) are used with *pros hymas*, meaning "with you" in 1 Corinthians 16:6-7.[59] To me, this evidence unambiguously suggests that in Pauline usage *menō* with *pros hymas* can only mean "to remain with you."

In order to clarify the claimed linguistic obscurity of Galatians 2:5, Martyn claims that the best guide is Galatians 1:21. He insists that, had Paul been in Galatia during this period, he should have written, "Then, I went to the regions of Syria and Cilicia, far removed from Jerusalem, coming even to the cities of Galatia, as you yourselves well remember."[60] As I pointed out in the above article, however, this would be to confuse the *narratio* with the *probatio*, a point that Martyn does not deign to discuss.

On the positive side, I can only applaud Martyn when he writes, "If one is concerned to fix absolute dates, the safest point from which to take one's bearings may be Gal 1:18." Paul would have left Damascus about AD 38 to make his first visit to Jerusalem.[61]

After many years when no scientific commentaries on the New Testament appeared in French, two have recently been devoted to Galatians.

Apropos of Paul's founding visit among the Galatians, S. Légasse writes:

> on pourrait localiser l'évangélisation des Galates au cours du voyage missionnaire décrit aux chaptres 13 et 14 des Actes des Apôtres, où l'on voit Paul fonder des communautés en Pisidie, en Phrygie et en Lycaonie. Toutefois, dans le récit de ce voyage, il n'est jamais question de Galates ou de Galatie. On sait d'autre par que Paul a effectué deux visites chez les Galates. Le première est la visit de fondation, occasionnée par la maladie de l'apôtre (Ga 4,13-14). On peut l'identifier avec le passage 'à travers la Phrygie et le pays galate' mentionné en Ac 16,6, au cours du deuxième voyage missionnaire.[62]

On the basis of Galatians 2:5, Légasse correctly concludes that this visit took place before the Conference at Jerusalem (Gal 2:1-10)[63] and identified the Galatians with the Celtic inhabitants of North Galatia.[64]

---

[59] *Galatians*, 198 note 17.
[60] *Galatians*, 184.
[61] *Galatians*, 182 note 237. Similarly Witherington, *Grace in Galatia*, 118 note 86.
[62] *L'épître de Paul aux Galates*, 29.
[63] *L'épître de Paul aux Galates*, 34.
[64] *L'épître de Paul aux Galates*, 30.

J.-P. Lémonon agrees that Galatians 2:5 necessarily implies that the Galatians had been evangelized before the Jerusalem Conference but gives it little importance because those addressed in Galatians were the churches founded during Paul's first missionary voyage with Barnabas, sometime between 42 and 45.[65] His justification for this option is twofold: (1) "Identifier les Galates de Paul aux Galates du sud, et non point aux Galates-Celtes, rend beaucoup plus compréhensible l'importance accordée à la tradition juive, en particulier à l'Écriture, dans la lettres aux Galates. En effet, par Flavius Josèph (*AJ* 12.147-53), nous savons qu'à la fin du IIIᵉ s. av. JC, Antiochus III find déplacer deux mille familles juives de Babylonie en Phrygie."[66] (2) 'il n'est point étonnant de trouver des communautés parlant grec dans la région phrygio-galatique; ce serait plus surprennant au nord où, au Iᵉʳ s. l'influence gréco-romaine est moins marquée, bien que, pour des raisons liées au maintien de la *pax romana* dans la région, le gouverneur de la province réside a Ancyre."[67]

The second point is far from conclusive, because we have no knowledge of how much Greek was spoken in the province of Galatia. The text of Josephus, to which Lémonon refers in his first point, needs to be controlled rather more tightly. The occasion of the transfer of population was an uprising in Lydia and Phrygia. In consequence, one would have expected the Jews to be located farther to the west where the two regions meet. This is confirmed by the meager physical evidence of Jewish presence, which suggests that their main centers were at Laodicea and Apamea.[68] In 62 BC there were at least eleven thousand adult male Jews in the Lycus valley.[69]

Lémonon also forgets that the Galatians were not the only ones to hear the letter read aloud. The Judaizing intruders would also have been present (Gal 1:7; 5:10), and it was to them that Paul's arguments based on

---

[65] *L'épitre aux Galates*, 89, 33. This is also the position of F. Vouga, *An die Galater*, HNT 10 (Tübingen: Mohr Seibeck, 1998), 10.

[66] *L'épitre aux Galates*, 31.

[67] *L'épitre aux Galates*, 32.

[68] E. Schürer, *The History of the Jewish People in the Age of Jesus Christ (175 B.C.–A.D. 135)*, rev. ed. G. Vermes and F. Millar (Edinburgh: Clark, 1973), 3.27. Similarly Mitchell, *Anatolia*, 2.31–37.

[69] J. B. Lightfoot, *Saint Paul's Epistles to the Colossians and to Philemon* (London: Macmillan, 1904), 20, which is based on the twenty pounds of gold confiscated by Flaccus; see Philo, *Flacc.* 68.

a detailed knowledge of Jewish tradition were directed.[70] The Galatians of Pessinus no doubt listened, but he wanted the intruders to really *hear*. They could still create a lot of trouble for him when they moved on from Galatia, and he needed to subvert their mission. With his usual perspicacity, Martyn observes that Paul accomplishes his objective in Galatians "by allowing his speech to Peter [Gal 2:11-14] to become without notice a speech addressed to the Teachers [= intruders] in Galatia."[71]

Even though Lémonon opts for the South Galatian hypothesis, he leaves the door open to a mission in North Galatia.

> L'Apôtre pass sous silence son premier voyage avec Barnabas et indique le point de départ de son deuxième grand voyage, placé par l'auteur des Actes après l'Assemblée de Jérusalem pour des raisons ecclésiologiques : c'est après avoir eu l'accord de la communauté de Jérusalem que Paul entreprendrait ce grand voyage missionaire qui le conduit en Macédonie et Achaïe. Or, en fait, l'Assemblée de Jérusalem, quel qu'en soit l'objet précis, eut probablement lieu au terme du second voyage, en raison de difficultés soulevées par la conversion, en nombre important, de gens des nations à la foi en Christ.
>
> Cependant, une difficulté demeure. . . . au v. 21 [de Gal 1] Paul ne mentionne que Syrie et Cilicie, il ne cite même pas la Galatie ('la région phrygio-galatique'), il abrège. La brièveté s'explique par de données conventionelles d'écriture : la narration doit être 'clair, brève, vraisemblable', 'il y a souvent dans les détails une sorte de brièveté qui n'en allonge pas moins l'ensemble' (Quintilian, *Institution oratoire,* 4.2.31,41). . . . Mais, sourtout, Paul n'a pas à rappeler aux Galates ce qui'ils savent parfaitement, puisque, au cours de ce voyage, il est passé chez eux.[72]

Having made precisely the same rhetorical point in the above article, I can only applaud Lémonon's argument.

---

[70] See my *Paul: A Critical Life,* 200.
[71] *Galatians,* 230.
[72] *L'épitre aux Galates,* 78.

2

Paul in Arabia

(Gal 1:17)

One of the most intriguing asides in the Pauline letters is "I went away into Arabia; and again I returned to Damascus" (Gal 1:17).[1] The brevity is a challenge, but the response of the commentators is disappointing. The location of the area is rarely adequately justified,[2] and no one, to the best of my knowledge, has attempted an explanation of what happened there.

Where was Arabia? Strabo gives the geographers' answer: "Arabia Felix is bounded by the whole extent of the Arabian Gulf [= Red Sea] and the Persian Gulf."[3] The extent of this huge land mass underlines the need for a more tightly focused question. What would the term "Arabia" have suggested to a Jew who lived in first-century Judaea?

Josephus provides a very precise answer. Arabia could be seen to the east from the tower Psephinus in Jerusalem.[4] Thus, it was on the desert side of the three easternmost cities of the Decapolis, Damascus, Raphana, and [733] Philadelphia.[5] More specifically, it was contiguous to Hero-dian territory running along the southern border of the Roman province

---

[1] Originally published in *CBQ* 55 (1993): 732–37, whose pagination appears in the text in **bold**. A popular version appeared in *BAR* 10, no. 5 (1994): 46–47.

[2] H. D. Betz is far from untypical in writing, "We can assume, however, that he went to the cities of the Kingdom of Nabataea (called *provincia Arabia*)" (*Galatians: A Commentary on Paul's Letter to the Churches in Galatia*, Hermeneia [Philadelphia: Fortress, 1979], 73). The Roman province of Arabia was created in only AD 106; see G. W. Bowersock, *Roman Arabia* (Cambridge, MA: Harvard, 1983), 76.

[3] *Geography* 2.5.32, trans. H. L. Jones in LCL.

[4] *JW* 5.159–60, trans. H. St. J. Thackeray et al. in LCL.

[5] Pliny, *Natural History* 5.16.74, trans. H. Rackham in LCL. Cf. Strabo, *Geography* 16.2.20.

of Syria[6] and lay south and east of the great fortress Machaerus.[7] Petra was the royal seat of Arabia.[8] Whence the name "Arabia Petrea,"[9] or "Arabia belonging to Petra."[10] This mountain-encircled city, however, was the capital and chief city of the Nabataeans.[11] Whence another name, "Arabia of the Nabataeans."[12]

Since this, then, is what "Arabia" would have meant to a first-century Jew, Paul went into Nabataean territory,[13] which at that period ranged from the Hauran down through Moab and Edom and expanded on both sides of the Gulf of Aqaba.[14] What was his purpose? Some have thought that he sought a quiet place for reflection and study.[15] The law had ceased to be the centripetal force which held the different facets of his life together. That power was now exercised by the risen Lord and, it is suggested, he needed time and tranquility in order to assimilate a change of such magnitude.

Plausible as this suggestion is, it does not adequately account for what happened subsequently. Paul must have been doing something to draw attention to himself and arouse the ire of the Nabataeans because he had to return to Damascus, and even three years later the Nabataean authorities still wanted to arrest him (Gal 1:17; 2 Cor 11:32-33). The

---

[6] *AJ* 16.347, trans H. St. J. Thackeray et al. in LCL.

[7] *JW* 7.172.

[8] *JW* 1.125; cf. 1.159; 1.267; 4.454.

[9] *AJ* 18.109.

[10] Dio Cassius, *History* 68.14.5, trans. E. Cary in LCL.

[11] Strabo, *Geography* 16.4.21.

[12] Strabo, *Geography* 17.1.21. Similarly Plutarch, *Antonius* 36.2, trans. B. Perrin in LCL.

[13] 2 Cor 11:32-33 and the texts of Pliny and Strabo cited in note 5 exclude the hypothesis of H. Bietenhard that Paul preached in the Decapolis, possibly at Pella ("Die syrische Dekapolis von Pompeius bis Trajan," *ANRW* 2, no. 8 [1977]: 255).

[14] The most detailed single ancient treatment of the lifestyle of the Nabataeans is that of Strabo, *Geography*, 16.4.26. The classic study remains that of J. Starcky, "Pétra et la Nabatène," *DBSup* 7 (1966): 886–1017, but see also Bowersock, *Roman Arabia*, 45–75, and A. Negev, "The Nabataeans and the Provincia Arabia," *ANRW* II / 8 (1977): 549–635.

[15] Most recently, M.-F. Baslez, *Saint Paul* (Paris: Fayard, 1991), 101; R. N. Longenecker, *Galatians*, WBC 41 (Dallas, TX: Word Books, 1990), 34; but without suggesting, as J. B. Lightfoot did on the basis of Gal 4:25, that Arabia was Sinai (*Saint Paul's Epistle to the Galatians* [London: Macmillan, 1910], 87–90).

probable explanation is that Paul was trying to make converts.[16] Since he understood his [**734**] conversion as a commission to preach the gospel among pagans (Gal 1:16), it would have been out of character for him not to have acted upon it as soon as was feasible.

Nabataeans and Jews

In order to understand the violence of the Nabataean reaction, the salient points of their stormy relations with the Jews must be recalled. Things started well, when Antipater of Idumea sealed an alliance between Hyrcanus II and Aretas III by marrying Kypros, who came from an eminent Nabataean family and later became the mother of Herod the Great.[17] Against his will in 32–31 BC the latter was forced into a war with the Nabataeans, which he won after suffering heavy losses.[18] He again defeated them circa 9 BC.[19] It is not at all surprising, therefore, that the Nabataeans enthusiastically provided auxiliaries to aid P. Quinctilius Varus, the governor of Syria, in his brutal suppression of the revolt which followed the death of Herod around 4 BC.[20]

In order to calm the tensions between the two peoples, Herod Antipas married the daughter of Aretas IV,[21] possibly at the suggestion of the emperor, Augustus, if Suetonius' report of his policy is correct.[22] In time, however, he tired of her and divorced her in order to marry Herodias, the wife of his half-brother Philip.[23] This marriage is probably to be dated in AD 23.[24] Its criticism by John the Baptist is reported both by the gospels and Josephus.[25] Their divergent emphases (moral for the former;

---

[16] So, recently, F. F. Bruce, *Paul: Apostle of the Free Spirit* (Exeter: Paternoster, 1977), 81–82; Betz, *Galatians*, 74; S. Légasse, *Paul apôtre. Essai de biographique critique* (Paris: Cerf/Fides, 1991), 72.

[17] *JW* 1.181.

[18] *JW* 1.364–85.

[19] *AJ* 16.282–85.

[20] *JW* 2.68.

[21] *AJ* 18.109.

[22] *Augustus* 48, trans. J. C. Rolfe in LCL.

[23] *AJ* 18.110.

[24] C. Saulnier, "Hérode Antipas et Jean le Baptiste. Quelques remarques sur les confusions chronologiques de Flavius Josèphe," *RB* 91 (1984): 365–71.

[25] Mark 6:17-18 and par.; *AJ* 18.118.

political for the latter) are, in fact, complementary and adequately explain John's arrest and imprisonment in Machaerus, probably around AD 28.[26] Herod Antipas had moved there from Galilee in order to be prepared for an attack by Aretas in revenge for the insult to his daughter. The latter, in fact, made [**735**] a disputed area on his northern border a pretext for war.[27] In the battle, which probably should be dated circa AD 29,[28] the troops of Antipas were routed. Whereupon, according to Josephus, he indignantly complained to Rome.[29] The historicity of this complaint cannot be guaranteed, but a war could not be kept secret, and the news would certainly come to the ears of the emperor.

The Situation in Arabia when Paul Arrived

Aretas IV had every reason to feel anxious. The following are the essentials of a rather complicated story which took place some forty years earlier.[30]

With the authorization of C. Sentius Saturninus, the governor of Syria, Herod the Great went into Arabia to arrest criminals from his territory in Trachonitis. A skirmish ensued when the Nabataeans intervened to protect them, and some soldiers on both sides died. Syllaeus, representing the Nabataeans in Rome, presented the affair to Augustus as an unwarranted breach of the peace. The emperor's extreme displeasure explains why Herod had been careful to secure prior Roman approval for his military action. It did him no good, however, and he lost the impe-

---

[26] *AJ* 18.119. Although presented as the date of the beginning of John the Baptist's ministry, "the fifteenth year of the reign of Tiberius Caesar" (Luke 3:1) is more likely to be the date of his arrest. Only after John's incarceration did Jesus return to Galilee (Mark 1:14) and begin a mission which terminated in AD 30.

[27] The text of *AJ* 18.113 is defective, and Gabalis is the most probable restoration; see H. Hoehner, *Herod Antipas*, SNTSMS 17 (Cambridge: Cambridge University Press, 1972): 254–55; E. Schürer, *The History of the Jewish People in the Age of Jesus Christ (175 B.C.–A.D. 135)*, rev. G. Vermes and F. Millar (Edinburgh: Clark, 1973), 1:350. It is not impossible that the conflict inspired Jesus' parable of two kings going out to war (Luke 14:31-32). Were the allusion certain it would date the battle before AD 30, the year in which Jesus died.

[28] Saulnier, "Hérode Antipas," 375.

[29] *AJ* 18.115.

[30] *AJ* 16.271–355.

rial favor completely. As Augustus put it in a severe reprimand, Herod had been relegated from the status of a friend to that of a subject. The emperor refused a first embassy from Judea and only reluctantly heard a second embassy led by Nicolaus of Damascus, who, with the support of ambassadors from Aretas IV, proved Syllaeus' version of the episode to be false. Herod was restored to favor, but Aretas found himself in serious trouble, because on the death of Obodas he had assumed the throne of Arabia without the permission of Rome. Augustus had planned to entrust Arabia to Herod, and it was only the latter's refusal that enabled Aretas to succeed after being reproved for his rashness.

Aretas, therefore, knew from personal experience that Rome had little patience with warlike actions between the client kings who guarded the eastern frontier of the empire. It would be most surprising if he had not feared some reaction on the part of Tiberius as he had once dreaded the response [**736**] of Augustus. The retirement of Tiberius to Capri in AD 26 has been interpreted as a loss of interest in the affairs of state. While there may be some truth in this as regards internal matters, it is not so as regards the provinces.[31] Philo's judgment that in his twenty-three years of rule Tiberius "did not let the smallest spark of war smoulder in Greece or the world outside Greece,"[32] while not completely accurate,[33] is borne out (for the part of the world with which we are concerned) by his vigorous and effective responses in matters large, e.g., the Parthian occupation of Armenia in AD 34,[34] and small, e.g., when Pilate to annoy the Jews placed shields with the emperor's name in Herod's palace in Jerusalem.[35] His vigilance regarding the security of the eastern frontier is perfectly illustrated by the way he responded to the death of Herod Philip in AD 33/34. While leaving the revenues to accumulate for a successor, he immediately attached the territory to the province of Syria.[36]

---

[31] See M. P. Charlesworth, "Tiberius," in *CAH* 10:648–52.

[32] *Leg.* 141, trans. F. H. Colson et al. in LCL.

[33] There were uprisings in Africa (AD 17), in Thrace (AD 19, 21, 25), and in Gaul (AD 21). See H. H. Scullard, *From the Gracchi to Nero: A History of Rome from 133 B.C. to A.D. 68*, 5th ed. (London/New York: Methuen, 1982): 278–80.

[34] Josephus, *AJ* 18.96–105; Dio Cassius, *History* 58.26.1–4; 59.27.2–4; Tacitus *Annals* 6.31–37.

[35] Philo, *Leg.* 299–308; Josephus, *JW* 2.169–74.

[36] *AJ* 18.108.

Despite his age and weariness, Tiberius was perfectly capable of reacting quickly and decisively. In the case of Aretas it only needed an order to the governor of Syria, who had four legions at his disposition.[37]

As Aretas waited tensely for something to happen, his attitude toward Jews was certainly anything but benign. They (in the person of their king) were responsible for the desperate anxiety which weighed upon him. A Roman reprisal would be but the latest in the series of disasters which the Jews had brought upon his people. His subjects presumably shared his apprehension and his anger, both of which intensified as the years passed. By the time Paul arrived circa AD 33, the tension would have been building for three years. It was certainly not a propitious moment for a Jew to begin preaching what to an outsider was but a new variety of Judaism. To those Nabataeans who were the objects of his ministry it could only appear as an attempt to infiltrate, divide, and weaken them. What they saw as an invitation to betrayal [737] would have prompted an immediate and violent reaction. Paul escaped. Otherwise there would have been no point in drawing the authorities into the affair and painting him in such colors that he was remembered as dangerous three years later (cf. 2 Cor 11:32-33).

This reconstruction may not be the only one possible, but it integrates and maximizes the meager data available. If it is correct, it is unlikely that Paul penetrated very deeply into Arabia. He may not even have gotten as far as Bosra; there were three Nabataean towns further north, Phillopolis, Kanatha, and Suweida.[38] If Aretas contemplated armed resistance, he would certainly have had troops in that area, and Paul would have been a figure of suspicion once he opened his mouth. This makes it improbable that Paul stayed long. His silence about the duration suggests that it was very short, since he lists his two weeks in Jerusalem and his three years in Damascus (Gal 1:18). The impulsive gesture is important only insofar as it indicates that from the beginning Paul was convinced that his mission was to Gentiles. He no doubt chose Arabia because it is unlikely that there were any Jews there.

---

[37] Who precisely was in charge in Syria at this stage is problematic; see Schürer, *History*, 1:260–62, 362. It is improbable that L. Vitellius, who became governor of Syria in AD 35, was ever ordered by Tiberius to attack Aretas, as Josephus reports (*AJ* 18.115, 120–26). The latter gives a completely different explanation for the presence of Vitellius in Jerusalem in *AJ* 18.90–95. See Saulnier, "Hérode Antipas," 373–74.

[38] See the map in Negev, "The Nabateans," 550.

Postscript

I have strengthened my hypothesis that Paul went to Arabia to preach by adopting T. Donaldson's brilliant insight that Paul persecuted Christians precisely because they proclaimed Jesus to be the Messiah.[39] In traditional Jewish belief, the advent of the Messiah meant the end of the law; there would be no need for it because all his people would be just. Paul's acute intelligence saw clearly that Christians could not have it both ways. If they continued to insist that Jesus was the Messiah, then they were, in fact, rejecting the law. It could not be "both-and." It had to be "either-or." As a Pharisee Paul could not accept that the law had come to an end, principally because Jesus did not conform in any way to the Pharisaic vision of the Messiah described in the *Psalms of Solomon* 17 and 18. Christians, in consequence, were wrong, and Paul's "persecution" was designed to correct them (Gal 1:13).

Paul's "either-or" mentality meant that psychologically he was fully prepared to abandon the law completely once he had accepted Jesus as the Messiah. Thus, in the period immediately subsequent to his conversion Paul did not have to endure any agonizing struggle to get his mind around a new idea. He did not have to be weaned from a cherished belief. The recognition of the need for a choice had been well established in his mind. As a result, Jesus was simply substituted for the law. Thus, when Paul went to Arabia, it was not to pray for peace of mind but to proclaim Jesus as Savior.

Confirmation of this interpretation is provided by Carsten Burfeind, who argues from the formulation of Galatians 1:16. Paul is not commissioned as a missionary "to the Gentiles" but as a preacher of Christ "among the Gentiles" (ἵνα εὐαγγελίζομαι αὐτον ἐν τοις ἔθνεσιν), and this is precisely what he claims to have done (Gal 2:2). In other words, he was to seek out not individual pagans in the land of Israel but pagans in general in Gentile territory.[40] This interpretation of the grammatical structure is not new—"Undoubtedly then Paul means here to define the

---

[39] "Zealot and Convert: The Origin of Paul's Christ-Torah Antithesis," *CBQ* 51 (1989): 655–82.

[40] "Paulus in Arabien," *ZNW* 95 (2004): 129–30.

divinely intended sphere of his preaching as among Gentiles"[41]—but it was important to draw attention to it anew in the light of the uncontrolled speculation that has developed around Galatians 1:17. It provides the simplest explanation of why Paul went to Arabia soon after his conversion, because the historical circumstances outlined in the above article make it virtually certain that it was inhabited by Gentiles alone.

Gordon Fee begins with a dichotomy; Paul went to Arabia either to preach or to pray. If the former, Arabia would be the area south of Damascus. If the latter, which Fee prefers, Arabia would include Mount Sinai. His argument from what he considers the complicated structure of Galatians 1:16-17 is rather convoluted.[42]

> The purpose clause, "so that I might preach him among the Gentiles," is not the main point of the present sentence, but is rather anticipatory of what is to come. Paul's sentence itself indicates that his going away to Arabia was the flip side of his not consulting "with flesh and blood" (I didn't do the one but the other). In which case his reason for going to Arabia would be for the sake of "consulting" with the Lord about what had happened to him; and where better to go, given his deep and passionate love of his people and their history, than the mount of revelation itself.[43]

Were this, in fact, the case, one can legitimately ask why Paul did not mention Sinai (cf. Gal 4:25) rather than the vague and polyvalent "Arabia." It must also be kept in mind that in Galatians 1 Paul's concern is to minimize his contacts with Jerusalem and to stress the God-given character of his gospel (Gal 1:11-12), which was in no way dependent on the teaching of the Jerusalem community. There is not the slightest hint that he was so profoundly upset that he felt the urgent need to commune with God. Recognition that Jesus was the Messiah meant that the law was no longer relevant, and the door to salvation was open to Gentiles. The

---

[41] E. de Witt Burton, *A Critical and Exegetical Commentary on the Epistle to the Galatians*, ICC (Edinburgh: Clark, 1921), 53. This simple point completely undercuts the vain effort of A. Bunine ("Paul: 'Apotre des Gentiles' ou . . . 'des Juifs d'abord, puis des Grecs'?," *ETL* 82 (2006): 35–68) to show that Paul did not preach to Gentiles until the eve of the Conference in Jerusalem (Gal 2:1-10).

[42] G. D. Fee, *Galatians: Pentacostal Commentary* (Blandford Forum: Deo, 2007), 43. Similarly Burton, *Galatians*, 55.

[43] *Galatians*, 50–51.

purpose of the above analysis of the political situation in Nabatea was precisely to explain Paul's choice of Arabia as a Gentile mission field.

Unsatisfactory as it may be, the sobriety of Fee's suggestion contrasts vividly with the wild speculations of Hengel and Schwemer. They refuse my suggestion that in his enthusiasm Paul walked blindly into a dangerous political situation in northern Arabia on the grounds that the military conflict between Aretas IV and Antipas took place much later.[44] This is simply stated without argumentation, and not the slightest attempt is made to counter the chronological arguments of Saulnier, whom I was following in dating this conflict to AD 29. Such cavalier dismissal of anything "inconvenient" is unfortunately integral to their methodology. They want Paul to stay in Arabia for up to two years, which are to be counted among the "three years" of Galatians 1:18.[45] They opt for this not uncommon,[46] but unnatural,[47] interpretation in order to give Paul time both to go far into Arabia and to arrive at one of his most important theological insights.

The starting point for Hengel and Schwemer is that for Jews the Nabataeans were the descendants of Ishmael, the son of Abraham. In fact, they took their name from Nabaioth, Ishmael's eldest son. Thus, they were the closest pagan "relatives" of the Jews,[48] who no doubt had synagogues everywhere, notably in Petra.[49] Paul, however, pushed much further south, because the mother of Ishmael was Hagar, and her name made him think of Hegra (Madain Salih), which became the goal of his quest.

> Darauf, dass er im nabatäischer Arabien noch weiter in den Süden bis in die zweitwichtigste State Hegra (Madain Salih) vorgedrungen ist, *könnte* Gal 4,25 hinweisen, wo er Hagar mit dem Berg Sinai in Arabien identifiziert. . . . Dass Paulus von der an Hegra hafenden

---

[44] M. Hengel and A. M. Schwemer, *Paulus zwischen Damaskus und Antiochien. Die Unbekannten Jahre des Apostles*, WUNT 108 (Tübingen: Mohr Siebeck, 1998), 180 note 729.

[45] *Paulus zwischen Damaskus und Antiochien*, 175.

[46] Burton, *Galatians*, 59.

[47] G. Lüdemann, *Paul: Apostle to the Gentiles; Studies in Chronology* (London: SCM, 1984), 63.

[48] *Paulus zwischen Damaskus und Antiochien*, 180.

[49] *Paulus zwischen Damaskus und Antiochien*, 184, 190.

jüdischen Hagartradition wusste, könnte man am besten auf seinen längern Aufenthalt in der Arabia (Gal 1,17), d. h. in nabatäishchem Gebiet zurüchführen. Paulus muss gewusst haben, dass der Sinai in der Nähe von Hegra zu suchen ist.[50]

The most important point for Hengel and Schwemer, however, is that the Nabataeans were circumcised but did not belong to the Chosen People. This fact, they believe, directed Paul's thought.

Bei der Autorität Abrahams im nabatäischen Arabien ist es durchaus denkbar, dass der junge Schriftgelehrte [Paul] schon damals das Argument verwendet hat, die Beschneidung Abrahams mit 99 und seines Sohns Ismael mit 13 Jahren sei erst sehr spät erfolgt und die Rechfertigung Abrahams auf Grund seines Glaubensgehorsams gehe dieser zeitlich weit voraus, so dass Beschneidung schon bei Abraham zum blossen 'Siegel für die Glaubensgerechtigkeit' (Röm 4,11) wurde.[51]

It was in Arabia, therefore, that Paul reached the conviction that circumcision was irrelevant to salvation.

Hengel and Schwemer's elaborate reconstruction has the attractiveness of a good detective story. It is much simpler, however, to think that once Paul accepted Jesus as the Messiah all the prescriptions of the law became irrelevant. Moreover, a simple reading of Genesis would have informed him of the chronological relationship of Abraham's belief (15:6) and circumcision (17:23).

Schäfer also includes Paul's stays in Arabia and Damascus in the "three years" of Galatians 1:18 but hesitates as to the proportions to be assigned to each.[52] What did Paul do in Arabia? "Nach allem bisher Gesagten ist die annahme einer paulinischen Verkündigung in nabatäische geprägten Städten nich allzuweit entfernt von Damaskus am plausibelsten."[53] She would not have him go farther south than Bosra, which I believe is correct. This, in turn, would suggest that the duration of Paul's visit was not very long.

---

[50] *Paulus zwischen Damaskus und Antiochien*, 186.

[51] *Paulus zwischen Damaskus und Antiochien*, 191–92.

[52] R. Schäfer, *Paulus bis zum Apostelkonzil. Ein Beitrag zur Einleitung in den Galaterbrief, zur Geschichete der Jesusbewegung und zur Pauluschronologie*, WUNT 2.179 (Tübingen: Mohr Siebeck, 2004), 129–30.

[53] *Paulus bis zum Apostelkonzil*, 101; cf. 429.

This is also the view of Légasse[54] and Lémonon,[55] who both agree with me that Paul went to Arabia to preach and that his mission field was the northern part of the Nabataean kingdom. According to Martyn, "The fact that Aretas, king of Nabatea, became at one point very angry with Paul (2 Cor 11:32-33; cf. Acts 9:23-25) may be hint enough that Paul preached a message [in Arabia] that was in some way unsettling to public order."[56]

[54] S. Légasse, *L'épître de Paul aux Galates*, LD Comm. 9 (Paris: Cerf, 2000), 100–101.

[55] J.P. Lémonon, *L'épitre aux Galates*, CBNT 9 (Paris: Cerf, 2008), 72, 75.

[56] *Galatians*, 170 note 216.

3

The Names for Jerusalem in Galatians

(1:17-18; 4:25-26)

One of the minor mysteries of Galatians is the shift from Ἱεροσό-λυμα in 1:17-18; 2:1 to Ἱερουσαλήμ in 4:25-26.[1] The silence of most commentators betrays their conviction that the variation is without significance. In fact, there is a real problem if one thinks in terms of a single document and the absence of any explanation (e.g., a quotation in a foreign language).

No one writing in Gaelic will shift from "Baile Atha Cliath" to "Dublin." No one writing in English will shift from "London" to "Londres." No one writing in German will shift from "Basel" to "Bâle." No one writing in French will shift from "Genève" to "Geneva." No one writing in Italian will shift from "Bolzano" to "Bozen." No one writing in Polish will shift from "Gdansk" to "Danzig." No one writing in Portuguese will shift from "Lisboa" to "Lisbon." So why does Paul, writing in Greek, shift from the Greek form Ἱεροσόλυμα to the Semitic Ἱερουσαλήμ?

There are certain commentators who recognize that this is a real question but make no effort to answer it.[2] To the best of my knowledge only two scholars have formulated responses. For Theodor Zahn the variation "erklärt sich aber daraus, daß es sich dort [1:17-18; 2:1] um prosaische Angabe eines Reiseziels, hier [4:25-26] um eine theologische Betrach-

---

[1] Originally published in *ZNW* 90 (1999): 280–81. This article has also appeared as chap. 3 in my *Keys to Jerusalem* (Oxford: Oxford University Press, 2012).

[2] H. Schlier, *Der Brief an die Galater*, MeyerK (Göttingen: Vandenhoeck & Ruprecht, 1962), 221 note 4; H. D. Betz, *Galatians*, Hermeneia (Philadelphia: Fortress, 1979): 73 note 172; F. F. Bruce, *The Epistle of Paul to the Galatians*, NIGTC (Exeter: Paternoster, 1982), 94.

tung hohen Stils handelt, wofür dem Hebräer Pl die 'heilige Sprache' angemessener schien, als die hellenisirte Form."[3]

This explanation might claim support from Philo's usage. When speaking historically in the *Legatio ad Gaium*, Philo consistently uses Ἱεροσόλυμα (§156, 278, 288, 312, 313, 315), but when he speaks allegorically he employs Ἱερουσαλήμ (*Som.* 2.250).

Although independent of Zahn, Joachim Jeremias takes a similar approach, "Er gebraucht im Galaterbrief da die profane Form, wo er über seine Besuche in der Heiligen Stadt berichtet (1:17f; 2:1), und da die sakrale Form, wo er die irdische und die himmlische Gottesstadt einander gegenüberstellt (4:25f). An den restlichen Stellen (Röm 15:19, 25f, 31; 1 Kor 16:3) steht die feierliche Form, weil von Jerusalem als der Muttergemeinde und dem Zentrum der Mission die Rede ist."[4]

Central to both these hypotheses is the idea that Paul uses Ἱερουσαλήμ when it is question of what might be called elevated thought as opposed to prosaic information. The evidence does not bear this out. In Romans 15:25-31 Paul uses Ἱερουσαλήμ three times, plus once in 1 Corinthians 16:3, when passing on banal data regarding the collection for the poor of Jerusalem.

[281] A better founded hypothesis begins to emerges if we look more closely at Pauline usage. Ἱερουσαλήμ appears seven times distributed between three letters (Rom, 1 Cor, Gal), whereas Ἱεροσόλυμα is found three times and only in Galatians. These simple statistics suggest that Ἱερουσαλήμ was Paul's normal word for the Holy City, and that Ἱεροσόλυμα is an exception that demands explanation.

This is precisely what we should expect, given the general statistics established for the two names by Joachim Jeremias.[5] The LXX, the Bible of Diaspora Jews, uses Ἱερουσαλήμ exclusively, as do Jewish writers when they translate biblical texts into Greek. This is the environment in which Paul grew up, and the terminology thus acquired would have been reinforced by his years as a Pharisee. Ἱεροσόλυμα, on the other hand, was used by Jewish authors writing for a Gentile audience and was taken over by pagan writers as *hierosolyma*.

---

[3] *Der Brief des Paulus an die Galater*, KNT (Helsingfors: A. Deichert'sche Verlagsbuchhandlung Nachf, 1907), 235 note 45.

[4] "IEROUSALHM/IEROUSOLUMA," *ZNW* 65 (1974): 275.

[5] Jeremias, "IEROUSALHM/IEROUSOLUMA," 274.

Given the Gentile character of the Galatian churches (Gal 4:8),[6] it is most probable that the intruders would have used Ἱεροσόλυμα in their references to Paul's relationship to the Mother Church.[7] This led Paul to use the same term in his defense of his independence from Jerusalem in order to make it clear that both he and his opponents were talking about the same place. Not surprisingly, therefore, Ἱεροσόλυμα is limited to Galatians 1–2 in the Pauline letters.

Postscript

My suggestion won an immediate response from Michael Bachmann.[8] While agreeing that I might be right as regards Galatians 1–2, where the usage of his opponents affected Paul's own formulation, he felt that the shift back to Paul's usual Ἱερουσαλήμ was an inadequate explanation of Galatians 4:25-26. He insists that the singular and feminine form of the name was required here both because it was the usual way of referring to the heavenly Jerusalem (e.g., Heb 12:22; Rev 3:12; 21:2, 9-10) and because it corresponds to the evocation of women in the allegory of 4:21–5:2. Hence his conclusion, "So dürfte es richtig sein, das Nebeneinander von *Hierosolyma* and *Ierusalêm* im Galaterbrief doppelt zu begründen: die Verwendung von *Hierosolyma* eher formal, die von *Ierusalêm* inhaltlich."

The use of the meaningless "formal" is a little disingenuous, and Bachmann appears to have forgotten that *Hierosolyma* can also be feminine, e.g., *pasa Hierosolyma* (Matt 2:3).[9] Moreover, I suspect that those who go to "content" for an explanation of the two names in Paul are strongly influenced by the appearance of the two forms throughout Luke (*Hierso-*

---

[6] I have argued that the Galatians were natives of Pessinus; see my "Gal 4,13-14 and the Recipients of Galatians," *RB* 105 (1998): 202–7 = chap. 8 below. There were no Jews in that area; see S. Mitchell, *Anatolia: Land, Men, and Gods in Asia Minor* (Oxford: Clarendon, 1993), 2:31–37.

[7] A rather elaborate reconstruction of the criticisms of the intruders is given by Bruce, *Galatians* (note 2), 26. For a minimalist version see J. L. Martyn, *Galatians*, AB (New York: Doubleday, 1997), 178.

[8] "*Hierosolyma* and *Ierusalêm* im Galaterbrief," *ZNW* 91 (2000): 288–89. Curiously, Lémonon has the impression that Bachmann agrees with me (*Galates*, 75).

[9] See BDF §56(4).

loyma 4x; *Ierusalêm* 26x) and Acts (*Hiersoloyma* 25x; *Ierusalêm* 39x).
This phenomenon has intrigued commentators.[10] The most recent and most
thorough study is a Polish Habilitationsschrift, *Ierousalêm. Hierosolyma.
Old Testament and Hellenistic Roots of the Lucan Picture of the Holy City
in the Light of Greek Onomastics* by Krzysztof Mielcarek.[11]

As background to Luke-Acts, Mielcarek investigates the three books
of the LXX in which both forms appear (Tobit, 1 Macc, 1 Esd), and concludes that all use one form or the other in specific contexts. For example,
in all three *Hierosolyma* appears in contexts which speak of the punishment of the city. This, then, would seem to legitimize a content-oriented
approach to Luke-Acts. The Semitic form there, he argues, carries much
greater theological weight than the Hellenistic form, but the latter cannot
be dismissed as a mere geographical or profane category.

My difficulty with this approach is that it envisages only one way of
accounting for the phenomenon, namely, the connotation that the context
appears to affix to a particular form. Other possibilities are not taken
into account with the result that no determination of the most probable
explanation can be made.

Moreover, the content approach inevitably leads to formulations such
as "The author of Luke-Acts used a Hebrew-like form *Ierousalêm* to
establish a strong connection with the temple" (Mielcarek, 237; my emphasis). This implies that *Ierousalêm* carries this connotation whenever
and wherever it is used, which, of course, is nonsense, as one example
will illustrate. It has the further advantage of indicating a different way
of explaining the shift from *Hierosolyma* to *Ierusalêm* or vice versa.

[1] Now when Festus had come into his province, after three days he
went up to Jerusalem [*eis Hierosolyma*] from Caesarea. [2] And the
chief priests and the principal men of the Jews informed him against
Paul; AND THEY URGED HIM, [3] ASKING AS A FAVOR TO HAVE THE MAN SENT

---

[10] E.g., I. de la Potterie, "Les deux noms de Jérusalem dans l'évangile de Luc," *RSR*
69 (1981): 57–70; idem, "Les deux noms de Jérusalem dans les Actes des Apotres,"
Biblica 62 (1982): 153–87; D. D. Sylva, "*Ierusalêm* and *Hierosolyma* in Luke-Acts,"
ZNW 74 (1983): 207–21.

[11] *Ierousalêm. Hierosolyma. Starotestamentowe i hellenistyczne korzenie Łukaszoweo
obrazu świętego miasta w świetle onomastyki greckiej*, Studia Biblica Lublinensia 11
(Lublin: Wydawnictwo KUL, 2008); English summary, 237–41.

TO JERUSALEM [*eis Ierousalêm*], PLANNING AN AMBUSH TO KILL HIM ON THE WAY. [4] Festus replied that Paul was being kept in Caesarea, and that he himself intended to go there shortly. [5] "So," said he, "let the men of authority go down with me, and if there is anything wrong about the man, let them accuse him."

[6] When he had stayed among them not more than eight or ten days, he went down to Caesarea; and on the next day he took his seat on the tribunal and ordered Paul to be brought. [7] And when he had come, the Jews who had gone down from Jerusalem [*apo Hierosolymôn*] stood about him, bringing against him many serious charges which they could not prove. (Acts 25)

From a literary perspective, the shift from *Hierosolyma* to *Ierusalêm* and back contributes nothing to the narrative. Neither carries any weighty connotation. Both simply designate a place that is the beginning or end of a journey. The use of different terms for the same reality, however, can indicate a change of sources or an editorial retouch. I suggest that the words in small capitals are just such a retouch. *Ierusalêm* in v. 3 is the one exception in a narrative about Paul's appearances before Festus and before Agrippa and Bernice in Caesarea (Acts 25:1–26:32) which consistently uses *Hierosolyma* (25:1, 7, 9, 15, 20, 24; 26:4, 10, 20).

The original story line reflects an effort of the "Jews of Jerusalem" to succeed where the "Jews from Asia" (Acts 21:27) and the "Jews of Thessalonica" (Acts 17:13) had failed. They denounced Paul before the new procurator Festus in Jerusalem. His presence there, however, was simply a ceremonial visit of introduction, and Festus refused to do business until he was back in Caesarea. There, after a week or so, charges were formally brought, and Festus decided that Paul had no case to answer. He could have been released, had he not appealed to Caesar.

The purpose of the retouch is to graphically underline that the charges against Paul were baseless. If the Jewish authorities were prepared to murder him (cf. Acts 23:12), and thereby risk the displeasure of a Roman governor, it was because they knew that they did not have arguments that would stand up in court. Unconsciously, the editor used the form of the name of Jerusalem with which he was familiar (*Ierusalêm*) and failed to recognize that it clashed with the name used in his source (*Hierosolyma*).

In this case, redactional intention is certainly better than any explanation based on content and may possibly work equally well in other texts. It is a hypothesis that needs to be tried before a content-oriented approach can be accepted.[12]

---

[12] I regret that G.-H. Cho, *Die Vorstellung und Bedeutung von 'Jerusalem' bei Paulus*, Neutestamentliche Entwürfe zur Theologie 7 (Tübingen: Francke, 2004) was not available to me.

4

To Run in Vain
(Gal 2:2)

Ἀνεθέμην αὐτοῖς τὸ εὐαγγέλιον ὃ κηρύσσω ἐν τοῖς ἔθνεσιν, κατ' ἰδίαν δὲ τοῖς δοκοῦσιν, μή πως εἰς κενὸν τρέχω ἢ ἔδραμον ("I laid before them [though only in a private meeting with the acknowledged leaders] the gospel that I proclaim among the nations, in order to make sure that I was not running, or had not run, in vain"; Gal 2:2; *NRSV*). These words form part of Paul's introduction to his version of the meeting in Jerusalem, in the course of which the early church took the crucial decision that Gentile converts did not have to be circumcised.[1]

The verse is remarkable, not for its theological profundity, but for the ambiguity of three key terms—ἀνεθέμην, αὐτοῖς, and τοῖς δοκοῦσιν— which [**384**] are followed by a phrase that at first sight flatly contradicts what Paul has been saying up to this point in the letter, namely, μή πως εἰς κενὸν τρέχω ἢ ἔδραμον. Given the number of variables, which mean even more numerous possible combinations, it is hardly surprising that no consensus exists regarding either the translation or the meaning of the verse. In my view, if we can solve the problem of μή πως εἰς κενὸν τρέχω ἢ ἔδραμον, the ambiguity of the other terms can be easily resolved.

The first thing to be noticed about μή πως εἰς κενὸν τρέχω ἢ ἔδραμον is that the word-order is a little odd. One would have expected the positions of the two verbs to be inverted, as the paraphrase of J. B. Phillips illustrates, "to make sure what I had done, and proposed doing, was acceptable to them."[2] In a temporal sequence it is natural to mention

---

[1] Originally published in *RB* 107 (2000): 383–89, whose pagination appears in the text in **bold**.

[2] *Letters to Young Churches: A Translation of the New Testament Epistles*, Fontana Books (London: Collins, 1955), 112. Similarly Roland Y. K. Fung, *The Epistle to the Galatians*, NICNT (Grand Rapids, MI: Eerdman, 1998), 87 ("to make sure that the race I had run, and was running, should not be run in vain").

the past before the present and/or future. This is so deeply rooted in our psyche that it has influenced even scientific translations. Burton long ago demonstrated that in terms of Greek usage in general, and of Paul's use of μή πως in particular, τρέχω is most probably a present subjective referring to a continued fruitless effort in the future.[3] Thus, the phrase should be translated, "lest somehow I should run or had run in vain."[4]

Nonetheless, while agreeing that τρέχω is subjunctive, Betz translates as if it were a present indicative, "I may be running."[5] In this he is typical. The participle "running" appears in the *RSV* and *NRSV*, with synonyms in *NJB* ("the efforts I was making") and *NAB* ("the course I was pursuing"), and in an array of commentaries.[6] Such translations, however, absorb the past into the present, because Paul has just stated (Gal 2:2b) that he has not changed his [385] preaching. Thus, they offer only a halfhearted contrast with ἔδραμον, which explicitly emphasizes the past. The more accurate rendering of Burton and Longenecker offers a much more satisfactory contrast. This means that Paul, in a context dealing with both past and future, chose to highlight the latter at the expense of the former. This requires explanation.

Before examining the implications of μή πως εἰς κενὸν τρέχω ἢ ἔδραμον, we must recall that Paul in Jerusalem was in a severely disadvantageous position. "The Jerusalem leaders did not come to Paul, he went to them, and it is doubtful they would have feared their ministry was in vain if Paul had not approved of its character or direction. In other words, Paul *de facto* finds himself in a role socially inferior to the Jerusalem leaders in the social network of the church."[7] Whatever the

[3] E. de Witt Burton, *A Critical and Exegetical Commentary on the Epistle to the Galatians*, ICC (Edinburgh: Clark, 1921), 73–74.

[4] So, rightly, Richard N. Longenecker, *Galatians*, WBC 41 (Dallas, TX: Word Books, 1990), 43.

[5] H. D. Betz, *Galatians: A Commentary on Paul's Letter to the Churches in Galatia*, Hermeneia (Philadelphia: Fortress, 1979), 87 note 281.

[6] E.g., Frank J. Matera, *Galatians*, Sacra Pagina 9 (Collegeville, MN: Liturgical Press, 1992), 71 ("might be running"); James D. G. Dunn, *The Epistle to the Galatians*, BNTC (London: Black, 1993), 93 ("was running"); J. Louis Martyn, *Galatians*, AB (New York: Doubleday, 1997), 187 ("was running").

[7] Ben Witherington III, *Grace in Galatia: A Commentary on Paul's Letter to the Galatians* (Grand Rapids, MI: Eerdmans, 1998), 133.

strength of his convictions, Paul was fully aware that he was operating from a position of weakness according to the conventions of his age.

All agree that μή πως introduces a note of heightened apprehension.[8] With profound anxiety Paul contemplates a scenario that could mean the ruin of everything that he held dear. He clearly indicates that he came to the meeting with unnamed figures in Jerusalem as a highly nervous suppliant. His stressed use of the first-person singular unambiguously suggests that he feared the consequences *for himself* if the decision went against him. This further implies that he believed that the Jerusalemites had greater authority than he and that he was subject to that authority. He does not question their right to decide whether what he proposed to do, and what he had in fact done, was useless as regards salvation. We are given to understand that these mysterious personalities in the mother church were the ultimate court of appeal. In spiritual terms, they had the power of life and death over him.

This is the only way that an unbiased reader can understand μή πως εἰς κενὸν τρέχω ἢ ἔδραμον when it is read in and for itself. Two major problems, however, arise when it is read in context. (1) Up to this point in the letter Paul has been insisting that his gospel was God-given (Gal 1:11-12). It was not of human origin. Specifically, it had not been taught to him by the Jerusalem church. Hence, no one, and in particular the leaders of the church in Jerusalem, [386] had any authority to judge his gospel. (2) Hitherto Paul has exhibited no need or desire for anyone else's approval.

Thus, 1:11-12 and 2:2 contradict each other when taken literally. It is most unlikely, however, that Paul would have made such a mistake. In consequence, various efforts have been made to reconcile the two perspectives. In the proposals that have been made, however, this amounts to suppressing one or another of the sources of tension

According to Schlier, Paul did not believe that his encounter with Christ was sufficient to found his apostleship. The approval of the leaders of the mother church in Jerusalem was necessary.[9] Not only does this hypothesis effectively suppress chapter 1, but it makes Paul's seventeen-year delay (Gal 1:18 + 2:1) before seeking authorization inexplicable.

---

[8] BDF §370(2).

[9] Heinrich Schlier, *Der Brief an die Galater*, MeyerK (Göttingen: Vandenhoeck und Ruprecht, 1962), 68.

Why should he wait so long before getting cold feet regarding the truth of a gospel whose power he had experienced both in his own life and in that of all his converts?[10]

Betz takes a very different line: "'to run in vain' must reflect the present concern of the Galatians, who because of this concern are considering circumcision and obedience to the Torah. It is also the concern of the opposition who would have told the Galatians that without circumcision and Torah they are 'running in vain.'. . . Indeed, he would run 'in vain' if the Galatians' acceptance of the gospel and their faith in Christ were not sufficient for their eschatological redemption. . . . Influenced by the anti-Pauline opposition, they [the Galatians] have come to doubt whether Paul's gospel has any salvific validity and power." [11]

Plausible as this might be as a reconstruction of the struggle that the Galatians were going through, it is difficult to see how it could represent the meaning of Paul's actual words. If Paul thought of himself as speaking for the Galatians, why does he use the first-person singular? He could very easily have said something like "lest you had run in vain" (cf. v. 5), i.e., lest your struggle for faith was pointless. Moreover, what sense would the future connotation of τρέχω have in this perspective?

Betz, in sum, does the opposite to Schlier. He effectively suppresses 2:2. In this, he belongs to the majority, but other commentators go [**387**] about it in a different way. Burton speaks for many in writing "that the disapproval of his work by the leading apostles in Jerusalem would seriously interfere with that work and to a serious degree render it ineffectual" and that Paul feared the division of the Christian movement into "a Jewish and a Gentile branch."[12]

I cannot see how this explanation relates to what Paul actually said. If Paul feared a split in the church, why did he not say something like "lest the Jesus movement be split and Christ divided"? Unity was important to Paul, but if it was his concern here, he would have spoken about it as explicitly as he talked about divisions within the community at Corinth (1 Cor 1:11-14).

---

[10] C. K. Barrett, *Freedom and Obligation: A Study of the Epistle to the Galatians* (London: SPCK, 1985), 10.

[11] *Galatians*, 88.

[12] *Galatians*, 73. Similarly F. F. Bruce, *The Epistle to the Galatians*, NIGTC (Grand Rapids, MI: Eerdmans, 1982), 111; Dunn, *Galatians*, 93–94; Longenecker, *Galatians*, 49; Matera, *Galatians*, 80; Martyn, *Galatians*, 193.

The idea of Burton, who is followed by Bruce, that the disapproval of Jerusalem would render Paul's mission ineffective, or that it could not be executed effectively except in fellowship with Jerusalem, can hardly be correct. Jerusalem had not contributed in any way to Paul's highly successful missions, first in Asia and then in Greece. He had no reason to think that the absence of approval in the future would make his work any more difficult.

Finally, it should not be forgotten that at Jerusalem the representatives of the two sides did not work out a common position. They affirmed the unity of the church only insofar as *they agreed to differ*. Thereafter, throughout the world two groups of missionaries were demanding different things of the same converts (see v. 9)![13] Both groups accepted both Jews and Gentiles as members (Gal 3:28), but under different conditions. One demanded the circumcision of Gentiles, while the other did not. At no stage did the Jesus movement present a unified front to the world.

Since the proposed solutions are unsatisfactory, let us look at the problem from a different angle. When Paul wrote Galatians, the issue of the circumcision of Gentile converts had been resolved in his favor. Seen from this perspective, it was in Paul's interest to insinuate the greater status and authority of the Jerusalem leaders. He wanted to give the impression that the Jerusalem leaders were exactly what the intruders in Galatia said they were because he could go on to say that they agreed with Paul rather than with the intruders. The God-given [**388**] character of Paul's gospel was acknowledged by the very people whom the intruders had sworn would condemn him.

In other words, "lest I should run or had run in vain" is a very conscious literary sleight of hand carefully designed to hoist the intruders with their own petard. It might be judged a rather cynical ploy, but it is precisely the sort of clever misdirection that a well-trained orator would employ. It is, in fact, the rhetorical device of *concessio*, which Quintilian defines as "that in which we seem to allow something damaging, just to show our confidence in the cause [*concessio, cum aliquid etiam inicum videmur cause fiducia pati*]" (Quintilian, *Institutio Oratoria* 9.2.51).[14] With the slight emphasis on the future in τρέχω the words lead the reader

---

[13] With regard to the interpretation of the agreement in Gal 2:9, see my *Paul: A Critical Life* (Oxford: Clarendon, 1996), 142–44.

[14] Text D. Russell, *The Orator's Education 9–10*, LCL (Cambridge, MA: Harvard, 2001).

in a false direction until the trap is sprung. Paul's simulated nervousness in anticipation of a negative result gives great dramatic impact to the positive outcome, which is immediately stated without introduction. Titus was not circumcised (Gal 2:3)! The principle of freedom was established.

Now it becomes possible to see why Paul uses such ambiguous terms as ἀνεθέμην and τοῖς δοκοῦσιν. They were part of his rhetorical strategy to put the intruders off balance.[15] Paul could not say flatly that Jerusalem had authority over his gospel. That would have been untrue. If he could not lie, however, he could so set things up that the bias of at least some of his readers, i.e., the intruders, would lead them to a false conclusion. He had to choose terms that for him carried meanings that were consistent with the position he had taken in chapter 1 but that could be understood in another way by his readers. He certainly employed ανατίθημι in the sense of communication among friends or equals,[16] but his readers could understand that he had submitted his program for judgment.[17] Paul used δοκοῦντες ironically, as will become clear in Galatians 2:6, 9, but the term could give the impression that he was both impressed by, and deferred to, the authority of the Jerusalem leaders.[18]

Thus, two renderings of Galatians 2:2 are possible: one expressing Paul's real thought, the other articulating what he hoped his opponents would hear. Paul *said*: "I explained the gospel which I preach [**389**] among the nations to those supposed to be important." The intruders *heard*: "I submitted the gospel which I preach among the nations for evaluation to those in power." Manifestly, Paul intended "lest perhaps I should run, or had run, in vain" to direct attention to what he wanted the intruders to hear. It made their false interpretation inevitable. They could not see that he had his tongue firmly in his cheek!

Postscript

In an article that I know only through the abstract in *NTA* vol. 49, n. 1110, D. F. Tolmie astutely points out that that the phrase "lest perhaps

[15] It is clear from Gal 1:7 and 5:10 that the intruders were still in Galatia.
[16] As in Acts 25:14 and Plutarch, *Moralia* 772D.
[17] As in the historian Polybius, 21.46.11.
[18] See the lists of references in Betz, *Galatians*, 87 notes 276 and 277.

I should run, or had run, in vain" is inconsistent with Paul's literary approach in Galatians 1:1–2:10 but concludes only that it should be considered an unfortunate weak point in his argumentative strategy.[19] Even Homer nods! In the light of the ambiguity of the first part of the phrase, as I have shown in the above article, it is, in fact, a clever rhetorical device to ensure that the intruders took the meaning that Paul did *not* intend.

The partial character of Légasse's translation of Galatians 2:2, "je leur exposai l'Évangile que je prêche parmi les Gentils, mais en privé aux notables, de crainte d'avoir couru en vain,"[20] unconsciously betrays his awareness of the problem of the word order. Regrettably, he does not discuss it. His attention is focused on "le verbe *anatithenai* dont il faut bien préciser le sens. Ce sens n'est pas 'soumettre', en vue d'une approbation, mais 'exposer', dans un climat d'égalité. Les parallèles le font clairement ressortir."[21] The trouble is that *anatithēnai* is also well attested in the sense of "submit."[22] This means that an explanation must be found for Paul's choice of an ambiguous term. I suggested that, as an expert orator, he was preparing the intruders for what they hoped would be his capitulation and then sprang the trap of his assertion that Titus was not circumcised. It must not be forgotten that, although the letter is ostensibly addressed to the Galatians, its real audience was the Judaizing intruders. To have them appear disconcerted in public was a rhetorical victory.

Lémonon agrees that Paul is using the oratorical device of the *concessio*. "Alors qu'il a remporté la victoire, c'est de bonne stratégie de faire une entrée en matière sous le mode de l'humilité, de la concession," but he continues, "en insistant sur l'enjeu de l'Assemblée, c'est l'occasion de souligner l'importance de la communion."[23] He forgets that there was no real communion. Paul and Barnabas on one side and James, Kephas, and John on the other simply agreed to differ with regard to how Gentiles were to be received into the church.

---

[19] "Bang waarvoor? Die betekenis ἀν μή πως εἰς κενὸν τπέχω ἤ ἔδραμον in Galastërs 2:2 (Afraid of what? The meaning of ἀν μή πως εἰς κενὸν τπέχω ἤ ἔδραμον in Gal 2:2)," *HTS Teologiese Studies* (Pretoria) 60 (2004): 487–502.

[20] S. Légasse, *L'épître de Paul aux Galates*, LD Comm. 9 (Paris: Cerf, 2000), 116.

[21] *Galates*, 120, with reference to J. D. G. Dunn, "The Relationship between Paul and Jerusalem according to Galatians 1 and 2," *NTS* 28 (1982): 466–67.

[22] So, rightly, Martyn, *Galatians*, 190.

[23] J.-P. Lémonon, *L'épitre aux Galates*, CBNT 9 (Paris: Cerf, 2008), 85.

5

Nationalism and Church Policy
Reflections on Galatians 2:9

The New Testament mentions a number of shadowy figures whose impact on events was in inverse proportion to our knowledge of their life stories.[1] Barnabas, for example, played a critical role in the missionary outreach of the church of Antioch (Acts 13–14) and in the crucial debate in Jerusalem regarding the admission of Gentiles (Acts 15), but we know only that his real name was Joseph and that he was the scion of a levitical family settled in Cyprus (Acts 4:36).[2] How and why he was converted and what drove him to a mission among Gentiles remain mysteries.

Slightly more is known of James, the brother of the Lord. His early life paralleled that of Paul. Initially hostile to Jesus' mission (John 7:1-9), he owed his conversion to a post-resurrection appearance of Jesus (1 Cor 15:7; cf. Acts 1:14). Thereafter, the resemblances cease. In contrast to the peripatetic and ever-evolving Paul, James never moved from Jerusalem and remained totally faithful to the law.[3] Nonetheless, he was martyred by the Jewish authorities in the interval between the departure of the procurator Festus and the arrival of his successor Albinus.[4]

---

[1] A preliminary version of this paper was delivered at the Annual General Meeting of the Catholic Biblical Association held in Atchison, Kansas (14–17 August 1993). Originally published in *Communion et Réunion. Mélanges Jean-Marie Roger Tillard*, BETL 121, ed. G. R. Evans and M. Gourgues (Leuven: Peeters, 1995), 283–91, whose pagination appears in the text in **bold**.

[2] Late and unreliable traditions make Barnabas one of the seventy sent out by Jesus (Clement of Alexandria, *Stromata* 2:20), a missionary in Rome who converted Clement of Rome (*Pseudo-Clementine Recognitions* 1.7–13), and the author of the *Epistle of Barnabas*.

[3] Eusebius, *History of the Church* 2.23.

[4] Eusebius, *History of the Church* 2.23; Josephus, *AJ* 20.200.

The tensions brought to light by this simple juxtaposition of facts indicate that many aspects of James' character merit exploration, but here I intend to focus on one brief segment of his long career, the period between the Conference in Jerusalem and the incident at Antioch, during which he made two decisions that had a profound influence on the ministry of Paul. He sided with Paul in rejecting the view that Gentile converts to Christianity should be circumcised (Gal 2:1-10) but subsequently opposed him by insisting on the application of Jewish dietary laws in the Christian community at Antioch (Gal 2:11-14). What motivated him to take such apparently contradictory stances?

One would not have expected James to agree with Paul regarding circumcision. If his subsequent career is any indication, James should have been sympathetic to the strong case made by those in the church who insisted on the necessity of circumcision for all believers. At this stage in the history of the church, it was taken for granted by all, including Paul, that salvation was related to the chosen people, who worshiped the one God and to whom he had sent his Messiah. The [284] salvation question, as far as Gentiles were concerned, was: how could they be integrated into God's messianic people?[5] The simple obvious answer was: through observance of God's law signaled by acceptance of circumcision.

There is no real evidence from first-century Judaism that there was a significant body of opinion opposed to circumcision. No one had any doubt about the mandatory character of circumcision,[6] even if there were those who attempted to hide it[7] or who spiritualized it for converts.[8] When conversion without circumcision was contested, circumcision was imposed.[9] As far as Jewish Christians were concerned, circumcision was

---

[5] K. Stendahl, "The Apostle Paul and the Introspective Conscience of the West," *HTR* 56 (1963): 199–215.

[6] Gen 17:10-14; 1 Macc 2:46; Jubilees 15:25-34; Philo, *Mig.* 89–92; Josephus, *AJ* 13.257–58, 318; N. McEleney, "Conversion, Circumcision and the Law," *NTS* 20 (1973–74): 319–41; J. Nolland, "Uncircumcised Proselytes?," *JSJ* 12 (1981): 173–94; J. J. Collins, "A Symbol of Otherness: Circumcision and Salvation in the First Century," in *"To See Ourselves as Others see Us": Christians, Jews and "Others" in Late Antiquity*, ed. J. Neusner and E. Frerichs (Chico, CA: Scholars Press, 1985), 163–86.

[7] 1 Macc 1:15; Josephus, *AJ* 12.241; 1 Cor 7:18; Martial, *Epigrams* 7.35, 82. See R. G. Hall, "Epispasm and the Dating of Ancient Jewish Writings," *JSP* 2 (1988): 71–86.

[8] Philo, *Quaest. in Exod.* 2.2; *Som.* 2.25; *Spec. Leg.* 1.305; *Sibylline Oracles* 4.163–70.

[9] Josephus, *AJ* 20.38–48.

the traditional sign of belonging to the covenant people, which was seen as the divine channel of salvation.

They could point to the fact that Jesus had been circumcised (Luke 2:21) and highlight situations in which Jesus not only obeyed the law (as when he went on pilgrimage to Jerusalem and ate the Passover) but proclaimed its eternal value (Matt 5:18-19) and recommended obedience to it (e.g., Mark 1:40-45). Not unnaturally, therefore, they took it for granted that converts to Christianity should accept the same obligations as converts to Judaism. This point of view is documented in the Jewish-Christian pseudepigraphic *The Epistle of Peter to James* :

> Some from among the Gentiles have rejected my [Peter's] lawful preaching and have preferred a lawless and absurd doctrine of the man who is my enemy [Paul]. And indeed some have attempted, while I am still alive, to distort my words by interpretations of many sorts, as if I taught the dissolution of the law and, although I was of this opinion, did not express it openly. But that may God forbid! For to do such a thing means to act contrary to the law of God which was made known by Moses and was confirmed by our Lord in its everlasting continuance. For he said, "The heaven and the earth will pass away, but one jot or one tittle shall not pass away from the law." (2:3-5)[10]

This theological perspective was given force and actuality by practical considerations. Given the intense eschatological expectation of the beginnings, it is most unlikely that anyone among the first generation of Christians thought that Jerusalem would ever lose its centrality in determining the orientation of Christianity. The imminence of the Parousia, it was felt, guaranteed that the authority of Jerusalem would not be overwhelmed. Traditionally, Jews had thought that [285] a massive influx of Gentiles would take place only in the eschaton.[11] In the present, Jewish Christians believed, there simply would not be enough time for great numbers of pagans to be converted.

This projection, based on the painful slowness of the mission to Jews, failed to take into account the appeal the gospel would have for

---

[10] Translation from E. Hennecke and W. Schneemelcher, *New Testament Apocrypha* II (London: Lutterworth, 1965), 112.

[11] Isa 2:2-4; 49:6; 56:6-7; 60:4-7; Zech 2:11; 8:20-23; Tobit 14:6-7.

pagans. The tremendous success of the missionary effort of the church at Antioch, which demanded only faith in Jesus Christ for conversion, brought home to some law-observant Jewish Christians in Jerusalem that their vision of the church as the flowering of Judaism was in serious danger. If things were permitted to continue as they were, they foresaw themselves becoming an ever-smaller minority in an institution whose only ties to Judaism were the racial identity of its founder and his immediate disciples and recognition of God's preparatory work in the Old Testament. This, they decided, must not be permitted to happen.

Were genuine concern for the safety of Paul's converts lacking, the self-interest of Jewish Christians, of whom James was the leader, should have excluded any compromise on the matter of circumcision. The logic of their inheritance and social role should have made them enthusiastic supporters of the slogan "Unless you are circumcised according to the custom of Moses, you cannot be saved" (Acts 15:1). Yet James did not take this line, nor did a significant number of Jewish Christians in Jerusalem. It would be politically naive to assume that the troika of James, Cephas, and John (Gal 2:9) acted as they did without solid backing in the Jerusalem church. What motivated them?

Haenchen is one of the few commentators to address the issue, but his response can hardly be considered satisfactory. In his view, James and the others started from the premise that "the Law was given solely to Israel," from which they drew the conclusion that it could not be applied to Gentile converts.[12] Not only does such facile logic contradict Jewish conversion practice, but it makes the position of Paul's opponents inexplicable. If the matter was that clear and simple, why should they ever have thought of imposing the law on Gentiles?

If no explanation for James' attitude can be found within the religious framework of Judaism, perhaps an examination of the political situation might be more illuminating. This is, in fact, the case, and the thesis of this article is that Gentile hostility to Jews is the key to understanding the apparently conflicting decisions of James.

In the Roman Empire the Jews had certain rights which were clearly and precisely defined in law.[13] Such privileges, however, were enjoyed at

---

[12] *The Acts of the Apostles* (Oxford: Blackwell, 1971), 468.

[13] C. Saulnier, "Lois romaines sur les Juifs selon Flavius Josèphe," *RB* 88 (1981): 161–98.

the good pleasure of the emperor and never stood in the way of imperial action against Jews. Thus, in AD 19 Tiberius expelled the Jews from Rome.[14] When the [286] Nabataeans attacked and routed the troops of Herod Antipas, probably in AD 29,[15] Rome exacted no vengeance.[16] The situation deteriorated seriously when Gaius (Caligula) came to power in AD 37. His weakness permitted a violent outburst of anti-Semitism in Alexandria in the middle of AD 38.[17] Synagogues were burnt or desecrated, and the mob persuaded A. Avillius Flaccus, the prefect of Egypt, to change the status of Jews in Alexandria from that of resident aliens to that of aliens without right of domicile. Many were massacred, and those who survived were forced into an overcrowded ghetto. Violence ceased with the arrest of Flaccus and the arrival of a new prefect, C. Vitrasius Pollio, in October, but traditional Jewish rights were not immediately restored.

Jews in Palestine can hardly have been unaware of what was happening to their coreligionists in Egypt and feared for themselves. They had good reason. In the spring of AD 40, in reprisal for Jewish destruction of an altar of the imperial cult set up in Jamnia, Gaius ordered the legate of Syria, P. Petronius (AD 39–41), to transform the temple in Jerusalem into an imperial shrine by erecting a giant statue of the emperor as Jupiter in the holy of holies. He was authorized to use two of his four legions to enforce the decision.[18] Petronius managed to delay implementation of his orders until the Jewish king, Agrippa I, in late summer persuaded Gaius to change his mind. For the Jews of Palestine it must have been a nerve-racking six months as they prepared to sacrifice themselves rather than submit. They could never be fully at ease while Gaius lived. In fact, he was planning to go back on his word when he was assassinated on

---

[14] Josephus, *AJ* 18.65–84; Tacitus, *Annals* 2.85.5; Suetonius, *Tiberius* 36.1; Dio Cassius, *History* 57.18.5. These texts are discussed in detail by M. Smallwood, *The Jews under Roman Rule from Pompey to Diocletian: A Study in Political Relations*, SJLA 20 (Leiden: Brill, 1981), 202–10.

[15] C. Saulnier, "Hérode Antipas et Jean le Baptiste. Quelques remarques sur les confusions chronologiques de Flavius Josèphe," *RB* 91 (1984): 365–71.

[16] Josephus, *AJ* 18.109–15.

[17] The detailed documentation furnished by Philo in *Leg.* and *Flacc.* is discussed by Smallwood, *Jews under Roman Rule*, 235–42.

[18] Philo's report—*Leg.* 188, 198–348—is preferable to those of Josephus, *AJ* 18.261–309; *JW* 2.184–87, 192–203. See Smallwood, *Jews under Roman Rule*, 174–80.

24 January 41. Even that did not put an end to Jewish anxiety. Apropos of the imperial statue, Tacitus records that "there remained fears that a later emperor would repeat it."[19]

On his accession to the imperial purple Claudius (AD 41–54) moved quickly to undo the damage caused by the madness of Gaius.[20] The emperor made it very clear, however, that he considered the Jews a disruptive ferment through the empire and that the retention of their privileges was conditional on good behavior.[21] Thus, though the right of religious assembly was guaranteed, when a disturbance broke out in a Roman synagogue in AD 41, Claudius closed the synagogue and expelled the agitators from the city.[22] The Jews were served unambiguous notice that they were on probation.

[287] In the spring of AD 45 the procurator of Judea, Cuspius Fadus (AD 44–?46), ordered that the vestments of the high priest (without which he could not function), which had been released to the Jews by Vitellius in AD 36,[23] should be restored to Roman custody and housed in the Antonia.[24] The Jews persuaded Claudius to rescind the order, but once again they were made to feel fortunate. Whatever their rights, the decision could very easily have gone against them. Their awareness of the fragility of their position was intensified by two episodes which took place when Ventidius Cumanus (AD 48–52) was procurator of Judea.[25] Both involved senseless, deliberate provocation by individual soldiers. The first was permitted to escape unscathed, even though a great many Jews died. The second was executed, but a scroll of the law had been ripped apart and burnt.

---

[19] *Annals* 12.53.

[20] See, in particular, D. R. Schwartz, *Agrippa I: The Last King of Judaea*, TSAJ 23 (Tübingen: Mohr, 1990), 90–106.

[21] The *Letter to Alexandria* (*P. Lond.* 1912) is conveniently available as n. 48 in C. K. Barrett, *The New Testament Background: Selected Documents*, rev. ed. (San Francisco: Harper, 1987), 47–50. See Smallwood, *Jews under Roman Rule*, 245–50, 360–61.

[22] Suetonius, *Claudius* 25; Dio Cassius, *History* 60.6.6; Orosius, *History* 7.6.15–16. For detailed discussion, see G. Lüdemann, *Paul: Apostle to the Gentiles; Studies in Chronology* (London: SCM, 1984), 164–71; J. Murphy-O'Connor, *Saint Paul's Corinth: Texts and Archaeology*, 3rd ed. (Collegeville, MN: Liturgical Press, 1992), 152–60.

[23] Josephus, *AJ* 18.90; cf. 15.405.

[24] Josephus, *AJ* 20.6–14.

[25] Josephus, *AJ* 20.105–17; *JW* 2.223–31.

The inevitable consequence of such repeated incidents—many others may not have been recorded—was a profound sense of insecurity among Jews. If the Romans could not be trusted, then there was nothing for it but for Jews to take matters into their own hands. This is precisely what happened on one of the pilgrimage feasts in AD 51.[26] When Cumanus did not arrest the Samaritans who had slaughtered Galileans en route to Jerusalem, their friends and other Jews took their own vengeance on the Samaritans.[27] Things had reached such a pass that any perceptive observer could have predicted growing tension between the Jews and Rome with an ever-increasing potential for violence. Clearly, it was imperative for Jews to stand together. Only if they were totally united could they survive. Any diminution of commitment could be fatal.

The dilemma in which this placed politically conscious Jewish Christians is obvious. They were first and foremost Jews. All that separated them from their brethren was their acceptance of Jesus of Nazareth as the Messiah. Even without pressure from their coreligionists, their own instincts would have told them that the beginning of the 50s was a time to affirm, not to dilute, Jewish identity. Which end would the circumcision of Gentile converts achieve? Manifestly the latter. To circumcise Gentile converts was to accept them publicly as Jews, even though they had no attachment to Judaism; they were followers of Christ, not of Moses. What loyalty to the Jewish people could be expected of such individuals when hostile pressures began to take their toll? In a crisis, could any nationalistic Jew really trust them? Would such nominal Jews be prepared to sacrifice their lives for the temple and the law?[28]

Questions such as these, I suggest, lay behind James' acceptance of Paul's position on circumcision. James was swayed, not by theological reasons, but by practical considerations. Those who demanded the circumcision of Gentile converts [**288**] might be correct in theory, but it was not the moment to insist on principle. Whatever his personal inclinations, historical circumstances conspired to make James want to

---

[26] Smallwood, *Jews under Roman Rule*, 265 note 29.

[27] Josephus, *AJ* 20.118–24.

[28] These questions highlight the implausibility of R. Jewett's hypothesis that Jewish-Christian concern with circumcizing Gentile converts was motivated by the desire to avoid reprisals from Zealots, who insisted on complete separation from non-Jews ("The Agitators and the Galatian Congregation," *NTS* 17 [1970–71], 205).

find justification for not circumcising Gentile believers. It was this need which made him receptive to Paul's personality and arguments. No more than he had fourteen years earlier (Gal 1:19) could he doubt the sincerity with which Paul explained the implications of his conversion. Nor could he deny the grace manifested in the number of Gentiles who accepted the Pauline gospel (Gal 2:9a). Similar success presumably was duplicated by Barnabas elsewhere. Political expediency, however, was the concrete channel by which grace reached James and enabled him to see such success as evidence of the presence of the Holy Spirit manifesting the divine will that Gentiles should be admitted to the church as Gentiles.[29]

If this interpretation is correct, it should have as a corollary a concern on the part of James to strengthen the identity of Christians who were of Jewish origin by insisting on more exacting observance of Jewish practices. This is precisely what we find at Antioch (Gal 2:11-14).

As in other cities where converts were numerous, the Christian community at Antioch ("the whole church"; Rom 16:23; 1 Cor 14:23) was made up of a number of house churches ("the church in the home of X"; Rom 16:5; 1 Cor 16:19; Col 4:15; Phlm 2).[30] Such an arrangement had the advantage of offering converts a choice. While in theory they were joining a single community, in practice they had to opt for one particular house church among a number. Many and highly diverse factors no doubt influenced selection, but it would be unrealistic to assume that it was normal for individual house churches to have both Jewish and Gentile members. The trend must have been toward the creation of Gentile and Jewish house churches, which were grouped together under the umbrella of one *ekklēsia*. Unless the umbrella was to be a complete fiction, however, there had to be strong and regular links between the different house churches.

The most important of such links was table fellowship. In the ancient Near East a formal meal was the prime social event. To share food was to initiate or reinforce a social bonding which implied permanent commitment and deep ethical obligation.[31] In the eyes of their contemporaries there would have been no genuine community among Christians unless, in addition to the ritual of the Eucharist, they gathered around a common table.

---

[29] This is also the argument used by Luke in Acts 15:8, 12.
[30] R. Banks, *Paul's Idea of Community* (Exeter: Paternoster, 1980), 38.
[31] See D. E. Smith, "Table Fellowship," *ABD*, 6:302-4.

Nowhere was the significance of the meal more accentuated than in Judaism. Sixty-seven percent of Pharisaic legislation which can be dated with some plausibility to the pre–AD 70 period is concerned with dietary laws, 229 specific rulings out of 341.[32] Not all Jews would have been as scrupulous as the Pharisees. It is equally certain, however, [289] that the vast majority would have observed the fundamental distinction between clean and unclean food and would have insisted on the former being entirely drained of blood (cf. Acts 10:14). It was a matter of principle for which their ancestors had died (1 Macc 1:62-63), and it was one of the most obvious identity markers of the Jewish religion. "Separate yourselves from the nations, and eat not with them" (*Jubilees* 22:16). What this meant for relations between Jews and Gentiles is well spelled out by G. Schramm: "The effects of practicing kashruth, from a socio-religious standpoint, are clear: the strictures of kashruth make social intercourse between the practicing Jew and the outside world possible only on the basis of a one-sided relationship, and that is on the terms of the one who observes kashruth."[33]

How, then, did the Jewish and Gentile house churches of Antioch maintain any semblance of unity? Dunn rightly dismisses the two extreme possibilities, namely, that the Jews created no difficulties for Gentiles by ignoring their own laws, or that the Gentiles created no problems for Jews by adopting a Pharisaic level of dietary observance. In this latter case, Peter could not have been said to have "live[d] like a Gentile" (Gal 2:14) simply because he ate with believers of pagan origin. The most probable scenario, he claims, lies somewhere in the middle: "The Gentile believers were already observing the basic food laws prescribed by the Torah: in their table-fellowship with the Jewish believers, in particular,

---

[32] J. Neusner, *The Rabbinic Traditions about the Pharisees before 70*, vol. 3 (Leiden: Brill, 1971), 304. Criticism of the relevance of such statistics are met by J. D. G. Dunn, "Jesus, Table-Fellowship and Qumran," in *Jesus and the Dead Sea Scrolls*, ABRL, ed. J. H. Charlesworth (New York: Doubleday, 1992), 254–72, here 257–60.

[33] "Meal Customs (Jewish Dietary Laws)," *ABD*, 4:648–50, here 650. Similarly E. P. Sanders, "There was no barrier to social intercourse [for Jews] with Gentiles, as long as one did not eat their meat or drink their wine" ("Jewish Association with Gentiles and Galatians 2:11-14," in *The Conversation Continues: Studies in Paul and John in Honor of J. Louis Martyn*, ed. R. T. Fortna and B. R. Gaventa [Nashville: Abingdon, 1990], 170–88, here 178).

pork was not used, and when meat was served care had been taken to ensure that the beast had been properly slaughtered."[34]

In practical terms, when Gentile believers dined with Jews, they accepted the food offered them, even though bloodless kosher meat might not have been to their taste. When Jews dined in a Gentile house, they trusted their fellow believers to offer them food and drink acceptable to Jews.[35] From a Jewish perspective, such trust was a significant concession. Most if not all the meat available outside Jerusalem would have been part of a pagan sacrifice, and the common assumption was that Gentiles would pollute Jewish food and drink if they got the slightest chance (*m. Abodah Zarah* 5. 5). Hence, Jews regularly brought their own food when dining with Gentiles.[36]

The plausibility of this compromise is enhanced by the number of God-fearers at Antioch to which Dunn has drawn attention.[37] If, as seems probable, the majority of Gentile converts at Antioch were drawn from such people, whose attraction to Judaism found expression in the adoption of Jewish practices,[38] it would have been very easy for them to make the relatively minor concessions which made table fellowship with their Jewish fellow-believers possible.

This delicate balance was disturbed by a delegation from Jerusalem; "certain [people] came from James" (Gal 2:12). Prior to their arrival, Peter had had no difficulty eating regularly in Gentile house churches.[39]

---

[34] "The Incident at Antioch (Gal 2:11-18)," *JSNT* 18 (1983): 31.

[35] The king of Egypt said to his guests, the Jewish translators of the Hebrew Bible, "Everything shall be prepared in keeping with your usages, and for me also along with you" (*Letter of Aristeas* 181).

[36] When going out to dine with Holofernes, Judith "gave her maid a skin of wine and a flask of oil, and filled a bag with roasted grain, dried fig cakes, and fine bread; then she wrapped up all her dishes and gave them to her to carry" (Judith 10:5; cf. 12:2).

[37] Josephus, *JW* 2.463; 7.45.

[38] Esther 8:17 LXX and Josephus, *JW* 2.454 show that this is the sense of *ioudaizein* in Josephus' note, "Though believing that they had rid themselves of the Jews, still each city had its Judaisers (*tous ioudaizontas*) who aroused suspicion; while they shrank from killing offhand this equivocal element in their midst, they feared these neutrals as much as pronounced aliens" (*JW* 2:463); see Dunn, "The Incident at Antioch," 26.

[39] The use of the imperfect *synēsthien* "implies that he did this, not on a single occasion, but repeatedly or habitually" (E. Burton, *A Critical and Exegetical Commentary on the Epistle to the Galatians*, ICC [Edinburgh: Clark, 1921], 104).

He continued for a while, but he gradually drew back and ended up by stopping completely:[40] "and the rest of the [**290**] Jewish believers joined him in playing the hypocrite—so that even Barnabas was led astray by their hypocrisy" (Gal 2:13).[41] A barrier rose between the Jewish and Gentile house churches.

What had the people sent by James said to precipitate this crisis? Manifestly, they must have insisted on a more scrupulous observance of Jewish dietary laws than had been the case hitherto.[42] All they had to do was to insist that Jewish believers should no longer assume that Gentile Christians would offer them Jewish food. Such blanket and unwarranted criticism of their standards of honor and decency must have proved extremely offensive to Gentile church members. Those who were prepared to accept the slur and who believed that communion with Jews was essential to preserve the ideal of unity would have had to hand over control of their kitchens to Jews. In other words, they were compelled to "judaize" (Gal 2:14). In order to be faithful to the ideal of one church, they found themselves challenged to adopt a higher standard of Jewish practice than they had ever envisaged.

One's judgment about whether even this would have satisfied James depends on why he intervened at Antioch. The nationalistic reasons which led him to refuse the circumcision of Gentiles also obliged him to insist on the observance of dietary laws for Jewish converts.[43] In both cases it was a question of conserving Jewish identity, in one by refusing dilution and in the other by positive reinforcement. Whatever his personal feelings, such consistency would have been imposed on James by those in Jerusalem who had had to accept his position on the circumcision of Gentile converts.

Peter, another signatory to the Jerusalem agreement, found himself on the horns of a dilemma. His actions had declared the table fellowship of the church at Antioch unobjectionable, but he had sided with James

---

[40] *Hypestellen kai aphōrizen heauton* are also in the imperfect, "indicating that Peter took this step not at once, immediately on the arrival of the men from James, but gradually, under the pressure, as the next phrase implies, of their criticism" (Burton, *Galatians*, 107).

[41] The translation is from R. Longenecker, *Galatians*, WBC 41 (Dallas, TX: Word Books, 1990), 63.

[42] So, rightly, Dunn, "The Incident at Antioch," 31.

[43] Dunn, "The Incident at Antioch," 32.

at the meeting in Jerusalem, and he was responsible for the mission to Jews (Gal 2:8). He was now in a situation where he could not have it both ways. He had to make a public decision, and he opted for his Jewish roots. Not surprisingly, "fear" is the unworthy motive which Paul postulates to explain Peter's option (Gal 2:12).[44] It is entirely possible, however, that Peter read the situation clearly and in great agony of mind decided for those who needed him most. The strength of the Gentile church was apparent at Antioch, and it had dynamic leaders in Paul and Barnabas. The Jewish church, on the contrary, was struggling and would be shattered by the defection of one of its most revered figures.

James' nationalistic concerns served a providential purpose in Jerusalem by inducing him to open the church to Gentiles precisely as Gentiles. Is the same true of his intervention at Antioch? There, his intent was to drive a wedge between Jewish and Gentile believers in order to exclude any communion between Jewish and Gentile house churches. Compromise was by definition excluded. No matter what dietary restrictions Gentiles accepted for the sake of the unity of the community, there would always be further demands from the Jewish side. Radical division of [291] the church at Antioch (and presumably elsewhere) was not just an unfortunate by-product; it was the purpose of James' program to heighten Jewish Christians' awareness of their racial identity.

For Paul, this development was manifestly unchristian. It amounted to saying that Gentile believers were still "sinners" (Gal 2:15). James, on the contrary, did not see it as at all incongruous. In fact, he must have been surprised and offended at Paul's reaction. It is a tragic paradox that James' inherited conviction that separation was the only way to conserve Jewish identity was reinforced by the very argument on which Paul had insisted so passionately during the circumcision debate, namely, that belief in Jesus as the Messiah was *the one essential condition* for membership in the church. James could hardly be blamed for drawing

---

[44] Certain exegetes historicize Paul and debate whether it was Peter's fear of the political consequence of losing his position of power (so H. D. Betz, *Galatians: A Commentary on Paul's Letter to the Christians in Galatia*, Hermeneia [Philadelphia: Fortress, 1979], 109) or fear of the consequences for the Jerusalem church if he, one of its "pillars," were known to fraternize with Gentiles (so Longenecker, *Galatians*, 75, and Sanders, "Jewish Association with Gentiles," 186).

the conclusion that social contacts between Jewish and Gentile Christians were irrelevant.

The shock of being hoist with his own petard was the providential incentive for Paul to reevaluate his own vision of a mixed Jewish and Christian local church in at least two respects. First, what he had always acted on in practice he now was forced to articulate as a principle. Faith in Jesus was basic, but it alone did not make a Christian; what really mattered was "faith working through love" (Gal 5:6). A believer had to live the truth in love ("Without love I am nothing"; 1 Cor 13:2), and a believing community had to "put on love which is the bond of perfection" (Col 3:14). Second, whereas before Paul had been content to let Jewish members of the church continue to observe the law, he now recognized that if the law was given the tiniest toehold in a local church it would ultimately take over, as it had, in fact, done at Antioch. He became resolutely and radically antinomian (cf. Phlm 14).[45]

In the last analysis the nationalism of James had both good and bad consequences. On the positive side, it ensured that Christians did not have to assume the burden of the law and were freed from the constraints of obedience. On the negative side, however, it formally introduced into the church the age-old abyss separating Jew and Gentile and thereby sanctioned a vision of Christianity in which neighbors did not have to be loved.

Postscript

Any plausible reconstruction of the events lying behind Galatians 2:1-14 must deal with the fundamental issue of James' complete about-face. Within a limited space of time he publicly took contradictory positions. At the Conference in Jerusalem he was happy to dispense with the fundamental demand of the law, circumcision, whereas the delegation he sent to Antioch had the mandate to enforce the Jewish dietary laws. In other words, he is at once against the law and for the law. Presumably, he had good reasons for acting as he did, and these can only be brought into the open by asking two questions: (1) why did James agree with Paul

---

[45] See further my *Paul: A Critical Life* (Oxford: Clarendon, 1996), 152–57.

that Gentile converts did not need to be circumcised, and (2) why did James send a delegation to Antioch to enforce the Jewish dietary laws?

Esler is one of the few to pay close attention to the details of Galatians 2:9, δεξιὰς ἔδωκαν ἐμοι καὶ Βαρναβᾷ κοινωνίας ("they gave the right hand of fellowship to me and Barnabas").[46] After pointing out that in the Greco-Roman world verbal agreements were not sealed by a handshake, he draws attention to the fact that in 1–2 Maccabees the expression "to give right hands" occurs eleven times, and in virtually all these instances the gesture is made by a military superior to an inferior. In consequence, he interprets the agreement in Jerusalem thus, "James, Cephas and John condescend to Paul and Barnabas by acting as if they are in a superior position to them in a conflict and are graciously offering a cessation of hostilities."[47]

This is a perfect example of the triumph of erudition over common sense. It beggars belief to imagine that Paul intended his account of the most crucial event in his career to climax with a suppliant whimper, "The leaders in Jerusalem were really very nice to me and Barnabas." He was the winner.

Esler treats κοινωνίας as an appositive genitive. Paul and Barnabas were offered a peace "which consisted of friendship." What did κοινωνία mean in this context? By a process of exclusion he arrives at 1 Corinthians 10:16 as providing the only suitable parallel. Hence, it evoked eucharistic table fellowship. Thus, he maintains, the form of agreement reached in Jerusalem was precisely tailored to the problem of the mixed table fellowship that had brought the delegation from Antioch to Jerusalem. "Interpreting *koinōnia* in the way proposed here means that Peter's visit to Antioch constituted the specific implementation of the agreement" (p. 134). In other words, Peter's mission was intended as a practical demonstration of what the agreement meant—a Jew was fully entitled to share meals with Gentile Christians.

---

[46] P. F. Esler, *Galatians*, NT Readings (London: Routledge, 1998), 132–36.

[47] *Galatians*, 133. In the same context Esler finds it noteworthy that Paul and Barnabas did not receive any binding oaths from the Pillars. Perhaps they were influenced by the teaching of Jesus, who forbade the swearing of oaths; on the historicity of this teaching, see J. P. Meier, *A Marginal Jew: Rethinking the Historical Jesus*, vol. 4: *Law and Love*, AYBRL (New Haven, CT: Yale, 2009), 184–206.

This conclusion forces Esler to confront the question of what the delegation from James' people was doing in Antioch. A vague reference to Mediterranean culture leads him to speculate that the defeated "false brothers" took advantage of the absence of strong-minded principled people like Paul, Barnabas, and Peter to pressure James and John to reverse the agreement and so to save their honor.

In other words, Esler ignores my first question and fudges the second. In this he is in very good company. Witherington, for example, writes,

> It is believable that James, himself a devout Law-observant Jewish Christian, especially if there was threat of the dissolution of the church in Jerusalem due to persecution, might request his fellow Jewish Christians to be Law-observant. It is possible, however, that all he was really requesting was *Peter* be Law-observant since his mission was to Jews. . . . It is also possible that the men who came from James were indeed the false brothers, only James had not viewed them in the same way as Paul (later) did.[48]

Martyn is not very different:

> Peter has left Jerusalem, at least temporarily, and John is no longer mentioned. Political unrest in Judea that would eventually lead to a zealotic uprising may have caused the Jerusalem church to put at its head the man most strict in his zeal for the Law, James. And these developments may have encouraged the False Brothers and other members of the circumcision party to make another attempt to bring the Gentile mission of Antioch under the Law, at least to some degree.[49]

Lémonon follows the same line by suggesting that "'certains gens d'auprès de Jacques" ne sont pas sans rapport avec les faux frères."[50] According to Fee, "We cannot know whether these 'certain people' were

---

[48] B. Witherington, *Grace in Galatia: A Commentary on Paul's Letter to the Galatians* (Grand Rapids, MI: Eerdmans, 1998), 160–61.

[49] *Galatians*, 241–42.

[50] J.-P. Lémonon, *L'épitre aux Galates*, CBNT 9 (Paris: Cerf, 2000), 94, but in the corresponding note he speaks of James' people as an official delegation. His real position, however, is betrayed by the concluding words, "Il semble judicieux, comme Lagrange, ou Osty, de traduire par un formule qui laisse planer un certain ambiguïté comme le texte grec lui-même" (*Galates*, 95).

envoys from James, or whether they were simply itinerants" whom he identifies with those mentioned in Acts 15:24: "we have heard that some went out from us without our authorization and disturbed you."[51]

All push James into the background by focusing attention on the extreme wing of the circumcision party. In other words, it was not really the former who interfered at Antioch but the latter. Légasse explicitly excuses James by assigning only a very minor role to his delegation. Peter acted out of fear of the circumcision party (Gal 2:12), i.e., he was afraid that news of his eating with Gentiles would get to Jerusalem and would expose the community there to persecution by nonbelieving Jews. Hence the sending of the delegation by James, which by implication can only mean that it was directed to Peter (although Légasse does not say so). Following Dunn, however, his preference is for an alternative. "Mais on pourrait tout aussi bien songer aux Juifs d'Antioche, qui aurait considéré d'un mouvais œil leurs coreligionnaires qui en prenaient à leur aise avec les prescriptions de la Tora et qui auraient été prêts à leur charcher noise."[52]

In describing James as "a devout Law-observant Jewish Christian" (Witherington) or "the man most strict in his observance of the Law" (Martyn), these two authors illegitimately abstract completely from Galatians 2:9, where James agrees that circumcision is not necessary for salvation.

To put this into perspective it must be kept in mind that all elements of the law were equally binding. According to Deuteronomy, "You must neither add anything to what I command you, nor take away anything from it, but keep the commandments of the LORD your God with which I am charging you" (4:2; *NRSV*), which is repeated in 12:32, "You must diligently observe *everything* that I command you; do not add to it or take anything from it" (*NRSV*). Clearly it is question of "the *entire* law" (4:8). It is understandable, therefore, that the Essenes of Qumran should commit themselves to the perfect observance of "*all* that is revealed of

---

[51] G. D. Fee, *Galatians: Pentacostal Commentary* (Blandford Forum: Deo, 2007), 74. It goes without saying that those mentioned in Acts 15:24 evoke those mentioned in 15:1, who are to be identified with the "false brethren" of Gal 2:4 and who have nothing to do with James' people (Gal 2:12).

[52] S. Légasse, *L'épître de Paul aux Galates*, LD Comm. 9 (Paris: Cerf, 2000), 160, quoting Dunn, "The Incident at Antioch," 9–11.

all the law" (*1QS* 8:1-2). In the repeated *qôl* one might see a polemic allusion to the "Seekers after Smooth Things" (*4QpNah* 1:2, 7), whose interpretation of the law was less exigent than that of the Essenes. This view of the law as a totality is maintained in the refusal of the Mishnah to distinguish between major and minor precepts (*m. Aboth* 2:1; 3:12; 4:2).

The unity of the whole law is also maintained in first-century Christian sources. The formulation of James cannot be surpassed, "Whoever keeps the law but fails in one point has become guilty of all of it" (2:10). In Galatians 3:10 Paul quotes Deuteronomy 27:26 in a form closer to the LXX than to the MT, which does not have "all": "Cursed be every one who does not abide by *all* things written in the book of the law, and do them." We are fortunate in having evidence from Paul himself as to how seriously this was taken among his contemporaries. His respect for the law is underlined by the number of times he quotes it, but because he rejected circumcision and the dietary laws (Acts 21:21), he was considered a complete renegade worthy of death (Rom 15:31). No Jew would have described Paul as zealously law-observant.

In other words, James' agreement with Paul at the Jerusalem Conference (Gal 2:9) was completely out of character. It went against his character and training and cries out for explanation. I suggested that his motivation was nationalistic rather than religious; it was not the time for Jewish identity to be diluted by the incorporation of pagans into the Jewish people. The value of this hypothesis is enhanced by the fact that it also explains why the same James sent a delegation to promote Jewish observance at Antioch; it was the time to reinforce the Jewish identity of those who had converted to Christianity.

6

Galatians 2:15-16a

Whose Common Ground?

Ἡμεῖς φύσει Ἰουδαῖοι καὶ οὐκ ἐξ ἐθνῶν ἁμαρτωλοί· εἰδότες [δὲ] ὅτι οὐ δικαιοῦται ἄνθρωπος ἐξ ἔργων νόμου ἐὰν μὴ διὰ πίστεως Ἰησοῦ Χριστοῦ, καὶ ἡμεῖς εἰς Χριστὸν Ἰησοῦν ἐπιστεύσαμεν ("We Jews by birth and not Gentile 'sinners'—knowing that 'no one is justified by works of [the] law but only by [the] faithfulness of Jesus Christ'[1]—and we have believed in Christ Jesus . . ."; Gal 2:15-16).[2]

[377] G. S. Duncan said of these verses, "This is the text on which all that follows in the Epistles is commentary."[3] This statement of an exegetical consensus regarding the importance of Galatians 2:15-16 has won the support of all subsequent commentators, even if they are rather vague about why these verses are so crucial. This reason was first spelled out formally by Hans Dieter Betz, when he identified Galatians 2:15-21 as the rhetorical *propositio*, which commands the *probatio* in Galatians

---

[1] "The objective genitive, strictly defined, demands not only a verbal ruling noun but also one whose cognate verb is transitive. The verb *pisteuô* is itself transitive only with the meaning 'to entrust' followed by two accusatives. In the case of *pistis Christou* one may be well advised, then, to speak of genitive of authorship or of origin" (J. Louis Martyn, *Galatians*, AB [New York: Doubleday, 1997], 270 note 171). This is confirmed by a comparison of Gal 2:16 with Gal 2:21 and 3:22.

[2] Originally published in *RB* 108 (2001): 376–85, whose pagination appears in the text in **bold**.

[3] *The Epistle of Paul to the Galatians*, MNTC (London: Hodder & Stoughton, 1934), 64–65.

3–4.[4] This classification has been accepted by Richard N. Longenecker[5] and by James D. G. Dunn.[6] It is rejected by J. Louis Martyn,[7] more because of his conviction that neither Galatians nor any other Pauline letter can be stuffed into the straitjacket of a classical rhetorical outline[8] than because of any disagreement on the significance of the content, which he himself classifies as Paul's "second thesis."[9]

Whatever their terminological differences, both Martyn and Betz consider Galatians 2:15-21 to fall into two parts, namely, vv. 15-16 and 17-21, and identify the former as a statement of shared knowledge.[10] This is the clear implication of εἰδότες, "knowing," as many commentators have recognized[11] but which is given most detailed articulation [**378**] by Longenecker: "The perfect participle εἰδότες functions as an adverbial participle of attendant circumstance ('circumstantial participle') and so adds an associated fact or conception to what was stated in v 15. It is best translated as a coordinate verb with *kai* ('and we know'). Its use here suggests what follows is commonly held knowledge. In fact, the appearance of ὅτι, which is probably a ὅτι *recitativum*, signals that what follows could even be set in quotes as something widely affirmed."[12]

---

[4] *Galatians: A Commentary on Paul's Letter to the Churches in Galatia*, Hermeneia (Philadelphia: Fortress, 1979), 114. He gives credit for an undeveloped insight to Heinrich Schlier, *Der Brief an die Galater*, MeyerK (Göttingen: Vandenhoeck & Ruprecht, 1962), 87–88.

[5] *Galatians*, WBC 41 (Dallas, TX: Word Books, 1990), 82.

[6] *The Epistle to the Galatians*, BNTC (Peabody: Hendrickson, 1993), 132.

[7] J. L. Martyn, *Galatians*, AB (New York: Doubleday, 1997), 231 note 86

[8] *Galatians*, 20–23. This perfectly correct observation has little argumentative impact, because the rhetoricians themselves warn against slavish adherence to rules. See the discussion in my *Paul the Letter-Writer*, GNS 41 (Collegeville, MN: Liturgical Press, 1995), 83–86, in which I quote Quintilian, *Institutio Oratoria* 2.13.1–7, and *Rhetorica ad Herennium* 3.16.

[9] *Galatians*, 25.

[10] Betz, *Galatians*, 18; Martyn, *Galatians*, 249.

[11] Dunn, *The Epistle to the Galatians*, 134. The importance of the participle is ignored by J. B. Lightfoot, *Saint Paul's Epistle to the Galatians* (London: Macmillan, 1910); E. de Witt Burton, *A Critical and Exegetical Commentary on the Epistle to the Galatians*, ICC (Edinburgh: Clark, 1921); F. F. Bruce, *The Epistle to the Galatians: A Commentary on the Greek Text*, NIGTC (Exeter: Paternoster, 1982).

[12] *Galatians*, 83.

To the best of my knowledge, Martyn is the only one to attempt to establish in detail the tradition regarding justification shared by Paul, Peter, James, and Christians of Jewish origin in general. The basis of his reconstruction are three texts generally considered to reflect a pre-Pauline justification tradition, namely, 1 Corinthians 6:11b; Romans 3:25-26a; 4:25. The data they contain can be synthesized as follows: Justification is God's merciful act of pardon, made effective in Christ's death and resurrection, setting right what had gone wrong when his people transgressed his covenant.[13] Were Paul to have quoted this in Galatians 2:15-16 there would be no problem. It was a statement with which both sides were in perfect agreement. What Paul does quote, however, is completely different!

Martyn further notes that the law is not mentioned in this justification tradition because its enduring validity was taken completely for granted. The sins forgiven in justification are those so identified by the law and committed within the framework of the covenant.

Martyn then goes on to assert that the intruders in Galatia and Paul exploited this silence in different ways.[14] Paul interpreted the silence of the justification tradition regarding the law as meaning that the law was no longer relevant and found this confirmed in the response of Gentiles to God's gracious mercy as expressed in the gospel entirely apart from the law. The intruders, on the other hand, accepted the unspoken presupposition of the justification [379] tradition and made the continuing relevance of the law explicit in their demand for circumcision.

Here we touch the nub of the problem. Martyn is certainly right regarding the position of the intruders. "That rectifying transfer [from pagan existence into God's Law-observant people] clearly requires that Gentiles take up observance of the Law."[15] How, then, can Paul claim that οὐ δικαιοῦται ἄνθρωπος ἐξ ἔργων νόμου is agreed common ground

---

[13] This is a highly condensed version of the nine points made by Martyn, *Galatians*, 265–68.

[14] *Galatians*, 268–69.

[15] *Galatians*, 269. The obvious meaning of "works of the law" is "deeds demanded by the law" without any further qualifications; see especially Stephen Westerholm, *Israel's Law and the Church's Faith: Paul and His Recent Interpreters* (Grand Rapids, MI: Eerdmans, 1988), 106–21.

with the intruders? He attributes to these Christian Jews in Antioch and in Galatia a theological position that they explicitly deny.[16]

Only Franz Müssner has clearly seen this problem.[17] Some other commentators betray their awareness that something is not quite right, but only indirectly via an unacceptable solution. For Pierre Bonnard, for example, it is a question of knowledge shared by Paul and "certain" Jewish Christians.[18] Similarly, Frank J. Matera speaks of "Jewish-Christians like Paul."[19] This restriction of φύσει Ἰουδαῖοι is unwarranted. It has no basis in the text.

Unless we assume that Paul told a blatant lie in order to further his argument against the intruders in Galatia, we must ask in what sense he could claim that Jewish believers who insisted on observance of the law were, in fact, committed to the position οὐ δικαιοῦται ἄνθρωπος ἐξ ἔργων νόμου.

Just as he saw the problem clearly, Müssner had an intuition of the solution. The continuation of the citation in note 17 is "aber sich für den Apostel aus dem Urevangelium 'Christus ist gestorben für unsere Sünden' (1 Kor 15, 3; Gal 2, 20) mit logischer Notwendigkeit ergibt."[20] [380] In other words, in Galatians 2:15-16 Paul attributes to Christian Jews a theological position *that they should have defended*, not the one they actually maintained. This insight, however, needs to be developed. Two questions must be answered: (1) Why should Christian Jews, precisely as Jews, have drawn the conclusion that Paul here attributes to

---

[16] For the terminology "Christian Jew" and "Jewish Christian," see Martyn, *Galatians*, 118 note 96, and 588. In both cases the second word indicates the dominant attitude. Paul was a Jewish Christian, whereas James was a Christian Jew, and Peter at Antioch behaved first like one and then like the other.

[17] "ein Glaubessatz, den Paulus hier so formuliert, der jedoch in solcher Formulierung bisher sehr wahrscheinlich nicht zum ausdrücklichen Inhalt des christlichen Glaubenswissens und der Glaubenspredigt gehört hat" (*Der Galaterbrief*, HTKNT 9 [Freiburg: Herder, 1974], 168). For the confusion engendered by failure to see the problem, see, for example, Heikki Räisänen, "Galatians 2:16 and Paul's Break with Judaism," *NTS* 31 (1985): 543–53.

[18] "*Nous*, les judéo-chrétiens. Mais cette nette conscience de la vanité des privilèges juifs ne se rencontrait pas également ches tous les judéo-chrétiens" (*L'épitre de saint Paul aux Galates*, CNT 9, 2e éd. [Neuchatel: Delachaux & Niestle, 1972], 53).

[19] *Galatians*, Sacra Pagina 9 (Collegeville, MN: Liturgical Press, 1992), 99.

[20] F. Müssner, *Der Galaterbrief*, HTKNT 9 (Freiburg: Herder, 1974), 168.

them? Where is the logical necessity? (2) Why did they not, in fact, draw this conclusion?[21]

The most satisfactory basis for an answer to the first question is provided by Terence L. Donaldson, who has convincingly argued that Paul's persecution of Christians was inspired by his perception that their proclamation of Jesus the Messiah as the sole means of salvation was a radical threat to his Pharisaic understanding of the nature of the community of salvation.[22] Paul the Pharisee, of course, believed in the Messiah, but he was a being of the future who had nothing to do with the present, which was dominated by the law. Like other Jews, Paul lived comfortably with a *sequential* relationship: *now* the law, *then* the Messiah. The already/not yet structure of Christian messianism cut right across this belief. Christians were proclaiming that the Messiah had *already* arrived, even though there was no new heaven or new earth. To all intents and purposes the old world of the law continued intact.

The only way that Paul the Pharisee could reconcile the standard Jewish view with that of the followers of Jesus of Nazareth was to postulate the *coexistence* of law and Messiah. Once formulated, this hypothesis appeared absurd. It was blindingly obvious to Paul that a single effect demands one cause, not two. If the law defined the community of salvation, then the Messiah was irrelevant. If the Messiah defined the community of salvation, then the law was irrelevant.

The dichotomy was radical. No compromise was possible. The law and the Christian Messiah were opponents. Only one could survive. As a Pharisee Paul strove for the victory of the law by persecuting Christians in a bid to force them to deny that Jesus was the Messiah. His encounter with Christ in the moment of conversion, however, revealed that he was on the wrong side. Thereafter, Paul strove for the victory of the Messiah. "Because his zeal [as a persecutor] was based on a fundamental opposition between Christ and Torah, his conversion resulted not in a resolution

---

[21] Without specific reference to Gal 2:15-16, but in the context of the Christ/Law antithesis, E. P. Sanders raised the question, "Why did Paul draw conclusions which others in his situation, or in similar situations, did not?" (*Paul, the Law, and the Jewish People* [Philadelphia: Fortress, 1983], 153). He could find no convincing answer.

[22] "Zealot and Convert: The Origin of Paul's Christ-Torah Antithesis," *CBQ* 51 (1989): 655–82.

of the tension between them, but in a different perspective on what he continued to perceive as an unresolvable tension."[23]

The basis of Paul's conviction that Christian Jews should have seen the incompatibility between Christ and the law was that he had perceived it *even when he was still a Jew*. In consequence, he argued, it should be even more obvious to those who had accepted Jesus as the Messiah. As both Antioch and Galatia showed, however, Christian Jews did not draw the same conclusion. Why not?

A clue to the answer to this second question is to be found in Paul's treatment of the legitimacy of eating food offered to idols (1 Cor 8).[24] The community at Corinth was split. The Strong considered that there was nothing wrong with eating meat offered to idols. The Weak disagreed violently.[25] The argument of the Strong was incontrovertible. There was only one God. Idols, in consequence, did not really exist (1 Cor 8:4). Hence, food offered to them was not modified in any way.

Paul recognized that the Weak could not have refused this argument; πάντες γνῶσιν ἔχομεν ("we all have knowledge"; 1 Cor 8:1). Acceptance of monotheism was integral to their conversion. The behavior of the Weak, however, betrayed the superficiality of their assent. It was a purely notional acceptance of a theoretical point. Thus, Paul continued, οὐκ ἐν πᾶσιν ἡ γνῶσις· τινὲς δὲ τῇ συνηθείᾳ ἕως ἄρτι τοῦ εἰδώλου ὡς εἰδωλόθυτον ἐσθίουσιν ("this knowledge is not in everyone. Some through hitherto being accustomed to the idol eat as if it were really being sacrificed to the god"; 1 Cor 8:7).[26] Paul, in other words, makes a distinction "between having knowledge (v. 1) and its being *in* them as an effective and illuminating principle."[27]

---

[23] Donaldson, "Zealot and Convert," 680.

[24] For a detailed treatment, see my "Freedom or the Ghetto (1 Cor. 8:1-13; 10:23–11:1)," *RB* 85 (1978): 543–74 = chap. 8 in my *Keys to First Corinthians* (Oxford: Oxford University Press, 2009).

[25] Their familiarity with idol worship and the type of pressure brought to bear on the Weak (1 Cor 8:10) show them to have been of Gentile origin; see my "Freedom or the Ghetto," 554.

[26] For the justification of this paraphrase, see Gordon D. Fee, *The First Epistle to the Corinthians*, NICNT (Grand Rapids, MI: Eerdmans, 1987), 379.

[27] Archibald Robertson and Alfred Plummer, *A Critical and Exegetical Commentary on the First Epistle of St Paul to the Corinthians*, ICC (Edinburgh: Clark, 1911), 169.

[382] The intellectual conviction that there was only one God had not been fully integrated emotionally by the Weak. Having been conditioned from childhood to think of idols as enjoying a real existence, it was inevitable that there should be a time lag between intellectual and emotional acceptance of monotheism. The objection of the Weak to eating meat offered to idols was not rational but profoundly instinctive. It was a visceral aversion to what appeared to them as a return to a way of life which they had abandoned (perhaps at some cost).

If Paul could understand and sympathize with the emotional problem of Gentile converts, it is at first sight surprising that he refused to empathize with the predicament of Jewish converts, whose emotional attachment to the law had survived their acceptance of Jesus as the Messiah. Structurally the two problems were the same. In the case of Christian Jews, as in the case of the Weak at Corinth, long conditioning prevailed over logic.

We do not know if the Weak at Corinth attempted to disguise the fundamentally emotional nature of their response by appealing to rational argument. Christian Jews certainly did, as we can infer from Paul's words to the Corinthians, ὃ καὶ ἱκάνωσεν ἡμᾶς διακόνους καινῆς διαθήκης, οὐ γράμματος ἀλλὰ πνεύματος τὸ γὰρ γράμμα ("he who qualified us to be ministers of a new covenant not of the letter but of the spirit"; 2 Cor 3:6). Grammatically, "not of the letter but of the spirit" qualifies "new covenant," not "covenant" alone.[28] In a polemic situation Paul is making a distinction between *two types of new covenant*, which is best brought out by a paraphrase, "we are not letter-ministers but spirit-ministers of the new covenant."[29]

Paul is consciously reacting to an understanding of the new covenant which remained inextricably bound up with the law, a new covenant of the letter.[30] The proponents of this view at Corinth were the Christian

---

[28] So, rightly, Hans Windisch, *Der zweite Korintherbrief*, MeyerK (Göttingen: Vandenhoeck & Ruprecht, 1924), 110; Victor Paul Furnish, *II Corinthians*, AB (New York: Doubleday, 1984), 199; Hans-Josef Klauck, *2, Korintherbrief*, Neu Echter Bibel 8 (Würzburg: Echter, 1986), 37.

[29] This suggeston is based on A. Plummer, *A Critical and Exegetical Commentary on the Second Epistle of St Paul to the Corinthians*, ICC (Edinburgh: Clark, 1915), 88.

[30] So, rightly, Annie Jaubert, *La notion d'alliance dans le Judaïsme aux abords de l'ère chrétienne*, Patristica Sorbonensia 6 (Paris: Seuil, 1963), 447. In a similar vein, Ralph P. Martin, *2 Corinthians*, WBC 40 (Waco, TX: Word Books, 1986), 54.

Jews who had previously troubled the churches of Galatia.[31] **[383]** The new covenant theme, which was part of the eucharistic liturgy bequeathed by Jesus to his first followers (1 Cor 11:25),[32] furnished Christian Jews with a perfect argument for maintaining the validity of the law, while at the same time accepting Jesus as the Messiah. Jeremiah had written, "This is the *covenant* which I will make with the house of Israel after those days, says the Lord: I will put *my law* within them, and I will write it upon their hearts, and I will be their God and they shall be my people" (31:33). It would have been very easy for Christian Jews to see a fully internalized law as the explanation of why the people of the Messiah would be holy.[33] The function of the Messiah, in their eyes, was to introduce the eschaton; then it was business as before but in a cleaner, better world.

This devaluation of the role of the Messiah was possible for Christian Jews only because they abstracted from the reality of the Messiah who had, in fact, arrived. For them, as perhaps for Paul prior to his conversion, the Messiah was only a vague theological symbol. Paul's effort to reconcile the death of Jesus with his messianic office forced him to see Jesus as a highly specific individual.

No one expected the Messiah to die. To speak of the death of the Messiah was "an unprecedented novelty" which flew in the face of all popular expectation.[34] Sigmund Mowinckel explains, "It was only natural that in the specific, individual prediction or description of the Messianic kingdom, the kingly rule of the Messiah came as a glorious climax, beyond which neither thought nor imagination sought to reach.[35] . . . But, apart

---

[31] See my *Paul: A Critical Life* (Oxford: Clarendon, 1996), 193–94. The connotation of "the ministry of death, carved in letters on stone" (2 Cor 3:7; cf. 3:3) is unambiguous. The intruders (2 Cor 3:1) were members of a Christian Law-observant mission.

[32] Heinz Schürmann has argued that the Pauline and Lucan version of the word over the cup is more primitive than that of Mark and Matthew: *Der Einsetzungsbericht, Lk 22,19-20. II Teil. Eine quellenkritischen Untersuchung des lukanischen Abendmahlberichtes, Lk 22, 7-38*, NTA vol. 20, bk. 4 (Münster: Aschendorf, 1955), 104.

[33] Isa 60:21; Ezek 36:25; *PsSol* 17:26-27, 32, 43; 18:8; 1 Enoch 5:8-9.

[34] Martin Hengel, *The Atonement: The Origins of the Doctrine in the New Testament* (Philadelphia: Fortress, 1981), 40.

[35] This is confirmed for *PsSol* 17 by Gene L. Davenport, "The 'Anointed of the Lord' in Psalms of Solomon 17," in *Ideal Figures in Ancient Judaism: Profiles and Paradigms*, SBLSCS 12, ed. John J. Collins and George Nickelsburg (Chico, CA: Scholars Press, 1980), 79.

from the idea of an interim kingdom, the idea of the two aeons helped to make the Messiah not only a specific individual, [**384**] but an eternal being."[36] This instinctive assessment was reinforced by the recognition that, as sinless,[37] the Messiah was not subject to the punishment of death.[38]

Paul alone in the early church realized that a sinless Messiah (2 Cor 5:21), who was also a dead Messiah, posed a very serious problem.[39] Its resolution did not prove very difficult, because the possibilities of reconciliation were strictly limited. If someone on whom death had no claim, in fact, died, only one explanation was possible. Jesus *chose* to die. The uniqueness of this insight is highlighted by the fact that only Paul[40] and the so-called Pauline school,[41] which he influenced, insist that the death of Jesus was *self*-sacrifice.[42]

Once Paul had accepted this insight, the death of Jesus ceased to be a problem. The modality of his death then became the central issue:[43] why

---

[36] *He That Cometh*, trans. G. W. Anderson (Oxford: Blackwell, 1959), 324. There is only one explicit reference to the death of the Messiah, namely, 4 Ezra 7:28-30. The Hebrew original of this work must be dated in the early part of the second century AD; see Bruce Metzger in James H. Charlesworth, *The Old Testament Pseudepigrapha* (New York: Doubleday, 1985), 1:520. It is now clear that the Messiah in 4Q285 "is the subject of the verb to kill, not its object" (John J. Collins, *The Scepter and the Star: The Messiahs of the Dead Sea Scrolls and Other Ancient Literature* (New York: Doubleday, 1995), 58–59.

[37] Only *PsSol* 17:36, 38 explicitly mentions the sinlessness of the Messiah, but it is clearly implied in the repeated stress on the holiness of the messianic people (see note 33 above). Their leader could not be a sinner.

[38] On death as punishment for sin and not integral to the structure of the human person, see, in particular, Gen 2:17; 3:23; Wis 2:23-24; Sir 25:24; 1 Enoch 69:11; cf. 98:4. Many other texts could be cited to show the persistence of this belief in Judaism into the later rabbinic period, but my focus is on those which antedate Paul.

[39] Other NT writers proclaim the sinlessness of Jesus (John 8:46; Heb 4:15; 7:26; 9:14; 1 Pet 1:19; 2:22) but do not relate it to his death.

[40] Gal 1:4; 2:20; Phil 2:7-8.

[41] Eph 5:2, 25; 1 Tim 2:6; Titus 2:14; Heb 9:14; 12:2.

[42] Given Paul's rather detailed knowledge of the Jesus tradition, it is not at all impossible that he should have been influenced by Mark 10:45, provided, of course, that it is authentic, but this hypothesis is not at all necessary.

[43] Paul did not inherit his stress on the crucifixion of Jesus from his contemporaries in the early church. None of the fragments of the primitive kerygma that Paul quotes (1 Thess 1:9-10; 4:14; 5:9; Gal 1:3-4; 1 Cor 15:3-5; Rom 1:3-4; 4:24-25; 10:9) mentions the crucifixion.The eucharistic words (1 Cor 11:23-25) and two liturgical hymns (Phil 2:6-11; Col 1:15-20) are equally silent.

did Jesus choose crucifixion, the most horrible form of death? And Paul's answer is that Jesus willed it to demonstrate the extent of his love for sinners.[44] In consequence, [835] Paul could only think of the Messiah as the one "who loved me, that is, who gave himself for me" (Gal 2:20).[45]

This profoundly personal appropriation of the salvation brought by Jesus is the fundamental reason why Paul could not tolerate anything that in any way tended to diminish the salvific act of Christ. The over-whelming experience of Christ's love was the framework within which, for Paul, the logic of the Christian Jews should operate. It is entirely natural, therefore, that Paul should contrast doing "the works of the law" not merely with the advent, or the existence, of the Messiah but with "the faithfulness of Jesus Christ" (Gal 2:16), the ultimate self-sacrifice of the Messiah.[46]

Postscript

The ongoing debate on Galatians 2:15-16 has focused on two points: (1) who exactly are evoked by Ἡμεῖς φύσει Ἰουδαῖοι . . . εἰδότες? and (2) what is the precise force of ἐὰν μὴ? While following the ins and outs of the discussion, I was led to the realization that in 2:16 Paul employs the rhetorical technique of the *concessio*, which he had already used most effectively in Galatians 2:2 (see chap. 4 above).

As regards the first question, it is generally taken for granted that "we . . . know" englobes Paul and the intruders in Galatia. This is denied by W. O. Walker.[47] One of his arguments is taken from M. D. Nanos, who disagrees with the current consensus that Paul's opponents were Christian Jews.[48] On the contrary, he maintains, "they were members of the larger Jewish communities of Galatia entrusted with the responsibility of conducting Gentiles wishing more than guest status within the com-

---

[44] I have developed this point in a forthcoming article: "The Origins of Paul's Christology: From Thessalonians to Galatians" = chap. 10 below.

[45] The "and" here is explanatory; BDF §442(9).

[46] This is further confirmation of the already convincing arguments that πίστις Ἰησοῦ Χριστου here cannot be understood to mean "faith in Christ."

[47] "Does the 'We' in Gal 2:15-17 Include Paul's Opponents?," *NTS* 49 (2003): 560–65.

[48] The best presentation of the evidence is that of Martyn, *Galatians*, 120–26.

munities through the ritual process of proselyte conversion by which this is accomplished."[49]

Since Nanos' book was not available to me, I cannot say what arguments he invokes to support this conclusion. Two major objections, however, can be raised against his thesis. First, in the first century Jews were not aggressive proselytizers.[50] They welcomed those who sincerely wished to become members of their community, but they did not seek out Gentiles or try to persuade them to "judaize" (Gal 2:14). Philo's counsel of generous acceptance of converts (*Virt.* 102) would be pointless were Jews active missionaries. The principle that governed their attitude toward non-Jews is explicitly formulated by Josephus:

> Moses took the best of all measures to secure our own customs from corruption, and to throw them open ungrudgingly to any who elect to share them. To all who desire to come and live under the same laws with us, he gives a gracious welcome. . . . But he did not wish that those who come into contact with us accidentally should share our intimacy. (*Against Appion*, 2.209-10; see 2.261)

From this perspective, Matthew's "Woe to you scribes and Pharisees, hypocrites! for you traverse sea and land to make a single proselyte" (23:15) is best understood as meaning that the Pharisees, who had the Sadducees and the Essenes as competitors, did everything possible to win *Jews to their vision of Judaism.*

The second objection is that, to the best of our knowledge, there were no Jewish communities in North Galatia to sponsor or exercise the activity that Nanos postulates. Stephen Mitchell has shown that while there were Jewish communities on the western and southern fringes of Phrygia, there is no trace of any Jewish presence in northern Galatia.[51]

A further argument advanced by Walker is that when Paul has his opponents in view he speaks *about* them using the third person. He never addresses them in the second person. Thus, were 2:15-16 to include the intruders, it would be a complete departure from his usual practice.

---

[49] *The Irony of Galatians: Paul's Letter in First-Century Context* (Minneapolis: Fortress, 2002), 6. I owe this quotation to p. 564 of Walker's article.

[50] For details see my "A First-Century Jewish Mission to Gentiles," *Pacifica* 5 (1992): 32–42.

[51] *Anatolia: Land, Men, and Gods in Asia Minor* (Oxford: Clarendon, 1993): 2:31–37.

I can agree with this observation, but only up to a point. Even though the letter is addressed to the Galatians (1:2; 3:1), it is really directed to the Judaizers, who were still present (1:7; 5:10) and would have heard the letter when it was read aloud (cf. Col 4:16). Only this hypothesis does justice to Paul's assumption that some of his hearers would grasp the force of arguments which depended on a detailed knowledge of Jewish tradition. The Galatians were pagans (4:8), and since there were no Jewish synagogues in the area (see above), the presence of "God-fearers" among them is most improbable. Given his choice of this strategy, it is not surprising that on occasion Paul should address his opponents directly.

Walker's principal argument is derived from Paul's use of the first-person plural elsewhere in Galatians. "We/our" can englobe (1) all Christians indiscriminately be they of Jewish or Gentile origin; (2) primarily Jewish Christians but secondarily Gentile Christians; and (3) Paul plus one or more of his associates, thereby implicitly contrasting them with others.[52] He maintains that only the third usage is appropriate in Galatians 2:15-17 because the first two are excluded by the phrase "Jews by birth and not Gentile sinners," which makes it clear to Walker that the "we" of these verses refers to Jews but not to Gentiles. If "we" is used in the third sense, the implicit "they" can only be the intruders, who in consequence cannot be englobed in the "we." When this data is inserted into the context of Galatians 2:1-21, Walker concludes, "the 'we' of 2:15-17 refers in the first instance to Paul and Cephas, with possibly a secondary reference to Barnabas and 'the other Jews' in the Galatian churches."[53]

This objection would have been convincing, if I believed, as I once did, that the intruders in Galatia were accredited representatives of the Jerusalem church. The more I reflected, however, the more I failed to find any reason why this church would invest so much to disrupt a law-free mission that had first been approved privately by Peter (Gal 2:7b-8) and then formally by the leaders of the church in Jerusalem (Gal 2:9).

The only church that had a vested interest in the lifestyle of Pauline foundations was Antioch-on-the-Orontes.[54] It had commissioned his

---

[52] "Does the 'We' in Gal 2:15-17 Include Paul's Opponents?," 561.

[53] "Does the 'We' in Gal 2:15-17 Include Paul's Opponents?," 565.

[54] For more detail, see my *Keys to Second Corinthians* (Oxford: Oxford University Press, 2010), 46–50.

mission to the west (Acts 13:1-3; 15:40-41). Thus, when he founded churches in Galatia, Philippi, Thessalonica, and Corinth, he was acting as its agent, and Antioch reasonably considered his foundations daughter churches. Thus, when Cephas and Barnabas led Antioch to "judaize" (Gal 2:11-14), they felt it imperative to send a delegation to follow Paul's path to the west. His boastful nature (Gal 1:14; 1 Cor 15:10), which poured forth his success, guaranteed that they had all the necessary information, perhaps even to the names of those who had emerged as leaders in the various churches. If the mother church had changed its ethos from law-free to law-observant, then it was imperative that her daughters should do the same. The principle implicit in such assumption of authority is manifest in Antioch's submission to Jerusalem, from which it had been founded (Acts 11:19).[55] It was this that justified James' intervention (Gal 2:12).

When the situation in Galatia is viewed in this light, the intruders were the agents of the church of Antioch, whose leaders certainly numbered Barnabas and possibly Cephas. Thus, if Walker concedes that the "we" of 2:15-17 englobes Cephas and Barnabas, then it necessarily includes his opponents in Galatia!

Ian Scott implies an objection to this reconstruction in writing, "When the Apostle claims that 'we know' the contents of this verse, he is speaking about an agreement that he could take for granted in his argument with Peter and the others in Antioch. Yet the flow of Paul's argument in 2:15-21 and throughout 3:1–5:6 presumes that these ideas are controversial in the current Galatian setting."[56] This makes sense only on the assumption that Scott accepts the common view that the intruders in Galatia came from Jerusalem. I have already drawn attention to the improbability of this hypothesis. Only Antioch had an interest in changing the ethos of churches founded under its mandate.

Scott's article, however, alerted me to a question that I had not considered. In 2:15-17 is Paul going over the heads of the intruders to their masters in Antioch? He had once been in full agreement with Cephas and

---

[55] Thus, Jerusalem was the "grandmother church" of Galatia, Philippi, Thessalonica, and Corinth, but this does not mean that Jerusalem intervened directly in the affairs of these foundations. They were the responsibility of Antioch.

[56] "Common Ground? The Role of Galatians 2:16 in Paul's Argument," *NTS* 53 (2007): 425–35, here 433.

Barnabas regarding a law-free mission. They had turned against him in Antioch, but only on the matter of Jews eating with Gentiles. Nothing, apparently, was said about circumcision. Was it possible, therefore, that the intruders had exaggerated their mandate and had gone much further than the church of Antioch had intended by insisting on circumcision? In other words, had Cephas and Barnabas recognized their error and returned to their original liberal position on Gentiles and the law?

The answer, I am convinced, must be in the negative. Paul's identification of James' people as οἱ ἐκ περιτομῆς ("those of the circumcision"; Gal 2:12) reveals his conviction that their insistence on *kashrut* was only the thin end of the wedge. Moreover, the motives that he ascribes to Peter and Barnabas, namely, "fear" and "insincerity," respectively (2:12-13), make it rather unlikely that he is thinking of them charitably in 2:15. Finally, it is most improbable that the intruders (the only source of information) would have informed the Galatians that they were proposing the strictest possible interpretation of their mandate.

I must reiterate, therefore, that in 2:16 Paul is assuming as common ground what, in fact, was not agreed by his opponents. The issue was so clear to him that he could not believe that they could not see it also.[57] There is also the possibility, as we shall see below, that Paul was being rhetorically devious in precisely the same way that I have argued apropos of Galatians 2:2 (chap. 4 above).

Now we turn to the force of ἐὰν μή in the phrase οὐ δικαιοῦται ἄνθρωπος ἐξ ἔργων νόμου ἐὰν μὴ διὰ πίστεως Ἰησοῦ Χριστοῦ (Gal 2:16), which has generated significant debate. In what follows I leave aside the question of whether "faith of Jesus Christ" should be treated as a subjective or objective genitive, because it is not germane to the point at issue, and for convenience accept the translation of the authors cited.

The major translations render ἐὰν μὴ by "but" and so understand the relationship between "works of the law" and the "faith of Jesus Christ" as adversative; they are mutually exclusive. Hence, "we know that a person is justified not by the works of the law *but* through faith in Jesus Christ"

---

[57] This was not uncommon. For example, he told the Corinthians that they were "free from the Law" without explaining any of the nuances and was astounded to find that they had taken him literally and now believed that they were free to do whatever they liked (1 Cor 6:12; 10:23).

(e.g., *NRSV*, *NJB*, *NAB*). This interpretation has the report of virtually all the most authoritative commentators.[58]

This is rather surprising, since the adversative use of ἐὰν μὴ is not Pauline usage. Apart from Galatians 2:16, the phrase occurs eleven times in the undisputed letters of Paul, and in each case it must be translated by "unless, except," as A. Das' brief survey demonstrates.[59] This had been pointed out ninety years ago by Burton, who at the same time introduced an important distinction:

> ἐὰν μὴ is properly exceptive, not adversative (cf. on 1:19), but it may introduce an exception to the preceding statement taken as a whole or to the principal part of it—in this case to οὐ δικαιοῦται ἄνθρωπος ἐξ ἔργων νόμου or to οὐ δικαιοῦται ἄνθρωπος. The latter alternative is clearly to be chosen here, since the former would yield the thought that a man can be justified by works of the law if this be accompanied by faith, a thought never expressed by the apostle and wholly at variance with his doctrine as unambiguously expressed in several passages.[60]

It is noteworthy that Burton invokes no grammatical authority for the distinction between the whole of the preceding statement and one of its parts. Given his subsequent remarks, one can only infer that he invented the distinction because the natural understanding that the exception was to the statement taken as a whole yielded a meaning that he could not accept. There were two ways out of this dilemma. One was to give ἐὰν μὴ an adversative sense. The other was to limit the extent of the exception. The former offended Burton's refined grammatical sense, which left him with no alternative than to invent the limited application of ἐὰν μὴ.

W. O. Walker attempts to rescue Burton by explaining his solution as an ellipsis [in square brackets] within a parenthesis (in round brackets), and thus translates: "knowing that a person is not justified by works of the law ([a person is not justified] except through faith in Jesus Christ)."[61] This does not read naturally; to balance the negative first part, one would

---

[58] E.g., Schlier, *Der Brief an die Galater*, 92, note 6; Betz, *Galatians*, 113, 115–17; Martyn, *Galatians*, 251.

[59] "Another Look at ἐὰν μὴ in Galatians 2:16," *JBL* 119 (2000): 530–31. He is also careful to note, however, that ἐὰν μὴ is definitely adversative in John 5:19 and 15:4a.

[60] *Galatians*, 121.

[61] "Translation and Interpretation of ἐὰν μὴ in Gal 2:16," *JBL* 116 (1997): 515–20.

have expected a positive second part, namely, "a person is justified only through faith in Jesus Christ." The very awkwardness of Walker's reconstruction discloses the extent to which the text has been forced to reveal the solution he desires.[62]

In an article, whose title proved to be programmatic, J. D. G. Dunn retained the exceptive force of ἐὰν μὴ but accepted that it applied to the whole of the preceding statement. Paul was indeed attributing a salvific effect to "doing the works of the law," provided, however, that one also had faith in Jesus Christ.[63] This interpretation, however, owed less to the objective laws of grammar than to Dunn's conviction that the law is still binding on Christians with the exception of those precepts that served to found Jewish identity. Dunn recognized that his interpretation of 2:16a was contradicted by the second part of that verse, ἵνα δικαιωθῶμεν ἐκ πίστεως Χριστοῦ καὶ οὐκ ἐξ ἔργων νόμου ("that we might be justified by the faith of Christ and not by works of the law"), where the relationship is clearly adversative. He got around this difficulty, however, by claiming that in 2:16 Paul revealed a little of the evolution of his thought. He once accepted that obedience to the whole law and faith in Christ were complementary but eventually concluded that one was saved only by faith in Christ.

Not only is it difficult to find a reason why Paul would act in this way,[64] but it is extremely improbable that Paul gave any salvific value to the law once he had accepted Jesus as the Messiah. One does not need two causes to produce a single effect. If the Messiah was the sole instrument of salvation, then the law was irrelevant, and vice versa. Undoubtedly, there was a stage in Paul's career when he tolerated obedience to the law on the part of his Jewish converts. He accepted their need to preserve their ethnic identity, but he attached no religious value to such obedience. This attitude, however, changed to radical antinomianism (Acts 21:21) after the incident at Antioch (Gal 2:11-14), which brought it home to him that, if the law is given the slightest foothold in a Christian community, it will eventually become a rival to Christ.

[62] For an incisive critique of Walker, see Das, "Another Look," 532 note 11.

[63] "The New Perspective on Paul," *BJRL* 65 (1983): 95–122, here 112, reprinted in his *Jesus, Paul, and Galatians* (Louisville: Westminster/Knox, 1998), 195, with additional comments, 206–14.

[64] So, rightly, Räisänen, "Galatians 2:16 and Paul's Break with Judaism," 543–53, here 547.

To date, the most important contribution to the ἐὰν μὴ debate has come from D. Hunn, because she confronts the fundamental question: does the grammar of Paul's time permit him the options that scholars have discerned in Galatians 2:16?[65]

As regards the NT, she makes two observations, " 'Εὰν μὴ as exceptive of an entire statement is the rule both inside and outside the NT" and agrees with A. Das that, out of the approximately fifty instances of ἐὰν μὴ in the NT, only John 5:19 and 15:4 use it adversatively (p. 283). She points out, however, that in both the Johannine instances ἐὰν μὴ can be read as exceptive of the main point in such a way that the result makes good sense. "However an exceptive interpretation renders 'on his own' in John 5:19 and 'of itself' superfluous, and thus loses the emphasis clearly intended in the text" (p. 286).

Moving outside the NT, Hunn finds ἐὰν μὴ as excepting only the principal part of a statement in Plutarch, *Moralia* 454A (LCL 6.96–99); Origen, *Contra Celsum* 4.26 (PG 11:1065b; *ANF* 4.507); Origen, *Comm. in ev. Matt.* 11.17 (PG 13:960b; *ANF* 10.445); and Epictetus, *Encheiridion* 31.2 (LCL 2.512–13). The time span of these authors covers the Pauline period.

As regards the use of ἐὰν μὴ in an adversative sense, it appears in Origen, *Comm. in ev. Matt.* 10.19 (PG 13:884d; *ANF* 10.426); Origen, *Contra Celsum* 4.3 (PG 11:1032c; *ANF* 4.498); Clement of Alexandria, *Stromates* 3.15 (PG 8:1197b); Dionysius of Halicarnassus, *Roman Antiquities* 10.31.5 (LCL 6.272–75). Again the time span is relevant to Paul.

From this data she concludes, "The list of examples is long enough to substantiate the flexibility of ἐὰν μὴ to state both a partial exception and an adversative relationship. The difference between the two functions is primarily one of emphasis." Then she formulates a crucial grammatical rule, "If the extra word or phrase in the main clause is important enough to serve as a point of contrast, ἐὰν μὴ is adversative. If not, it is exceptive" (p. 288).

She then examines Galatians 2:16 in the light of this rule: "we consider the phrase, ἐξ ἔργων νόμου, in verse 16a to see whether it serves as a contrast to διὰ πίστεως Ἰησοῦ Χριστοῦ or whether it is an extraneous phrase simply to be skipped over" (p. 289). Most reasonably, she goes on to say that to ask the question is to answer it. In the light of 2:19-21

---

[65] " 'Εὰν μὴ in Galatians 2:16: A Look at Greek Literature," *NovT* 49 (2007): 281–90.

and 3:2-5, "works of the law" is clearly integral to the context of 2:16; it is not adventitious. Hence, in that verse ἐὰν μὴ can only be adversative.

The simplicity of this conclusion is possible only because of her initial assertion that "ἐὰν μὴ in Gal 2:16 cannot be exceptive of the entire main clause" (p. 289). In the light of what she has said above, this cannot be a rule of grammar. Her basis, therefore, must be interpretative, namely, that Paul would defeat his own purpose if 2:16a was intentionally ambiguous. "Paul clearly does seek to establish common ground. Reinterpreting to his own advantage the statement on which all had agreed, however, is a bait-and-switch that destroys the common ground he built, and his opponents would easily shoot down such an argument" (p. 289).

Here, I part from Hunn because she fails to deal adequately with the circumstances of the letter.[66] As I have argued earlier in this postscript, the letter was formally addressed to the Galatians but was in fact directed to the Judaizing intruders. One of Paul's tactics was to disconcert them in public, as we have seen above apropos of Galatians 2:2. The Galatians might not have understood the details of the debate, but they were shrewd enough to recognize when the intruders were knocked off balance. To show the Galatians that the Judaizers were unsure of themselves was one of the most convincing arguments that Paul could use against a possible change of allegiance on the part of his converts.

If the intruders understood Galatians 2:16a in the sense that Dunn proposes, Paul would seem to have given them everything they wanted.[67] It appeared to legitimize a law-observant mission to Gentiles, and the Judaizers would have basked complacently in the concession, perhaps superior glances flickered from one to the other. They had only heard, however, what they wanted to hear, and failed to recognize that the words could carry a very different meaning. They had been subtly led astray.[68] Once they had taken the bait and the hook was well set, Paul struck with

---

[66] This is also true of Das, who rightly remarks on the intentional ambiguity of 2:16a ("Another Look," 537) but without seeing how it served Paul's purpose.

[67] This is the rhetorical technique of the *concessio*, "in which we seem to allow something damaging, just to show our confidence in the cause [*concessio, cum aliquid etiam inicum videmur cause fiducia pati*]" (Quintilian, *Institutio Oratoria* 9.2.51; text D. Russell, *The Orator's Education 9–10*, LCL [Cambridge, MA: Harvard, 2001]).

[68] On the rhetorical technique of the *ductus subtilis*, see Quintilian, *Institutio Oratoria* 9.2.59–66.

vigor in words that carried not the slightest hint of ambiguity, ἡμεῖς εἰς Χριστὸν Ἰησοῦν ἐπιστεύσαμεν ἵνα δικαιωθῶμεν ἐκ πίστεως Χριστοῦ καὶ οὐκ ἐξ ἔργων νόμου, ὅτι ἐξ ἔργων νόμου οὐ δικαιωθήσεται πᾶσα σάρξ ("we believed in Christ Jesus in order that we might be justified by faith of Christ and not by works of the law, because by works of the law no one shall be justified"; 2:16b). No doubt the Judaizers jerked upright, and the smiles were wiped from their faces to the great satisfaction of Paul's partisans among the Galatians.

7

The Irrevocable Will
(Gal 3:15)

Ἀδελφοί, κατὰ ἄνθρωπον λέγω· ὅμως ἀνθρώπου κεκυρωμένην διαθήκην οὐδεὶς ἀθετεῖ ἢ ἐπιδιατάσσεται ("Let me give you, friends, an example that everyone will understand. Once a person's will has been ratified, no one can set it aside or add to it"; Gal 3:15).[1] Paul's purpose in introducing this example is to clarify the relationship between the promise to Abraham and the Mosaic law, by insisting that the latter cannot annul or significantly modify the former.

[**225**] Some commentators simplify the argument by claiming that οὐδείς is someone other than ἄνθρωπος, and so should be translated "no one else."[2] No one but the owner has any rights over his property. The justification for stating something so obvious can only be the assumption that Paul actually attributed the law to someone other than God. Martyn is formal, "Paul intends to preclude the thought that the *angels* responsible for the Law can have changed the covenant that *God* made with Abraham."[3]

---

[1] Originally published in *RB* 106 (1999): 224–35, whose pagination appears in the text in **bold**.

[2] So Marie-Joseph Lagrange, *Saint Paul. Épitre aux Galates*, EBib (Paris: Gabalda, 1925), 76; George S. Duncan, *The Epistle of Paul to the Galatians*, MNTC (London: Hodder & Staughton, 1934), 154; F. F. Bruce, *The Epistle of Paul to the Galatians: A Commentary on the Greek Text*, NIGTC (Exeter: Paternoster, 1982), 168; J. D. G. Dunn, *The Epistle to the Galatians*, BNTC (Peabody: Hendrickson, 1993), 182; J. Louis Martyn, *Galatians: A New Translation with Introduction and Commentary*, AB 33A (New York: Doubleday, 1997), 338.

[3] *Galatians*, 338. Elsewhere Martyn insists, "God had no role of any kind in the genesis of the Law. . . . The angels—not God—instituted the Sinaitic Law through the hand of Moses" (*Galatians*, 366–67). His sole argument is that Gal 3:20 necessarily implies

In Galatians 3:19 Paul does speak of the law as διαταγεὶς δι' ἀγγέλων ("ordained by angels"), but would any contemporary have thought for a moment that angels were the originators of the law, even though διά can carry that sense?[4] The association of angels with the giving of the law at Sinai is well documented,[5] and, given the postexilic emphasis on the transcendence of God, it was inevitable that eventually they should be inserted as mediators between God and Moses. God did not intervene directly in history but through his "messenger(s)." Hence the popular belief that the law was given by angels, which is attested by Josephus (*AJ* 15.136), by the New Testament (Acts 7:38, 53; Heb 2:2), and by early Christian works such as *Hermas* (Sim. 8.3.3). The reaction of *Abot Rabbi Nathan* shows that there were those who took this theological fiction literally,[6] [**226**] but this is a far cry from the idea that someone other than God, namely, angels, was the author of the law. It was always *the law of God* (cf. Rom 3:2; 7:22, 25; 8:7), as the divine passive προσετέθη ("it was added"; Gal 3:19) confirms.[7] Finally, would Paul have risked his entire credibility by ascribing the origin of the law to angels when his opponents could draw on the whole of Jewish tradition to show that its author was God?[8]

---

a plurality of givers, who can only be angels, since there is only one God. This verse, however, simply points out that the very notion of mediator demands two parties and says nothing about the composition of either party; see E. Burton, *A Critical and Exegetical Commentary on the Epistle to the Galatians*, ICC (Edinburgh: Clark, 1921), 191.

[4] BAGD dia, III, 2, b.

[5] See, in particular, H. D. Betz, *Galatians: A Commentary on Paul's Letter to the Churches in Galatia*, Hermeneia (Philadelphia: Fortress, 1979), 169; and Richard Longenecker, *Galatians*, WBC 41 (Dallas, TX: Word Books, 1990), 139–40.

[6] "'Moses received Torah from Sinai.' Not from the mouth of an angel and not from the mouth of a Seraph, but from the mouth of the King over the Kings of Kings, the Holy One" (Anthony J. Saldarini, *The Fathers according to Rabbi Nathan* [Leiden: Brill, 1975], 25). In addition, see the texts collected by Longenecker, *Galatians*, 142–43.

[7] So, rightly, Charles H. Cosgrove, "Arguing Like a Mere Human Being: Galatians 3:15-18 in Rhetorical Perspective," *NTS* 34 (1988): 536–49, here 540. Note a similar divine passive in the immediate context, "the promises were spoken" (3:16).

[8] In Martyn's brilliant reconstruction of the intruders' argument in Galatia, he has them say, "Later, when God handed down the Law on tablets of stone at Sinai, he spoke once again by the mouths of his glorious angels, for they passed the Law through the hand of the mediator, Moses (Gal 3:19). And now the Messiah has come, confirming for eternity God's blessed Law, revealed to Abraham and spoken through Moses" ("A

The exclusion of the possibility that anyone other than God authored the law forces us to recognize that the principle enunciated in Galatians 3:15 concerns the limitation of a testator's freedom. Once he has ratified his will, Paul claims, he cannot change it.[9] All commentators, however, agree that this principle has no basis in any legal code in the ancient world. A testator could change his will at any time.[10]

In desperation, commentators have favored the hypothesis of Ernst Bammel that although Paul uses διαθήκη in 3:15 he was actually thinking of the Jewish legal instrument called *mattenat bari*.[11] This was an irrevocable deed of gift which permitted the donor to retain the usufruct during his lifetime. Similar legal instruments existed in Greek and Roman law, and both contained explicit mentions of the death of the testator.[12] The fact that the beneficiary acquired full use of the property only after the death of the testator appeared to legitimize the assumption that each of these documents was in some sense a διαθήκη.

In fact, of course, a deed of gift, which is effective immediately, is completely different from a will, which becomes effective only at [227] some future date. The deed of gift is irrevocable because, once transferred, the property no longer belongs to the original owner. A will, on the other hand, can be revoked because the testator retains absolute control over his property. The distinction between the two types of document is a matter of elementary common sense. It is abundantly confirmed by the use of a *mattenat bari* to circumvent the testamentary regulations of Deuteronomy 21:15-17.[13]

Law-Observant Mission to Gentiles," in *Theological Issues in the Letters of Paul* [Edinburgh: Clark, 1997], 21).

[9] So Heinrich Schlier, *Der Brief an die Galater*, MeyerK (Göttingen: Vandenhoeck & Ruprecht, 1962), 144.

[10] See the references in Betz, *Galatians*, 155 notes 18 and 19.

[11] "Gottes ΔΙΑΘΗΚΗ (Gal. III, 15-17) und das jüdische Rechtsdenken," *NTS* 6 (1959–60): 313–19.

[12] References in Longenecker, *Galatians*, 129.

[13] "If a man says, 'Such-a-one, my first born son, shall not receive a double portion', or 'Such-a-one, my son, shall not inherit with his brethren', he has said nothing, for he has laid down a condition contrary to what is written in the Law. If a man apportioned his property to his sons by word of mouth, and gave much to one and little to another, or made them equal with the firstborn, his words remain valid. But if he had said that so it should be 'by inheritance', he has said nothing. If he had written down, whether

A new element was introduced into the debate by Timothy Lim.[14] *PYadin* 19 comes from the Babatha archive found in a cave in Nahal Hever near En Gedi on the Dead Sea and is dated to 16 April 128 AD. The relevant portion reads,

> Judah son of Elazar Khthousion, an En-gedian domiciled in Maoza, willed to Shelamzious, his daughter, all his possessions in En-gedi, viz. half of the courtyard across from(?) the synagogue(?) . . . including(?) half of the rooms and upper-storey rooms therein, but excluding the small old court near the said courtyard, and the other half of the courtyard and rooms Judah willed to the said Shelamzious [to have] after his death . . . so that the aforesaid Shelamzious shall have the half of the aforesaid courtyard and rooms from today, and the other half after the death of the said Judah, validly and securely for all time.[15]

This document, which is ratified by at least six witnesses, is exceptional in that it is both a deed of gift and a testament.[16] Lim tries to suggest that the irrevocability of the deed of gift carries over to the testament and in consequence that we have here a precise parallel to the διαθήκη of Galatians 3:15.[17] There is no hint in the document, however, that such is the case. Just because they are [228] juxtaposed does not transform a testament into a deed of gift. What Shelamzious has she holds. But she can only hope for what she is promised.

If the deed-of-gift hypothesis has proved to be a blind alley, do we have to admit that we simply do not know what Paul was thinking of when

---

at the beginning or in the middle or at the end [of his testament] that thus it should be as a gift', his words remain valid" (*m. Baba Bathra*, 8:5; trans. H. Danby, *The Mishnah* [Oxford: Oxford University Press, 1933], 377).

[14] *Holy Scripture in the Qumran Commentaries and Pauline Letters* (Oxford: Clarendon, 1997), 58–62.

[15] N. Lewis, Y. Yadin, and J. C. Greenfield, *The Documents from the Bar Kokhba Period in the Cave of Letters: Greek Papyri, Aramaic and Nabatean Signatures and Subscriptions*, Judean Desert Studies 2 (Jerusalem: IES, 1989), 85.

[16] A parallel oral declaration is found in Tobit, "Then Raguel called for Tobias and swore on oath to him in these words: '. . . Take at once half of what I own and return in safety to your father; the other half will be yours when my wife and I die'" (8:20-21).

[17] Esler concurs with Lim but concludes a little disingenuously, "Fortunately it is unnecessary to reach a conclusion as to exactly what sort of document Paul had in mind since the point he makes is reasonably clear" (*Galatians*, NT Readings [London: Routledge, 1998], 192).

he wrote Galatians 3:15? Not necessarily. Just a century ago Sir William Ramsay advanced a very different hypothesis. He argued that this verse should be understood against the background of the Greek law of adoption.[18] Generally, commentators content themselves with mentioning this opinion as one of the curiosities of the history of exegesis.[19] Rarely do they attempt a refutation, and, when they do, they tend to focus, not on the data, but on how Ramsay handled his material. In this he is certainly vulnerable. Not only did he rely heavily on a "Roman-Syrian Law-Book" which reflects the jurisprudence of an age some four hundred years later than that of Paul,[20] but he confused the picture by setting his exegesis of Galatians 3:15 in the context of an argument that the recipients of the letter lived in South Galatia.

These weaknesses, however, should not blind us to the value of Ramsay's essential contribution. He introduced into the debate a reference to *Disowned* by Lucian of Samosata (born c. AD 120). This has received much less attention than it deserves, principally because Ramsay failed to exploit it appropriately. The purpose of this article is to do justice to a brilliant intuition.

In Greek law possessions could be willed only to a relative. Thus, a man who had no legitimate sons had only one way to acquire an heir, namely, through adoption, whereby the law recognized his choice of an heir as a "son." "Aussi les Grecs n'ont-ils qu'un mot, ποιητός, pour désigner soit le fils adoptif, soit l'héritier institué; ils emploient les expressions εἰσποιεῖσθαι, adopter, et διατίθεσθαι, tester, comme synonyms."[21] **[229]** The effect of adoption was that the adoptee "devient héritier légitime et nécessaire de l'adoptant."[22]

---

[18] William M. Ramsay, *A Historical Commentary on St. Paul's Epistle to the Galatians*, 2nd ed. (London: Hodder & Stoughton, 1900), 350–53.

[19] So, for example, Theodor Zahn, *Der Brief des Paulus an die Galater*, KNT (Leipzig: Deichert, 1907), 164 note 20; Lagrange, *Saint Paul. Épitre aux Galates*, 76; Bruce, *Galatians*, 170–71; Longenecker, *Galatians*, 128.

[20] Ramsay does not hide the date (*A Historical Commentary*, 338).

[21] P. Gide and E. Caillemer, "Adoptio," in *Dictionnaire des antiquités grecques et romaines*, ed. C. Daremberg and E. Saglio (Paris: Hachette), I/1, 76. For a detailed study of the vocabulary used in reference to adoption, see James M. Scott, *Adoption as Sons of God: An Exegetical Investigation into the Background of UIOQESIA in the Pauline Corpus*, WUNT 2.48 (Tübingen: Mohr, 1992), 13–60.

[22] Gide and Caillemer, "Adoptio," 77. "The adoptee became legally the son of the adopter and so inherited the property" (D. M. MacDowell, "Inheritance (Greek)," in *The*

There were three types of adoption: *inter vivos*, testamentary, and posthumous.[23] For our purpose the last mentioned is irrelevant because the decision is taken by the family after the death of the adoptive father, who has no say in the matter. The difference between the first two is simply when the adoption takes effect and is perfectly brought out by the Athenian speechwriter Isaeus (c. 420–340 BC) in speaking about an adoption *inter vivos*:

> The law thus allowing Menecles, because he was childless, to adopt a son, he adopted me (ἐμὲ ποιεῖται), not by a will made at the point of death (οὐκ ἐν διαθήκαις) as other citizens have done, nor during illness; but when he was sound in body and mind, and fully aware of what he was doing, he adopted me, and introduced me to his fellow-wardsmen in the presence of my opponents and enrolled me among the demes-men and the members of his confraternity. (2.14; cf. 7.1)[24]

Isaeus is equally clear with respect to testamentary adoption: "the introduction of adopted children is always carried out by a will, the testator simultaneously devising his estate and adopting the son" (10.9);[25] "having bequeathed to him his property and having adopted him as his son" (6.3).[26]

Since testamentary adoption was simply a provision in a will, its effectiveness was entirely conditioned by the validity of the will. If the testator changed his will—as he was perfectly free to do—then the contemplated adoption did not take place. Equally, adoption *inter vivos* could be revoked by common consent, like any other contract. It could also be revoked unilaterally by either party. No condition was imposed on the adopter, but the adoptee could not opt out without leaving a legitimate son in his place.[27]

Oxford Classical Dictionary, 3rd. ed., ed. S. Hornblower and A. Spawforth [Oxford: Oxford University Press, 1996], 757).

[23] Theodore Thalheim, "Adoption," in PW 1 (1894), 397.

[24] E. S. Forster, trans., *Isaeus*, LCL (Cambridge, MA: Harvard, 1983), 49.

[25] Forster, *Isaeus*, 367, cf. 205.

[26] Forster, *Isaeus*, 205.

[27] Gide and Caillemer, "Adoptio," 78; Thalheim, "Adoption," 398. "The law does not allow the return of an adopted son to his original family, unless he leaves a legitimate son in the family which he quits" (Isaeus 6.44; Forster, *Isaeus*, 229).

[230] If it was theoretically possible to renounce an adoption, how frequently was it actually done? To the best of my knowledge none of our meager sources answers this question. It is at this point that the importance of Ramsay's reference to Lucian's *Disowned* becomes evident. From this work it emerges that in practice an adopted son should never be disinherited. In the popular mind the adopter's choice of a "son" was definitive. When it is recalled that that adoptee becomes the necessary heir of his adoptive father, this is as close as we can get to an irrevocable will.

In Greek law a natural son could be disinherited if a court accepted the validity of the charges laid by the father. Lucian succinctly states the basis of this legal provision:

> When that son was born there was no way, of course, to ascertain whether he would turn out to be bad or good, and on that account the privilege of repudiating children who are unworthy of their family has been allowed to their parents, since they determined to bring them up at a time when they were unaware of this. (*Disowned* 9)[28]

The uncertainty that justifies the repudiation of a natural son has no place in the case of an adopted son. He was not forced upon the father by birth but freely chosen as an adult with a well-defined character. The act of adoption, therefore, is a public affirmation of the virtues of the adoptee. In consequence, there could be no moral justification for a subsequent change of mind on the part of the father. As Lucian puts it,

> A son who seemed to you unworthy of his lineage need never have been taken back, but one whom you have pronounced good and taken back again you will not thereafter be able to disown; for you yourself have borne witness that he does not deserve to undergo this again, and have acknowledged that he is good. It is fitting, therefore, that his reinstatement should be irrevocable and the reconciliation binding. . . . Even if I were not your own son, but adopted, and you wished to disown me, I should not think you could; for what it was possible not to do at all, it is unjust to undo once it has taken place. (*Disowned* 11)[29]

---

[28] A. M. Harmon, trans., *Lucian*, LCL (Cambridge, MA: Harvard University Press, 1936), 5:491.

[29] Harmon, *Lucian*, 5:493–95. In the case at issue a natural son had been repudiated by his father and then reinstated. Effectively, the natural son was adopted; "he annulled

[**231**] The assumption that an adopted son was a known and stable quantity is also attested by Isaeus:

> Would he have done better if he had chosen a child from the family of one of his friends and adopted him and given him his property. But even such a child's own parents would not have known, owing to his youth, whether he would turn out to be a good man or worthless. On the other hand he had experience of me, having sufficiently tested me; he well knew what had been my behaviour towards my father and mother, my care for my relatives and my capacity for managing my own affairs. He was well aware that in my official capacity as thesmothete I have been neither unjust nor rapacious. It was then not in ignorance, but with full knowledge that he was making me master of his property. Further I was no stranger but his own nephew. . . . Since I was his kinsman, his friend, his benefactor, and a man of public spirit, and had been approved as such, who could maintain that my adoption was not the act of a man of sound judgement. (7.33–36)[30]

Two phrases in this quotation are of particular importance, "adopted him and given him his property" (ἐποιήσατο . . . καὶ τούτῳ ουσίαν ἔδωκεν) and "making me master of his property" (ἐποίει με τῶν αυτοῦ κύριον). They underline the necessary relationship between adoption and inheritance.[31] To be adopted as an adult was in a certain sense to enter into possession of the inheritance. This, of course, did not mean that the adopted son actually took control of his adoptive father's property. The law expressly forbade a son (a) to alienate or mortgage his father's goods and (b) to insist that they be shared. The need for such a law, however, highlights the sense of ownership of which every son, including an adoptee, was conscious. Moreover, if an impecunious son incurred a fine, the law specified that it should be taken out of his expected inheritance. "Il a donc, même du vivant de son père, une sorte de copropriété dans le patrimoine de la famille, analogue à celle que Gaius à Rome reconnaissait aux *sui heredes*."[32]

---

the disownment and made me his son once more" (*Disowned* 5; cf. 16). It was a matter of "choice and decision" (*Disowned* 12).

[30] Forster, *Isaeus*, 271. For a similar list of good qualities, see *Disowned* 21.

[31] See also Philo, *Mos.* 32.

[32] L. Beauchet, "Patria potestas," in Daremberg and Saglio, *Dictionnaire des antiquités grecques et romaines*, 4:344. The *sui heredes* were "those in the paternal power of

[**232**] In Galatians 3:16 Paul applies the principle of the irrevocable will to Abraham; "the promises were spoken to Abraham and to his seed." These promises concerned an "inheritance"; "God gave it [ἡ κληρονομία] to Abraham by a promise" (Gal 3:18). From this juxtaposition, any contemporary of Paul could conclude that Abraham was God's adopted son, since he could not be his son by nature.

This understanding of Abraham is attested in Hellenistic Judaism by Philo. After quoting Genesis 18:17, "Shall I hide from Abraham, my friend?" Philo comments,

> But he who has this inheritance (ὁ δὲ ἔχων τὸν κλῆρον τοῦτον) has passed beyond the bounds of human happiness. He alone is nobly born, for he has registered God as his father, and become by adoption his only son (θεὸν ἐπιγεγραμμένος πατέρα καὶ γεγονὼς εἰσποίετος αὐτῷ μόνος υἱός),[33] the possessor not of riches, but of all riches. (*Sobr.* 56)[34]

Scott has correctly seen that we have here a specific reference to Abraham[35] and not merely a generalized evocation of the wise man as such, as some scholars have thought.[36] This latter dimension, of course, is not excluded, because in Philo's system Abraham is "the standard of

---

the deceased who by his death became independent" (D. E. L. Johnston, "Inheritance (Roman)," in Hornblower and Spawforth, *The Oxford Classical Dictionary*, 758). According to Scott, "when Greek children became legal adults they were entitled to their inheritance" (*Adoption*, 67). This, however, is a misunderstanding of the sources. In opposition to Roman children, Greek children, during the lifetime of their father, had full control over what they earned and what they inherited from their mother (see Beauchet, "Patria potestas," 344; E. Sachers, "Potestas patria," *PW* 22, no. 1 (1953), 1135–37).

[33] Scott draws attention to the fact that the same construction appears in Isaeus 5.6 (*Adoption*, 89 note 138).

[34] F. H. Colson and G. H. Whitaker, trans., *Philo*, LCL (Cambridge, MA: Harvard University Press, 1938), 3:473. The relevance of this Philonic passage for the interpretation of Paul is enhanced by the fact that many of the terms also occur in 1 Cor 4:8-10; see R. A. Horsley, "Wisdom of Word and Words of Wisdom in Corinth," *CBQ* 39 (1977): 233.

[35] *Adoption*, 89–96.

[36] For example, Martin Hengel, *Der Sohn Gottes, Die Entstehung der Christologie und die jüdisch-hellenistische Religionsgeschichte*, 2nd ed. (Tübingen: Mohr, 1977), 86; Brendan Byrne, *"Sons of God"—"Seed of Abraham": A Study of the Idea of the Sonship of God of All Christians in Paul against the Jewish Background*, ABib 83 (Rome: Biblical Institute Press, 1979), 58.

nobleness" (*Virt.* 219) for all proselytes. Abraham, however, was the
first to see God; "'God appeared to Abraham' (Gen 12:7), to whom,
therefore, it is plain that he was not visible before" (*Abr.* 77). Moreover,
Abraham was the first to ascribe his paternity to one God, in contrast to
polytheists who ascribed their paternity to many gods, e.g., "the son of
a whore is a polytheist, being in the dark about his real father, and for
this reason ascribing his paternity to many, instead of to one" (*Mig. Abr.*
69; cf. *Conf.* 144; *Spec. Leg.* 1.332; *Fug.* 114).

[**233**] The understanding of Abraham as the adopted son *par excellence* confirms the proposed interpretation of Galatians 3:15 in light of
the contemporary conviction that there should be no reason to repudiate
an adopted son chosen for his exemplary character. The principle and its
application fit together perfectly. By his fidelity Abraham fully justified
God's choice.

Only now does it become possible to appreciate what Paul intended
to convey by κατὰ ἄνθρωπον λέγω (Gal 3:15). On the basis of a rather
thorough study of the phrase in Greek literature, Cosgrove concludes,
"Whether it is used adverbially or adjectivally, κατὰ ἄνθρωπον tends
to suggest the 'merely' human. The idea is not always distinctly negative . . . , but there appears to be a relatively consistent usage of the
phrase in expressions where the human forms the lesser part in a stated
or implied comparison."[37] While maintaining this basic line, Paul nonetheless gives the formula a distinctive nuance, which Cosgrove fails to
appreciate because he does not give adequate attention to what for Paul
was the antithesis of κατὰ ἄνθρωπον, namely, κατὰ θεόν, which appears
four times in his letters.

The *RSV* rightly translates the formula in Romans 8:27 as "according
to the will of God."[38] The other three instances occur in Paul's reaction
(2 Cor 7:9-11) to the reception of the Severe Letter (2 Cor 2:4), and
these enable us to go a step further because there we find κατὰ θεὸν
λύπη contrasted with τοῦ κόσμου λύπη (2 Cor 7:10). In Paul's lexicon
to be "in the world" is a simple statement of facticity without any moral

---

[37] "Arguing Like a Mere Human Being," 545–46.

[38] See, in particular, Marie-Joseph Lagrange, *Saint Paul. Épitre aux Romains*, EBib
(Paris: Gabalda, 1922), 213, but also William Sanday and Arthur C. Headlam, *A Critical
and Exegetical Commentary on the Epistle to the Romans*, ICC (Edinburgh: Clark, 1902),
214; Victor P. Furnish, *II Corinthians*, AB 32A (New York: Doubleday, 1984), 387.

judgment.[39] To be "of the world; belonging to the world" is a very different matter. The "spirit of the world" is contrasted with "the spirit which is from God" (1 Cor 2:12) and "the wisdom of this world is folly with God" (1 Cor 3:19). The pejorative connotation is confirmed by 1 Corinthians 11:32, "so that we may not be condemned along with the world." Grief that is "of the world," therefore, is grief that makes sense to fallen humanity, a grief that mimics repentance in order to avoid punishment or to secure advantage, or a grief that bewails the [234] loss of position or possessions. On the contrary, grief that is "according to the will of God" is a radical transformation of the personality through genuine sorrow.

This approach suggests that κατὰ θεόν means "according to divine revelation," whereas κατὰ ἄνθρωπον means "according to the common estimation," the "common sense" of fallen humanity.

Paul's usage confirms this hypothesis. When Paul speaks according to the conventions of everyday rhetoric, he says, ὃ λαλῶ, οὐ κατὰ κύριον λαλῶ ἀλλ᾽ ὡς ἐν ἀφροσύνῃ ("what I say is not in accordance with the Lord's standard, but in foolishness"; 2 Cor 11:17). What is foolish by the revealed standard is what the world expects (note κατὰ σάρκα in the following verse). There is some uncertainty as to whether κύριος here means God or Christ. That the latter cannot be excluded is strongly suggested by κατὰ Χριστόν in Romans 15:5, where believers must live according to the example of Jesus Christ, who did not please himself, as those in the world do (Rom 15:3).[40] Authenticity is revealed by God and exemplified by Christ.

Turning now to κατὰ ἄνθρωπον which appears in Romans 3:4; 1 Corinthians 3:3; 9:8; 15:32; and Galatians 1:11. The gospel that Paul preaches is not "according to the common estimation" (Gal 1:11). It was not simply a reflection of the values of the world (Gal 1:12a) but came through "a revelation of Jesus Christ" (Gal 1:12b). Neither in content nor form did Paul's message meet the expectations of the world (cf. 1 Cor 2:4-5).[41] The Corinthians were not perturbed by the fact of jealously, strife, and

---

[39] Rom 5:13; 1 Cor 1:27; 8:4; 14:10; 2 Cor 1:12; Phil 2:15; Col 1:6.

[40] See, in particular, J. D. G. Dunn, *Romans*, WBC 38 (Dallas, TX: Word Books, 1988), 840.

[41] Schlier (*Galater*, 44 note 2) wrongly rejects Luther's explanation, *tunc enim non esset evangelium, sed mendacium, quia "omnis homo mendax"*; "it would not be the gospel but a lie, because 'all men are liars.'" Paul's point is that the origin of his message makes a fundamental difference.

party factions in the community (1 Cor 3:3) because "according to the common estimation" these vices were endemic to humanity everywhere. In dealing with support for pastors, Paul classifies a series of arguments with which everyone would agree (1 Cor 9:8) as κατὰ ἄνθρωπον. In the common estimation, those who worked deserved to profit by their labors. Exceptionally in this case, the common estimate is confirmed by the law of Moses (1 Cor 9:9). Finally, Paul indicated that he had not really fought with wild beasts in Ephesus by specifying that he was speaking κατὰ ἄνθρωπον (1 Cor 15:32). He adopted a popular [235] perception of the human passions as ravening beasts[42] or of enemies as savage animals.[43] Once again he was speaking "according to the common estimation," according to the conventions of the society in which he lived.

If in 1 Corinthians 15:32 Paul uses κατὰ ἄνθρωπον to indicate that he should not be taken literally, why should the formula not have the same sense in Galatians 3:15? Paul knew perfectly well that what he was going to say did not accurately reflect the letter of the law regarding last testaments. He explicitly based his argument on the common estimate, the popular perception, of what were the rights of an adopted son. With admirable precision he wrote, εἰ δὲ υἱός καὶ κληρονόμος ("if a son [then] also an heir"; Gal 4:7).

Postscript

In this article I argued that a deed of adoption, in which the testator conferred all his goods on his adopted son, was in the popular estimation considered an irrevocable will. Paul used the phrase "in the popular estimation" because a testator who adopted a young adult of excellent character *should have* no reason to disinherit him. It was in no way parallel to a disinheritable natural son, who might mature badly. Legally, however, a will could be revoked at any time during the testator's life.[44] Only after his death was any change impossible.

[42] For texts, see Abraham J. Malherbe, "The Beasts at Ephesus," *JBL* 87 (1968): 71–80.

[43] Ps 22:20-21; Acts 20:29; Phil 3:2; 2 Tim 4:17; Titus 1:12; Ignatius, *Rom* 5:1; *Eph* 7:1; *Smyrn* 4:1.

[44] Mika Hietanen's contribution to the discussion is limited to "Perhaps Paul counts on no one to examine the argument critically" (*Paul's Argumentation in Galatians: A Pragma-Dialectical Analysis*, Library of NT Studies 344 [London: Clark, 2007], 122).

This interpretation has been challenged by Timothy Lim.[45] I had criticized his hypothesis that Galatians 3:15 referred to an irrevocable deed of gift because I read *PYadin* 19 as both a deed of gift and a last testament and considered this combination "exceptional." In order to demolish the second point Lim introduces two new documents into the debate (p. 367), one from Elephantine (dated 404 BC), the other from the Babatha Archives at Ein Gedi. Lim says that the former is comparable to *PYadin* 19 in two ways: "it is evident from the document that half was given now . . . and the other half after Anani's death" (p. 376). Unless we are speaking a different language, I persist in understanding this as a gift *and* a will. The two are clearly distinguished and are not merged or blurred in any way. There is no hint that the irrevocability of the gift is communicated to the will. Whatever the force of their expressed intention, Judah or Anani could have changed his mind subsequently regarding the half he intended to will to his daughter. Nothing in any law prevented him from doing so. In fact, it appears probable that an adulterous daughter could not inherit.[46] Obviously, therefore, I cannot consider convincing Lim's description of the document, "a two-stage process of the deed of gift, one half now, and the other half after death" (p. 374). On one hand there is a gift *and* on the other a promise, whose fulfilment is in no way guaranteed.

As regards adoption, Lim takes exception to my use of Lucian's *Disowned*, on grounds that the text is concerned with the reinstatement of a natural son and not the adoption of a son born of a different father (p. 372). I had made it perfectly clear, however, that the adoptee was a natural son, but I also stressed what seemed to be obvious, namely, that the recuperation of an alienated natural son was in effect a legal act, to which the only parallel was adoption. In both cases, he who was "nobody" in family terms became "somebody." In other words, the natal status of the adoptee was irrelevant. (Note also the remarks of Marc Rastoin below.)

Lim devotes considerable space to my treatment of κατὰ ἄνθρωπον λέγω. He makes a big thing of methodology but immediately tries to

---

[45] "The Legal Nature of Papyrus Yadin 19 and Galatians 3:15," in *When Judaism and Christianity Began: Essays in Memory of Anthony J. Saldarini*, JSJSup 85, ed. A. Avery-Peck et al. (Leiden/Boston: Brill, 2004), 361–76. In order to lessen the number of footnotes, pagination in the postscript refers to this article

[46] On the complicated issue, see E. A. Goodfriend, "Adultery," *ABD*, 1:83–84.

have his cake and eat it. He insists that the only valid parallels must contain the verb λέγω. Thus, he sets aside 1 Corinthians 3:3 ("to walk around with"), 1 Corinthians 15:32 ("to fight with beasts"), and Galatians 1:1 ("to be"). Such a material criterion might be more convincing had he offered translations of these verses in which he demonstrated that κατὰ ἄνθρωπον *should not be understood* as "according to the common estimation."

To object to my interpretation, Lim brings forward Ἀνθρώπινον λέγω (Rom 6:19) and μὴ κατὰ ἄνθρωπον ταῦτα λαλῶ (1 Cor 9:8). Unfortunately, he cannot have it both ways. By his criteria, these are not exact parallels. Therefore, they are irrelevant. The only exact parallel to Galatians 3:15 is Romans 3:5, and there Lim agrees that the meaning is "I speak according to the common estimation" (p. 372), which would seem sufficient to prove my point.

Lim concludes,

> Even if it is granted, for argument's sake, that in practice an adopted son is never disinherited, what Paul says in Gal 3:15 is that it is the διαθήκη, which Murphy-O'Connor translates as "will", once ratified that cannot be set aside or added to. The testamentary adoption (in Greek ποιητός), as he readily recognizes, is "a provision in a will". What he does not explain is how a provision within it can change the nature of a will and make it irrevocable. (p. 373)

Clearly, Lim has missed the point completely. Neither Paul nor I ever said that a will was *legally* irrevocable. What we both did say was that *in the popular mind* (κατὰ ἄνθρωπον) an act of adoption *was commonly considered* to be an irrevocable will because property was involved. And that is sufficient for Paul's argument.

Marc Rastoin helpfully refines my position:

> Certes, l'expression paulinienne ne comporte pas le verb ποιεῖν généralment utilisé pour l'adoption. J. Murphy-O'Connor donne par ailleurs un sense un peu forcé pour l'expression κατὰ ἄνθρωπον, celui de "selon l'opinion commune". Bref, il veut garder le sens de "testament" au sens grec, mais, pour ôter la difficulté de l'irrévocabilité, il choisit une spécificité du droit grec et de la naissance du testament grec. J. Murphy-O'Connor semble considérer qu'il s'agit d'une exception en la seule absence de descendants vivants. Ce n'est pas le cas. L. Gernet a montré que l'origine du

testament grec se trouvait dans le droit de l'adoption: "Pendant toute la période classique, l'institution d'héritier se présente sous la form d'une adoption de l'héritier".[47] Et l'adoption est possible même lorsque vivent des descendants charnels. Adopter quelqu'un était le meilleur moyen pour lui transmettre un héritage. Dans la culture grecque, être adopté, c'était être "fait fils" (εἰσ-ποεῖν + υἰός). . . . [Here he quotes Isaeus 7.1-3]. Murphy-O'Connor insiste à juste titre sur le fait qu'il y a relation nécessaire entre adoption et héritage. Il est donc logique que Paul introduise le thème de l'héritage en 3:18.[48]

In his discussion of *PYadin* 19 Llewelyn made a point which was not taken up by Lim but which would appear to support his thesis.

> Greek-speaking Jewish communities may have called the deed of gift a διαθήκη. For example, Rabban Simon b. Gamaliel (*t. B. Bat.* 9.14) states, "He who writes διεθέμην in Greek, behold this is a gift". It seems to be a reasonable assumption then that in the second century AD the Jewish deed of gift when made in Greek used the expression διεθέμην or διέθετο and thus could have been called a διαθήκη. If the same practice and terminology can be assumed to have been in use in the first century, then it is to such an instrument that Paul, a Greek-speaking Jew, referred at Gal 3:15. . . . The term διαθήκη could designate both a will and a gift.[49]

The artistry with which one possibility is built upon another is impressive but does not even remotely amount to probability. Rastoin also notes that Lim's hypothesis "tend à construire l'objet qu'elle recherche plus qu'elle ne le 'trouve'. Elle se heurte à la même objection que celle de Bammel: faire référence à 'une nuance juridique sophistiquée.'"[50] The intruding Judaizers may have understood the legal allusion, but not the Galatians, who knew nothing of Judaism.

---

[47] "La création du testament," *REG* 33 (1920): 123–68, here 125.

[48] *Tarse et Jérusalem. La double culture de l'Apôtre Paul en Galates 3:6–4:7*, ABib 152 (Rome: Pontifical Biblical Institute, 2003), 180–82.

[49] *New Documents Illustrating Early Christianity: A Review of the Greek Inscriptions and Papyri Published in 1980–81*, vol. 6 (Macquarie University: Ancient History Documentary Research Center, 1992), 47.

[50] *Tarse et Jerusalem*, 175 note 19.

My point has been taken up by Lémonon. After pointing out that a will can always be modified during the lifetime of the testator, he continues:

> Le texte paulinien viserait en fait la pratique de l'adoption qui, selon l'opinion commune (κατὰ ἄνθρωπον), serait irrévocable; *il faudrait distinguer entre le légal et l'opinion commune*. . . . [Lim] croit pouvoir identifier διαθήκη et donation entre vifs qui, elle, est irrévocable. Mais cette interprétation est difficile à admettre en raison de l'emploi de διαθήκη au v. 17.[51]

S. W. Hahn sets aside this whole line of argument by insisting that in Galatians 3:15-17 διαθήκη cannot be understood as "will" or "testament" but must mean "covenant."[52] The three points he makes against the current consensus are as follows (p. 81).

First, elsewhere in Paul διαθήκη is always used in the sense of "covenant." This observation carries argumentative force only on the untenable assumption that Paul was somehow constrained to use all terms univocally. As 2 Corinthians 2:16 shows, he was capable of changing the meaning of a term within the same verse. Moreover, Hahn goes a step further by assuming that the Galatians' familiarity with Paul's preaching meant that they would have understood the sense in which he usually used "covenant" (p. 83). Given his complete rejection of the law, I strongly doubt that Paul would have mentioned its necessary correlative "covenant" to Gentile converts. Why complicate matters? When "covenant" appears in Paul's letters, it is dictated either by tradition (1 Cor 11:25) or the needs of controversy with Judaizers (2 Cor 3:6, 14; Gal 3:17). Only in Romans 9:4 and 11:27 does "covenant" flow naturally from his pen, both because of the composition of the audience and the nature of the subject.

Second, both before and after 3:15 Paul is operating in the conceptual sphere of Jewish law, and an analogy from Greco-Roman law would have no rhetorical force or relevance. Here, Hahn mistakenly assumes that the entire audience of Galatians could have followed a subtle argu-

---

[51] J.-P. Lémonon, *L'épitre aux Galates*, CBNT 9 (Paris: Cerf, 2008), 134–35, my emphasis.

[52] "Covenant, Oath, and the Αθεδαη" Διαθήκη in Galatians 3:15-18," *CBQ* 67 (2005): 79–100. The page numbers in the text refer to this article.

ment based on Jewish tradition. This was true for the Judaizing intruders alone. Only a reference to secular law would be clear to the Galatians, who were pagans (Gal 4:8) without any admixture of "God-fearers."[53]

Third, if διαθήκη in 3:15 is understood as "testament," then what Paul says about it is nonsense because a "will" can be changed at any time during the life of the testator. This is precisely the objection to which I have replied in the above article.

Now we turn to Hahn's treatment of διαθήκη as such. The first major point he makes is that "Because a covenant was ratified by oath before the gods (or God), the obligations to which the parties had sworn could not be subsequently annulled or supplemented by either party" (p. 85). If this is correct, and Hahn takes διαθήκη in Galatians 3:15 in this sense, then what Paul says of it, οὐδεὶς ἀθετεῖ ἤ ἐπιδιατάσσεται ("no one sets aside or makes additions to it") is completely tautological. Yet one wonders if Hahn is right in ascribing such enduring validity to a "covenant." Unfortunately, he does not discuss a crucial text, namely, "Look, the days are coming, Yahweh declares, when I shall make a new covenant with the House of Israel (and the House of Judah), but not like the covenant I made with their ancestors . . . a covenant which they broke" (Jer 31:31-32). A "new covenant" necessarily implies an "old covenant" that has been superseded. The contrast is explicit in the text. In other words, God can unilaterally set aside a covenant, just as the human party had done.

Hahn's principal argument, however, is that, "In the heart of the unit, vv. 15-18, Paul uses a *qal wahomer* argument [which is] only valid if διαθήκη means 'covenant' in *both* v. 15 and v. 17" (p. 100). On the contrary, it is sufficient for the argument, if the two elements are analogously the same, as he implies more accurately on page 88. A human will or testament, which irrevocably promises a benefit (inheritance) to an adopted son, is certainly analogous to a divine covenant, which irrevocably promised blessings to Abraham and his offspring.

Not only does Paul's argument work equally well if διαθήκη is understood as "will/testament," but this meaning is much more appropriate to the context than "covenant." Hahn, for example, insists that a "covenant" was always ratified by an oath; it was its *sine qua non* (p. 85). There is no mention of an oath in the context of Galatians 3:15. On the contrary,

---

[53] See p. 50 in chap. 6 above.

what that context stresses is "the inheritance" (ἡ κληρονομία) given to Abraham by promise (3:18). An "inheritance," however, is related not to "covenant" but to "will/testament," which is not ratified by an oath.

Hahn concludes, "The coherence of Paul's argument in Gal 3:15-18, though subtle, is recognizable when we acknowledge *his contextual use and typological reading of biblical texts*" (p. 100; my emphasis). No Galatian would have been capable of following, let alone appreciating, Paul's line of argument. They totally lacked the required biblical background. The argument would have had force only for the intruders, who were no doubt steeped in the Old Testament. Hahn's article is a perfect illustration of what I have said already. Though addressed to the Galatians, the letter was, in fact, directed to the Judaizers, the only ones in the audience capable of recognizing Paul's mastery of the complex nuances of the Abrahamic tradition.

8

Galatians 4:13-14
and the Recipients of Galatians

The debate regarding the recipients of the epistle to the Galatians continues unabated. Were they the ethnic Galatians of the area to the west of modern Ankara, or the inhabitants of the southern part of the Roman province of Galatia who were evangelized by Barnabas and Paul according to Acts 13–14?[1]

The commentary of Betz opted for the ethnic (or North Galatia) hypothesis,[2] **[202]** whereas the recent commentaries of Longenecker[3] and Matera[4] prefer the province (or South Galatia) hypothesis. Dunn, for his part, concludes that "the evidence briefly reviewed is actually decisive on neither side,"[5] but Stephen Mitchell is categorical that "Paul did not visit N. Galatia."[6] The latter is perhaps the greatest contemporary expert on central Anatolia, and his view reflects that of those who are familiar with the area. Bruce approvingly quotes J. A. Findlay, who wrote, "It is significant that all those who know the geography of Asia Minor well are 'South Galatianists' to a man."[7]

---

[1] Originally published in *RB* 105 (1998): 202–7, whose pagination appears in the text in **bold**.

[2] H. D. Betz, *Galatians: A Commentary on Paul's Letter to the Churches in Galatia*, Hermeneia (Philadelphia: Fortress, 1979), 5.

[3] Richard N. Longenecker, *Galatians*, WBC 41 (Dallas, TX: Word Books, 1990), lxxii.

[4] Frank Matera, *Galatians*, Sacra Pagina 9 (Collegeville, MN: Liturgical Press, 1992).

[5] James D. G. Dunn, *The Epistle to the Galatians*, BNTC (Peabody MA; Hendrickson, 1993), 7.

[6] *ABD*, 2:871a. See also his *Anatolia: Land, Men, and Gods in Asia Minor*, vol. 2: *The Rise of the Church* (Oxford: Clarendon, 1995), 3.

[7] F. F. Bruce, *The Epistle to the Galatians: A Commentary on the Greek Text*, NIGTC (Exeter: Paternoster, 1982), 8 note 32.

It is regrettable that such experts have not read Paul with the same attention that they give to the terrain, because the abyss between the two is a decisive objection to the South Galatia hypothesis. This becomes clear from a close reading of Galatians 4:13-14, whose relevance to the identity of the recipients appears to have escaped the notice of all commentators.

The verses contain no serious textual problems: οἴδατε δὲ ὅτι δι' ἀσθένειαν τῆς σαρκὸς εὐηγγελισάμην ὑμῖν τὸ πρότερον, καὶ τὸν πειρασμὸν ὑμῶν ἐν τῇ σαρκί μου οὐκ ἐξουθενήσατε οὐδὲ ἐξεπτύσατε, ἀλλὰ ὡς ἄγγελον θεοῦ ἐδέξασθέ με, ὡς Χριστὸν Ἰησοῦν. Versions and commentators, however, differ about whether πειρασμός should be translated "test/trial" or "temptation" and whether this substantive, or "me" understood, is the direct object of the verbs ἐξουθενήσατε and ἐξεπτύσατε. Important as these questions are, they are not pertinent to the point at issue. For my purpose, only two aspects of the text need to be highlighted.

First, the evangelization of the Galatians was the result of an accident. It was not the purpose with which Paul began his journey.[8] Second, the pronouns and verbs are in the second-person plural. The implications of this were not lost on the most eminent partisan of the South Galatia hypothesis, Sir William Ramsay, who, however, viewed [204] them from the wrong perspective because he was entirely focused on demonstrating that Paul's ἀσθένεια τῆς σαρκὸς was malaria. He writes:

> First, the disease was active during Paul's residence in Galatia, and yet it was quite compatible with long journeys. That is implied alike on the North and South Galatian theories. The disease was active, because the Galatians saw it and did not despise the sufferer; it is implied that the Galatian Churches in general, and not some single one alone, witnessed the Apostle's condition. Yet he was able to make long journeys; on the North Galatian theory he went about between Ancyra, Tavium and Pessinus, then proceeded towards Bithynia (or, as some say, Pontus), then went through Mysia to Troas; and all these journeys must have been made very quickly, for no chronological system leaves free a long period for this work. On the South Galatian theory Paul went from Perga to Syrian Antioch and then to Iconium etc. These journeys need

---

[8] So, explicitly, J. B. Lightfoot on the basis of "the strictly grammatical interpretation of Gal. iv. 13, δι' ἀσθένειαν τῆς σαρκὸς" (*Saint Paul's Epistle to the Galatians* [London: Macmillan, 1910], 22). See BDF §223(3).

not have been performed with the speed and exertion implied in the
North Galatian theory, but still one of them is very long.

It follows that the disease did not take the form of one single attack of illness. It was intermittent. At one time Paul was prostrated
by an attack, at another he was able for considerable exertion, both
in travel and in preaching.[9]

We can leave aside what Ramsay says about Paul's route in North
Galatia. It is entirely speculative and in no way required by the North
Galatia hypothesis. The situation is quite different with regard to the
South Galatia theory because the proponents of this hypothesis identify
"the churches of Galatia" as Antioch in Pisidia (Acts 13:14), Iconium
(13:51), and Lystra and Derbe (14:6).

These cities, as Ramsay implicitly recognizes, cannot in any sense be
considered near each other. Derbe through Lystra to Iconium is 144 kms,
whereas Iconium is 142 kms from Antioch in Pisidia.[10] In order to have
Paul address the believers in these widely dispersed cities as a unity (which
is implied by "you" in Gal 4:13-14), we have to assume as a minimum
that the circumstances of his arrival in each city were exactly the same.

This, in fact, is exactly what Ramsay invites us to do. How preposterous his scenario is, however, becomes clear only when it is spelled
out in detail. Paul, he suggests, had no intention of evangelizing Antioch in Pisidia, but an attack of malaria forced him to stop there. On
his recovery, he headed east but, contrary to his plans, another attack
[205] obliged him to rest in Iconium, where he profited by the occasion
to preach the gospel. When he was well again, he moved south toward
some unknown destination, but a third bout of malaria gave him the opportunity to convert some inhabitants of Lystra. His strength restored,
he drifted to the southeast only to be felled again in Derbe where more
converts were made.

Is this really a plausible interpretation of Acts 13–14? Could Luke
have passed over in silence the extraordinary coincidence that unusually
frequent attacks of malaria explained the evangelization of South Galatia? Would not Paul himself have mentioned the impact of his recurrent

---

[9] *A Historical Commentary on St. Paul's Epistle to the Galatians* (London: Hodder
& Stoughton, 1900), 422–23.

[10] R. Jewett, *Dating Paul's Life* (London: SCM, 1979), 59.

illness on the direction of his ministry, in addition to the sufferings that were the result of persecution, in his allusion to the same journey in 2 Timothy 3:11? Is it serious to consider Galatians a circular letter in the most literal sense, the autograph (Gal 6:11) being passed on from one community to the other?[11] What could Paul's strategy have been, since the letter was coming from the west and the Judaizers from the east? What guarantee did he have that the letter would not reach a community prior to the arrival of the Judaizers? Would it not have been more intelligent to send a separate letter to each church?

Galatians 4:13-14 contains no hint of repetition with different groups. The natural meaning of the text is that Paul's illness had an impact on a relatively small number of people at the same time. Their warm reception of him, despite his illness, was a concerted action.

This both excludes the South Galatia hypothesis and forces us to abandon the version of the North Galatia hypothesis evoked by Ramsay (see above), which goes back to Lightfoot, who identified "the churches of Galatia" with Ancyra (modern Ankara), Pessinus (modern Balahissar), Tavium (modern Böyük Nefez Kjöi), and perhaps Juliopolis (modern Ömer Schischla).[12] According to Robert Jewett, the Galatian churches were Ancyra, Pessinus, and perhaps Germa (modern Dümrek).[13] This latter hypothesis is a slight improvement but equally impossible. Ancyra was 160 kms from Tavium, 112 kms from Germa, and 160 kms from Pessinus.[14] These distances are comparable to those in the South Galatia hypothesis and are equally incompatible with Galatians 4:13-14.

The problem of the distances in Lightfoot's hypothesis was noted by [206] James Moffatt, who approvingly quotes Schmiedel: "It is sufficient to suppose that during his illness, or during his convalescence, Paul founded a few churches, none of them very far apart, and all situated in the W. of North Galatia."[15] Once again, however, this greatly improved interpretation

---

[11] So Bruce, *Galatians*, 74; Longenecker, *Galatians*, 6.

[12] *Galatians*, 20. The modern names are taken from the map in *PW* 7:530.

[13] *Dating Paul's Life*, 138 note 52.

[14] Estimated from W. M. Calder and G. E. Bean, *A Classical Map of Asia Minor* (Ankara: British School of Archaeology, 1958).

[15] *An Introduction to the Literature of the New Testament*, 3rd ed. (New York: Scribner's, 1918), 94. Betz also notes that the churches must have been close geographically (*Galatians*, 40).

fails to do justice to Galatians 4:13-14. Were some of the churches founded when Paul was well enough to move around, he could hardly speak of his illness being a burden to those communities (τὸν πειρασμὸν ὑμῶν ἐν τῇ σαρκί μου). His reception would have been unrelated to his physical condition. It appears that we have to think on a much smaller scale.

The clue to understanding "the churches of Galatia" is the expression ἡ ἐκκλησία ὅλη "the whole church" (1 Cor 14:23; Rom 16:23). Robert Banks has astutely pointed out that the adjective "whole" would be redundant if all the believers in a given village, town, or city regularly met as a single group.[16] Its use necessarily implies subgroups which came together occasionally to constitute "the whole church." These, of course, are the believers who usually met in smaller houses or workplaces, "the church in the home of X" (Rom 16:5; 1 Cor 16:19; Col 4:14; Phlm 2). If we think of "the churches of Galatia" in terms of house churches in a small poor village, the formulation of Galatians 4:13-14 makes perfect sense. The resources of one house were inadequate to succour Paul and aid had to be sought from others.

One might object that this is to go too far to the other extreme. Is there not a radical disproportion between the extensive territory implied by "Galatia" and a single village? Yes, there is, but this gap between word and reality is the very stuff of irony. According to Quintilian,

> On the other hand, that class of allegory in which the meaning is contrary to that suggested by the word, involves an element of irony, or, as our rhetoricians call it, *illusio*. This is made evident to the understanding either by the delivery, the character of the speaker or the nature of the subject. For if any one of these is out of keeping with the words, it at once becomes clear that the intention of the speaker is other than what he actually says.[17]

[207] The recognition of irony is instinctive; "every reader learns that some statements cannot be understood without rejecting what they

---

[16] *Paul's Idea of Community* (Exeter: Paternoster, 1980), 38.

[17] *Institutio Oratoria* 8.6.54; cf. 9.2.44–47; trans. H. E. Butler in LCL. On irony in general, see Heinrich Lausberg, *Handbuch der literarischen Rhetorik. Eine Grundlegung der Literaturwissenschaft*, 3rd ed. (Stuttgart: Steiner, 1990), §§ 582–85, 902–4. For a specific instance of Pauline irony, see Karl A. Plank, *Paul and the Irony of Affliction*, SBL Semeia Studies (Atlanta: Scholars Press, 1987).

seem to say."[18] The discrepancy between their impoverished condition and the grandiose address employed by Paul should immediately have alerted the Galatians to the fact that something alien was stirring beneath the surface of Paul's calm words. A latent anger was working itself out. They were being mocked. This interpretation is reinforced by the fact that Galatians is the only letter in which εκκλησία is not qualified in such a way as to bring it into the religious sphere.[19] No doubt that Paul had spoken to the Galatians of the εκκλησία as the community of the faithful, but here he uses it in the secular sense of "assembly," another ironic shift.[20] He has grave doubts regarding their committment to the true God: "I am astonished that you are so quickly deserting him who called you in the grace of Christ" (Gal 1:6).

Postscript

Commentaries written subsequently to those mentioned in the above article reflect the same division as their predecessors. Witherington (1998), Vouga (1998), Jervis (2000), and Lémonon (2008) place the recipients of Galatians in the cities of South Galatia evangelized by Paul and Barnabas (Acts 13–14). Fee (2007) very hesitantly opts for North Galatia, as does Martyn, but much more resolutely. The "churches of Galatia" (Gal 1:2) are located in Ancyra, Pessinus, and possibly Tavium.[21] Esler follows me in narrowing Paul's mission area to Pessinus.[22] What is remarkable is that none of these authors perceives the slightest tension between Galatians 1:2 and Galatians 4:13-14. Their exegesis of the latter presents Paul as having operated in only one place and completely fails to account for the plurality of churches in the address of the letter.

The one commentator to have had an inkling of the problem is Légasse. He rightly opts for the North Galatia hypothesis but has taken some of my observations on board:

---

[18] Wayne C. Booth, *A Rhetoric of Irony* (Chicago: University of Chicago, 1974), 1.

[19] Contrast "to the church of the Thessalonians through God the [our] Father and the Lord Jesus Christ" (1 Thess 1:1; 2 Thess 1:1); "to the church of God which is at Corinth" (1 Cor 1:2; 2 Cor 1:1).

[20] So, rightly, Dunn, *Galatians*, 30.

[21] J. L. Martyn, *Galatians*, AB (New York: Doubleday, 1997), 16–17.

[22] *Galatians*, New Testament Readings (London: Routledge, 1998), 34.

> On retiendra toutefois qu'une évangélisation des grands centres tels
> qu'Ancyre, Pessinonte, Tavium, Julipolis, Germa s'accorde mal
> avec l'état de santé délabré que Paul évoque en Ga 4:13-14 étant
> donné la distance qui sépare ces villes les unes des autres. Il faut, de
> préférence, et malgré le bon réseau routier de la région, restreindre le
> rayon d'action où Paul quoique mal en point, fut accueilli avec chal-
> eur par les populations et put fonder quelques communautés. . . .
> One ne saurait suivre J. Murphy-O'Connor quant il comprend les
> "Églises de Galatie" (Ga 1:2) comme une désignation ironique de
> communautés domestiques réparties dans quelque pauvre village.[23]

One can only rejoice at the slight progress, but alas it seems to have been forgotten when Légasse comes to comment on Galatians 4:13-14.[24] Illness forces Paul to make a stop in Galatia, where he meets Galatians. The comment unambiguously suggests that Paul operated in only one place. But at the very end Légasse introduces a new element of great importance:

> L'expérience de Paul chez les Galates, quand ceux-ci l'accueillirent
> et posèr sous sa direction les fondements de leurs communautés,
> fut d'être l'objet de bénédictions enthousiastes de la par de ceux
> qu'il évangélisait.[25]

Here we have a hypothesis that resolves the tension between the plural and the singular. Paul stayed in one place, and those whom he converted themselves became apostles and founded other communities in Galatia. This is far from impossible. Under the direction of Paul, it was Epaphras who evangelized the Lycus valley, where he founded Colossae, and probably Laodicea and Hierapolis (Col 2:1; 4:12-13). Presumably, he had been converted by Paul in Ephesus, and Paul recognized that a traveler returning to his hometown did not have to worry about accomodation or a job. He was free to focus entirely on the gospel. The extent and the rapidity of the spread of Christianity in Asia meant that during his three years in Ephesus Paul himself could not personally have founded all the "churches of Asia" (1 Cor 16:19), which, in addition to the churches of the Lycus valley, included those in Thyatira (Lydia,

---

[23] S. Légasse, *L'épître de Paul aux Galates*, LD Comm. 9 (Paris: Cerf, 2000), 30.

[24] *Galates*, 324–26.

[25] *Galates*, 328.

Acts 16:14), Smyrna, Pergamum, Sardis, Philadelphia, Magnesia-on-the-Meander, and Tralles.[26]

I cannot escape the impression, however, that were Légasse concerned to propose an alternative to my hypothesis, he would have spoken otherwise and done so in the context of the first quotation above, which comes from his introduction to the letter. Nonetheless, for all its timidity, his suggestion is certainly viable and obviously would not demand the sort of irony that I was forced to postulate.

The one potential problem is the dating. Had Paul developed his missionary strategy of delegating founding missions to his converts when he evangelized Galatia, probably in AD 46 to 48?[27] We have no explicit evidence that he did so until he makes Ephesus his center in AD 52 to 54. Philippians was written to the first city evangelized by Paul after Galatia, and it contains a hint that at least merits examination. In Philippians 4:2 Paul publicly criticizes Euodia and Syntyche. This break with his custom of not singling out individuals for blame in public is explicable only if these were women with constituencies. This made the disagreement not a private dispute between two individuals but a quarrel between two groups in the church, which endangered its survival. The authority of Euodia and Syntyche can only have come from their role in the evangelization of Philippi. Such partnership is praised by Paul in the Thanksgiving: "thankful for your partnership in the gospel from the first day until now" (Phil 1:5; cf. 4:3). The possessive pronoun limits "the first day" to Paul's arrival in Philippi. In context, it cannot mean the beginning of his independent ministry. The joyful formulation gives the impression that such cooperation in evangelization was something new in Paul's experience. If this is correct, it is rather improbable that Paul's ministry in Galatia had been expanded by the same sort of cooperation.

---

[26] See my *Paul: A Critical Life* (Oxford: Clarendon, 1996), 173–75.
[27] See chap. 1 above.

9

The Unwritten Law of Christ
(Gal 6:2)

In all his letters Paul speaks only once of "the law of Christ" (Gal 6:2).[1] This uniqueness has meant that exegetes cannot draw on other contexts to define its meaning. Inevitably, suggestions have proliferated. J. L. Martyn recorded five major opinions,[2] which S. Légasse increased to six.[3] In recent years, however, something like a consensus has emerged insofar as commentators appear to have come to agree that by "law" Paul had in mind a body of binding precepts drawn from the Mosaic law and/ or another source.[4]

[214] R. N. Longenecker identifies the "law of Christ" as "those pre-scriptive principles stemming from the heart of the gospel (usually embedded in the example and teachings of Jesus), which are meant to be applied to specific situations by the direction and enablement of the Holy Spirit, being always motivated and conditioned by love."[5] The final clauses and the mention of "principles" do nothing to diminish the force of the adjective "prescriptive." The "principles" are as binding as legal precepts.

---

[1] Orginally published in *RB* 119 (April 2012) 213–31, whose pagination appears in the text in **bold**.

[2] *Galatians*, AB (New York: Doubleday, 1997), 548.

[3] *L'épître de Paul aux Galates*, LD Comm. 9 (Paris: Cerf, 2000), 452.

[4] This assessment is confirmed by T. A. Wilson, "Recently, however, an increasing number of scholars [among which he numbers himself] are exploring the possibility that the Law of Christ in fact refers to the Law of Moses" (*The Curse of the Law and the Crisis in Galatia: Reassessing the Purpose of Galatians*, WUNT 2.225 [Tübingen: Mohr Siebeck, 2007], 102). This is not to say, however, that there are not still those whose speculative suggestions evacuate "law" of all meaning, e.g., C. Pigeon, "La Loi du Christ en Galates 6:2," *Studies in Religion/Sciences Religeuses* 29 (2000): 425–38; W. Winger, "The Law of Christ," *NTS* 46 (2000): 537–46.

[5] *Galatians*, WBC 41 (Dallas, TX: Word Books, 1990), 275–76.

Similarly F. Adeyemi, who sees the law of Christ as composed of the commands and principles that direct the lives of believers.[6]

The same attitude is evident in those authors who speak of the "law of Christ" in terms of obedience. Légasse insists that the force of the genitive is to make Christ the author of the law, as in "law of God" (Rom 7:22,25; 8:7) or "law of Moses" (1 Cor 9:9), but denies that there is any question of Christ proclaiming a new law to take the place of the old. Nonetheless, the phrase evokes "un programme dont la formule n'est pas empruntée à la Tora, mais à la morale hellénistique," and which "s'impose au chrétien et doit régler toute son existence."[7] F. Mussner is no different. The "law of Christ" is not law in the OT sense, but "beide 'Gesetz' [Moses and Christ] der strengen Forderung nach Gehorsam an sich haben."[8]

Martyn makes much of the fact that up to this point in Galatians Paul has used νόμος in the sense of the Mosaic law thirty times. Thus, his readers would have been conditioned to give it the same meaning in 6:2.[9] Martyn then goes a step further by asserting that "possessive determination is not only a very frequent sense of the genitive but also the best reading of the genitive in Rom 3:27; 7:23,25; 8:2. One does well to translate the syntactical unit as 'the Law *in the possession of* A' or 'the Law *as it has been taken in hand by* A' or 'the Law *as it is determined by* A.'" In conclusion, he paraphrases Paul, "Christ brought the Law to completion, when he made it his own Law, by loving us and giving his life for us. Indeed, he did that precisely in accordance with the will of God our Father, whose promise and whose guidance are spoken by the scriptural Law that is now the Law in the hands of Christ."[10] Clearly, [**215**] eloquence does not guarantee clarity. How precisely has the law been

[6] *The New Covenant Torah in Jeremiah and the Law of Christ in Paul*, Studies in Bib. Lit. 94 (New York/Bern: Lang, 2006).

[7] *Galates*, 454.

[8] *Der Galaterbrief*, HTKNT 9 (Freiburg: Herder, 1974), 283, 286.

[9] Others who insist that Paul is speaking of the Mosaic Law in 6:2 are F. Matera, *Galatians*, Sacra Pagina 9 (Collegeville, MN: Liturgical Press, 1992), 221; G. Stanton, "The Law of Moses and the Law of Christ. Galatians 3:1–6:2," in J. D. G. Dunn, *Paul and the Mosaic Law: The Third Durham-Tübingen Research Symposium on Earliest Christianity and Judaism (Durham, September 1994)*, WUNT 89 (Tübingen: Mohr Siebeck, 1996), 99–116, here 114–16.

[10] *Galatians*, 555–58 (his italics).

changed by coming into the possession of Christ? Are its precepts still considered binding, or have they been reduced to the level of guidelines?

To the best of my knowledge, the only one to answer these questions is J. D. G. Dunn. Apropos of Galatians 6:2, he says, "Almost certainly Paul refers in this shorthand way to the Jesus-traditions as indicating how Jesus interpreted the law in his teaching and actions."[11] In commenting on Galatians 5:14, he explains how Jesus differed from his Jewish contemporaries: "For the one, 'doing the whole law' meant a complete package, a life within Judaism, a life-style marked out by the the Jewish distinctives. . . . For the other, 'fulfilling the law' meant an obedience not simply exemplified by, but conditioned throughout by love of neighbour, where the relative importance of other laws is determined by the love-command."[12] In other words, all the precepts of the law continue to be binding on Christians with the exception of those that founded the distinctive identity of Jews, e.g., circumcision, the dietary laws, sabbath rest, etc.[13]

The Force of Law

This is to turn Paul's thought completely upside down. Paul was radically antinomian; he rejected the law completely, not for what might be called "salvific" reasons, but because of what it did to people. This is clear in two texts which, to the best of my knowledge, are never brought into any discussion of Paul and the law, presumably because they do not appear in Galatians or Romans. Nonetheless, they establish a principle, which must command any view of the position of law in general and the Mosaic law in particular in the Christian church.

The purpose of the letter to Philemon is to persuade him to welcome Onesimus, who has injured him, as a brother and to release him into Paul's service. Paul claims that he has the authority to "command" Philemon to perform this act of charity, but because he loves him, he prefers to "appeal" to his generosity: πολλὴν ἐν Χριστῷ παρρησίαν ἔχων ἐπιτάσσειν σοι τὸ ἀνῆκον διὰ τὴν ἀγάπην μᾶλλον παρακαλῶ (Phlm

[11] *The Epistle to the Galatians*, BNTC (Peabody, MA: Hendrickson, 1993), 322.

[12] *Galatians*, 290–91.

[13] For further details of this distinctive vision, see J. D. G. Dunn, *The New Perspective on Paul: Collected Essays*, WUNT 185 (Tübingen: Mohr Siebeck, 2007).

8-9). Clearly, to "command" Philemon would be to injure him in [**216**] some way. Paul explains what he has in mind in v. 14: "I preferred to do nothing without your consent [γνώμη] in order that your goodness might not be by compulsion but of your own free will [ἵνα μὴ ὡς κατὰ ἀνάγκην τὸ ἀγαθόν σου ᾖ ἀλλὰ κατὰ ἑκούσιον]." In other words, compulsion destroys free will; if one is bound, as by a precept, one cannot act freely. The absolute opposition between ἀνάγκη ("force, constraint, necessity") and ἑκούσιος ("of one's own free will, voluntary") is well documented. Plutarch, for example, says that "true philosophers alone do willingly what all others do unwillingly because of the law" (μόνοι ποιοῦσιν ἑκουσίως ἃ ποιοῦσιν ἄκοντες οἱ λοιποὶ διὰ τὸν νόμον; *Moralia* 446E). The philosophers are persuaded by the merits of the act and so choose freely, whereas others believe that they have no choice but to obey the commands of the law. Such blind obedience may provide peace of mind, but at what a price!

The second text also concerns an act of charity, and the invocation of the same principle shows that it was integral to Paul's habitual thought. Paul wishes the Corinthians to contribute to the collection for the poor of Jerusalem. In his enthusiasm he bursts out, "See that you excel in this gracious work also" (2 Cor 8:7).[14] Once the words were out of his mouth, he recognized that this imperative would appear to the Corinthians as a binding precept, and immediately he corrects himself: "I say this not as a command" (οὐ κατ᾽ ἐπιταγὴν λέγω; 2 Cor 8:8; cf. 1 Cor 7:6). Why was the correction necessary? "Each one must do as he has made up his mind, not reluctantly or under compulsion, for God loves a cheerful giver" (ἕκαστος καθὼς προῄρηται τῇ καρδίᾳ, μὴ ἐκ λύπης ἢ ἐξ ἀνάγκης· ἱλαρὸν γὰρ δότην ἀγαπᾷ ὁ θεός; 2 Cor 9:7). The gift would have value only if freely chosen. To make it obligatory would be to introduce an element of compulsion that destroyed freedom.[15]

Perhaps the most succinct clarification of the principle at issue here is that of Thomas Aquinas in his commentary on 2 Corinthians 3:18:

---

[14] On the imperatival force of ἵνα with the subjunctive, see BDF §387(3).

[15] It is indicative of the myopia with which this subject is approached that neither Phlm 14 nor 2 Cor 9:7 are even mentioned in W. Coppins, *The Interpretation of Freedom in the Letters of Paul with Special Reference to the "German" Tradition*, WUNT 2.261 (Tübingen: Mohr Siebeck, 2009). Typically, he limits himself to the ἐλευθερ-texts of 1–2 Corinthians, Galatians, and Romans.

Whoever acts of his own accord acts freely, but one who is impelled by another does not act freely. *He who avoids evil, not because it is evil, but (merely) because a precept of the Lord forbids it, is not free.* On the other hand, he who avoids evil because it is evil is free.[16]

[**217**] The force of the emphasized sentence cannot be underestimated. If one acts in a particular way simply because a precept commands it, one is reduced to the status of a slave (cf. Gal 4:8-10).

It now becomes understandable why Paul refuses to recognize as binding precepts the two commands of the Lord that he quotes (1 Cor 7:10-11; 9:14). He shows his respect for the dominical logia by citing them, but in each case he does exactly what is forbidden; he permits a divorce and insists on earning his own living. Paul believed that he had good reasons for acting as he did and so made his choices in full freedom. It is unthinkable that he would expect his converts to do otherwise.

By his frequent references to the Old Testament, Paul shows his respect for it, but as with the commands of Christ, he refuses to treat its precepts as binding. How he understood Deuteronomy 25:5 is clear from the way he uses it as an argument in 1 Corinthians 9:9, yet in 1 Corinthians 9:15-18 he proclaims his freedom to do exactly the opposite.

It is also noteworthy that Paul, in order not to give his converts the possibility of avoiding a personal decision by blind obedience, never issues an order on moral matters but only on administrative ones.[17] The collection provides a perfect example. As we have seen above, he will not order the Corinthians to contribute, but once they have made that decision freely, he expects them to obey the organizational arrangements that he has made; they will do it his way and no other (1 Cor 16:1-4).

In order to perceive the relevance of this discussion to the "law of Christ" (Gal 6:2) one has only to look at Galatians 3:23 and confront it

---

[16] *Quicumque agit ex seipso, libere agit; qui vero ex alio motus, non agit libere. Ille ergo, qui vitat mala, non quia mala, sed propter mandatum Domini, non est liber; sed qui vitat mala, quia mala, est liber* (R. Cai, ed., *S. Thomae Aquinatis Doctoris Angelici super epistolas S. Pauli lectura* [Romae/Taurini: Marietti,1953], 1:464 note 112).

[17] For more details, see my *L'existence chrétienne selon saint Paul*, LD 80 (Paris: Cerf, 1974), 103–32. The same point is strongly made by S. Westerholm, *Israel's Law and the Church's Faith: Paul and His Recent Interpreters* (Grand Rapids, MI: Eerdmans, 1988), 215.

with Galatians 5:1. As might have been expected, in order to salvage his benign vision of the law, Dunn interpretes φπουρέω in 3:23 in the positive sense of "protective custody," i.e., "as providing some protection for Israel during the time when sin ruled supreme . . . Israel like a city garrisoned by the law within a larger territory ruled by sin."[18] The simple fact that ὑπὸ νόμον ἐφρουρούμεθα is continued by συγκλειόμενοι ("being shut up"), which takes up συνέκλεισεν ("shut up") in 3:22, demands Martyn's paraphrase: "In actuality the scripture locked up everything in the prison ruled over by Sin."[19] Martyn is also correct in pointing out that [218] "Paul's picture of the pedagogue is that of a man who confines and even imprisons his charge."[20] There is no freedom under the law.

Not surprisingly, therefore, Paul tells the believer "For freedom Christ has set us free [τῇ ἐλευθερίᾳ ἡμᾶς Χριστὸς ἐλευθέρωσεν]; stand fast, therefore, and do not submit again to a yoke of slavery [καὶ μὴ παλιν ζυγῷ δουλείας ἐνέχεσθε]" (Gal 5:1). Burton is entirely correct in claiming that "The sentence is, in fact, an epitome of the contention of the whole letter" because he rightly interprets the definite article before ἐλευθερίᾳ as "restrictive, referring to that freedom from the law with which the whole epistle from 2:1 on has dealt."[21] What is the force of the dative? For Burton it denotes "destination,"[22] which harmonizes with Martyn's "of place whither."[23] Betz is more explicit and forceful: "It is not a dative of cause and instrumentality, but one of 'destiny' and 'purpose,' and it must be interpreted in parallelism with ἐπ᾽ ἐλευθερίᾳ ('to freedom') in 5:13."[24] The need for such an unusual formulation is, in fact, made clear by Galatians 5:13, which shows that Paul's concept of freedom involves both an "already" and a "not yet." Through the saving grace of Christ it exists in embryo, but human effort in building community is necessary for it to become a reality, and without successful

[18] *Galatians*, 197.

[19] *Galatians*, 372. Similarly Burton, "a restrictive guarding" (*A Critical and Exegetical Commentary on the Epistle to the Galatians*, ICC [Edinburgh: Clark, 1921], 199); Betz, "kept imprisoned" (*Galatians*, Hermeneia [Philadelphia: Fortress, 1979], 176).

[20] *Galatians*, 363 note 225.

[21] *Galatians*, 270.

[22] *Galatians*, 271.

[23] *Galatians*, 447

[24] *Galatians*, 255–56.

achievement "freedom" is nothing but a consoling fiction.[25] If the community is such in name only, freedom is merely nominal.

Before leaving this topic, it must be recognized that Paul does, in fact, recognize that the Christian must accept one form of compulsion. In Galatians 5:14 he says that "the whole of the Law has been brought to completion in one sentence: You shall love your neighbour as yourself."[26] All that the law demanded has been reduced to this single imperative, which all believers must obey (cf. Rom 13:8-10). Essentially, the same thing is said in "The love of Christ constrains [συνέχει] us" (2 Cor 5:14). Theoretically, the genitive here is ambiguous; it can be either subjective or [219] objective. In Paul's thought, however, the two must be held closely together.[27] To bring this out C. Spicq invented the ingenious classification "génitif compréhensif ou simultané."[28] He also provides the most thorough analysis of the meanings of συνέχω and concludes that its use here carries the connotation of compulsion.[29]

The fundamental importance that Paul gives to love is explained by his conviction that "without love I am nothing" (ἀγάπην δὲ μὴ ἔχω οὐθέν εἰμι; 1 Cor 13:2). The expression οὐδέν εἰμι appears elsewhere only in 2 Corinthians 12:11, where the sense is clearly "I am a nobody, a worthless person" ("useless"; 1 Cor 7:19).[30] This meaning is manifestly

---

[25] For details, see my *Becoming Human Together: The Pastoral Anthropology of Saint Paul*, 3rd ed. (Atlanta: SBL, 2009), 154–74, 250–56. Dunn's vision of the Jewish Law is severely compromised by his failure to deal adequately with Paul's understanding of freedom; for example, there is no entry for "freedom" in the subject index of his magisterial *The Theology of Paul the Apostle* (Grand Rapids, MI/Cambridge, UK: Eerdmans, 1998); "liberty" fares only slightly better.

[26] For the translation, see Martyn, *Galatians*, 486–89.

[27] With regard to 2 Cor 5:14, M. Zerwick observes, "At hic cavendum est, ne in interpretando textu sacro sensus claritati sacrificetur aliquid ex sensus plenitudine" (*Graecitas Biblica*, SPIB, 3rd ed. [Rome: PIB, 1955], 11).

[28] *Agapè dans le Nouveau Testament. Analyse des textes*, EBib (Paris: Gabalda, 1959), 2:128.

[29] C. Spicq, *Notes de lexicographie néo-testamentaire*, OBO 22/2 (Fribourg: Éditions universitaires; Göttingen: Vandenhoeck & Ruprecht, 1978), 2:859–63.

[30] On the equivalence of οὐθείς and οὐδείς, see A. T. Robertson, *A Grammar of the Greek New Testament in the Light of Historical Research* (Nashville, TN: Broadman Press, 1934), 750–51.

inappropriate in 1 Corinthians 13:2.[31] One's social position is not conditioned by the quality of one's love. Thus, 1 Corinthians 13:2 should be translated, "without love I do not exist."[32] Loving is what brings the Christian into being (cf. 1 Cor 1:30). Loving is integral to the very idea of Christianity; one cannot conceive one without the other.

In 1 Thessalonians Paul had struggled to put across the same idea in an even more graphic way. "Concerning fraternal charity [φιλαδελφία] you have no need to have anyone write to you, because you yourselves have been taught by God to love one another [αὐτοὶ γὰρ ὑμεῖς θεοδίδακτοί ἐστε εἰς τὸ ἀγαπᾶν ἀλλήλους]" (4:8). Understandably, the proposals regarding the meaning of "taught by God" have been wide-ranging. It is highly improbable, however, that the phrase was intended to be taken literally. Paul has in mind an instinctive knowledge so profound and fundamental that it is most forcibly expressed by evoking a creative God who had put it in place from the first moment the Christian came into being. For Paul there was no possible alternative to love, which made it an imperative.

[220] Against this background, it is impossible that Paul should have given "law" in the phrase "law of Christ" any coercive force that would make it resemble the Mosaic law in the slightest degree.

A new possibility of meaning is opened up if the genitive is understood as explanatory, i.e., as a genitive of apposition or definition (BDF §167). In this case Galatians 6:2 should be rendered as "the law which is Christ." Despite a thorough search, I have not discovered anyone who has put forward the same hypothesis in similar language. This is not to say, however, that others have not come to substantially the same conclusion. B. Witherington's formulation is particularly noteworthy. "If we ask what image Gal 6:2 would have conjured up in the minds of the Galatians it would have been the story of Christ's life, death, and teach-

---

[31] *Pace* A. Robertson and A. Plummer, *The First Epistle of St Paul to the Corinthians*, ICC (Edinburgh: Clark, 1911), 289; R. F. Collins, *First Corinthians*, Sacra Pagina 7 (Collegeville, MN: Liturgical Press, 1999), 476, and the majority of commentators.

[32] With great insight Spicq writes, "Dans ce verset, [οὐθέν εἰμι] c'est presque l'équivalent du métaphysique *non-être* (τὸ μὴ ὄν, Platon, *Soph.* 238d; Aristote, *Métaph.* v, 2,1026b, 14)" (*Agapè*, 2:71 note 2).

ing that Paul had told the Galatians when he was with them."[33] This is a very significant point, which I shall develop below.

The translation "the law which is Christ" is certainly grammatically possible but questions remain. Is Paul likely to have used this construction, and if so, would it have made any sense to the Galatians? Both can be answered in the affirmative. According to A. T. Robertson, thirteen examples of the epexegetical genitive appear in the Pauline letters: 1 Thessalonians 1:3; 5:8; Colossians 1:5; 3:24; 1 Corinthians 5:8; 2 Corinthians 1:9; 2:14; 5:1, 5; Romans 3:27; 4:11; 8:23; 15:16.[34] Galatians 6:2, in consequence, is not a rare exception. The usage was part of his style. As regards the Galatians recognizing a man as a law, a fruitful approach is suggested by the assertion of Philo: "The lives of those who have earnestly followed virtue may be called unwritten laws" (νόμοι δέ τινες ἄγραφοι καὶ οἱ βίοι τῶν ζηλωσάντων τὴν ἀρετήν; *Virt.* 194).[35]

Unwritten Laws

The conventional Greek understanding of "unwritten laws" is set out succinctly by Aristotle:

> The law is particular or general. By particular, I mean the written law with which a state is governed; by general, the unwritten (laws) which appear to [221] be universally recognized [κοινὸν δὲ ὅσα ἄγραφα παρὰ πᾶσιν ὁμολογεῖσθαι δοκεῖ]. (*Art of Rhetoric* 1.10.3)
>
> There are two kinds of laws, particular and general [λέγω δὲ νόμον τὸν μὲν ἴδιον τὸν δὲ κοινόν]. By particular laws I mean those established by each people in reference to themselves, which again are divided into written and unwritten [τὸν μὲν ἄγραφον τὸν δὲ γεγραμμένον]; by general laws I mean those based upon nature. In fact, there is a general idea of just and unjust in accordance with nature, as all men in a manner divine, even if there is neither communication nor agreement between them. (*Art of Rhetoric* 1.13.2)[36]

---

[33] *Grace in Galatia: A Commentary on Paul's Letter to the Galatians* (Grand Rapids, MI: Eerdmans, 1998), 425.

[34] Robertson, *A Grammar*, 498–99. See also U. Holzmeister, "Genetivus Epexegeticus in NT," *VD* 25 (1947): 112–17.

[35] The καί is epexegetical; see BDF §442(9).

[36] Texts from J. H. Freese, *Aristotle: The Art of Rhetoric*, LCL (Cambridge, MA: Harvard, 1926).

The difference between these two texts reveals that "unwritten laws" were understood in two distinct senses. As general laws they represented the law of Nature, whereas as particular laws they enshrined the immemorial customs of individual peoples.

This distinction unfortunately controls the surveys of Philonic usage. As a result, they tend to focus on whether "unwritten laws" should be understood as references to the law of Nature or to the oral law of the Jews (*AJ* 13.297).[37] For H. L. Strack "unwritten laws" always meant the latter,[38] whereas R. Hirzel argued equally strongly that Philo's allusions were exclusively to the law of Nature.[39] Drawing on I. Heinemann,[40] E. R. Goodenough concludes that "it is demonstrated that Philo knows nothing of Jewish oral tradition."[41] Both opt firmly for the identification of "unwritten law" with the law of Nature. Much more reasonably H. A. Wolfson argues that, while there were occasional references to Jewish oral law, in the majority of cases the allusion was to the law of Nature.[42]

This approach to the problem of "unwritten laws" effectively obscures what in my view is Philo's most important contribution to the debate. [222] There are clearly two sets of "unwritten laws" in the works of Philo, namely, those that are "living," and those that are not. The latter includes such passages as:

> Customs are unwritten laws [ἔθη γὰρ ἄγραφοι νόμοι], approved by men of old, not inscribed on monuments nor on leaves of paper which the moth destroys, but on the souls of those who are partners in the same citizenship. For children ought to inherit from their parents, besides their property, ancestral customs which they were

---

[37] So E. M. Smallwood, *Philonis Alexandrini Legatio ad Gaium* (Leiden: Brill, 1961), 208–9, and A. Mosès, *De specialibus legibus III et IV*, Les Œuvres de Philon d'Alexandrie 25 (Paris: Cerf, 1970), 360–61. For the oral law, see E. Schürer, *The History of the Jewish People in the Age of Jesus Christ*, ed. G. Vermes et al. (Edinburgh: Clark, 1979), 2:330–55.

[38] *Einleitung in Talmud und Midrash* (München: Beck, 1982), 9.

[39] "Ἄγραφος νόμος," *Abhandlungen der philologisch-historischen Classe der Königlich Sachsischen Gesellschaft der Wissenschaften* 20, no. 1 (1900): 16–18.

[40] "Die Lehre vom ungeschriebenen Gesetz im jüdischen Schrifttum," *HUCA* 4 (1927): 149–71, here 152–59.

[41] *By Light, Light: The Mystic Gospel of Hellenistic Judaism* (New Haven, CT: Yale, 1935), 78.

[42] *Philo: Foundations of Religious Philosophy in Judaism, Christianity, and Islam* (Cambridge, MA: Harvard, 1948), 188–94.

reared in and have lived with even from the cradle, and do not despise them because they have been handed down without written record [παρόσον ἄγραφος αὐτῶν ἡ παράδοσις]. Praise cannot be duly given to one who obeys the written laws [τοῖς ἀναγραφεῖσι νόμοις], since he acts under restraint [ἀνάκῃ] and the fear of punishment. But he who faithfully observes the unwritten (laws) [τοῖς ἀγράφοις] deserves commendation, since the virtue which he displays is freely willed. (*Spec. Leg.* 4.149–50)[43]

It was only of the Jews that Gaius was suspicious, on the grounds that they were the only people who deliberately opposed him and had been taught from their very cradles, as it were, by their parents, tutors and teachers and—more than that—by their holy laws and even by their unwritten customs [πολὺ πρότερον τῶν ἱερῶν νόμων καὶ τῶν ἀγράφων ἐθῶν], to believe that the Father and Creator of the universe is one God. (*Leg.* 115)[44]

There are, besides these rules, ten thousand other precepts, which refer to the unwritten customs and ordinances of the nation. (*Hypothetica/Apologia pro Judaeis* 7.6)[45]

The title given to *Hypo.* by Eusebius is born out by the contents; it is a defense of the Jews.[46] Thus the "unwritten customs and ordinances" is an allusion to the Jewish oral law. The same is true of the "unwritten customs" of *Leg.* 115, as the context demonstrates.[47] Wolfson's careful exegesis of *Spec. Leg. IV*, 149-50 makes it very probable that Philo there had the Jewish oral law in view.[48]

Paul's critique of the "unwritten laws" of the Jews would be identical with his rejection of the written law; they destroyed freedom. It is noteworthy that in *Spec. Leg.* 4.149–50 Philo automatically associates law with "compulsion" (ἀνάκῃ), exactly as does Paul in Philemon 14. To be under the law, written or oral, is to have no choice but to obey. Thus, [223] we

---

[43] Text from F. H. Colson, *Philo*, vol. 8, LCL (Cambridge, MA: Harvard, 1989).

[44] Text from Smallwood, *Legatio ad Gaium*, 82–83.

[45] Text from C. D. Yonge, *The Works of Philo: Complete and Unabridged* (Peabody, MA: Hendrickson, 1993), 743.

[46] See E. Schürer, *The History of the Jewish People in the Age of Jesus Christ*, ed. G. Vermes et al. (Edinburgh: Clark, 1979), 3:866–68.

[47] So Smallwood, *Legatio*, 209.

[48] Philo, *Foundations*, 190–94.

turn to the second set of texts in Philo, which are also "unwritten laws" but in a very different sense.

Living Laws

In his treatment of Genesis Philo describes the order of nature as it came into being through creation. He then turns to those figures who existed before the law was given through Moses. Their righteousness is explained by the fact that they spontaneously and instinctively followed the unwritten laws. Thus, the title of Philo's study of Abraham is "On Abraham, that is, the life of the wise man made perfect through teaching, or the first book on unwritten laws [Βίος σοφοῦ τοῦ κατὰ διδασκαλίαν τελειωθέντος ἢ νόμων ἀγράφων [α´], ὅ ἐστι περὶ Ἀβράαμ]." The other lives treated are those of Isaac, Jacob, and Joseph. The first two were written (*Abr.* 52) but have not survived.[49]

The Patriarchs and Moses

Philo explains,

(3) Let us postpone consideration of particular laws, which are, so to speak, copies, and examine first those which are more general and may be called the originals of those copies. (4) These are such men as lived good and blameless lives, whose virtues stand permanently recorded in the most holy scriptures, not merely to sound their praises but for the instruction of the reader and as an inducement to him to aspire to the same; (5) for in these men we have laws endowed with life and reason [οἱ γὰρ ἔμψυχοι καὶ λογικοὶ νόμοι ἄνδρες ἐκεῖνοι γεγόνασιν], and Moses extolled them for two reasons. First he wished to show that the enacted ordinances are not inconsistent with nature; and secondly that those who wish to live in accordance with the laws as they stand have no difficult task, seeing that the first generations before any at all of the particular statutes was set in writing followed the unwritten law with perfect ease, so that one might properly say that the enacted laws

[49] Schürer, *History*, 3:847.

are nothing else than memorials of the life of the ancients, preserving to a later generation their actual words and deeds. (*Abr.* 3–5)[50]

Two points in this text are of particular importance for understanding "the law of Christ." First, the ideal is attainable. A clear distinction must be made between theoretical and real possibility. It is a real possibility [224] to walk on the moon because men have done it. To walk on Mars is only a theoretical possibility because no one has yet done it; it may be a dream never to be achieved. The insistence of the first Christians on the historicity of Jesus was to show that his gospel was not a vague ideal but a real possibility, a lifestyle that had actually been lived and that, in consequence, could be imitated by his followers. Second, knowledge of figures who are "unwritten laws" can be mediated; personal acquaintance is not required. Scripture preserved the virtuous lives of the Patriarchs for future generations.

Philo concludes his life of Abraham with these words:

Moses adds this crowning saying "that this man did the divine law and the divine commands" [τὸν θεῖον νόμον καὶ τὰ θεῖα προστάγματα πάντα ἐποίησεν; Gen 26:5]. He did them, not taught by written words, but unwritten nature gave him the zeal to follow where wholesome and untainted impulse led him. And when they have God's promises before them what should men do but trust in them most firmly? Such was the life of the first, the founder of the nation, one who obeyed the law, some will say, but rather, as our discourse has shown, himself a law and an unwritten statute [νόμος αὐτὸς ὢν καὶ θεσμὸς ἄγραφος]. (*Abr.* 275–76)

Philo here adapts the classical concept of the law of nature to express the idea of the "original" of the Mosaic law. His distinction between "divine law" and "divine commands" is most naturally understood as an allusion to the written and oral law, and this would appear to be confirmed by the last line of the quotation "a law and an unwritten statute."

Perhaps, too, since he was destined to be a legislator [νομοθέτης], the providence of God which afterwards appointed him without his knowledge to that work, causing him long before that day to be the

---

[50] All texts from *Abr.* are from F. H. Colson, *Philo*, vol. 6, LCL (Cambridge, MA: Harvard, 1984).

reasonable and living impersonation of law [νόμος ἔμψυχός τε καὶ λογικὸς]. (*Mos.* 1.162)[51]

The laws cannot have existed if Moses was the one to commit them to writing. It goes without saying that Colson must be using "impersonation" in its strict sense of "personification." Not unreasonably Philo associates Moses with the Patriarchs as a "living law":

> I have in my former treatises set forth the lives of Moses and the other wise men down to his time, whom the sacred scriptures point out as the founders and leaders of our nation, and as its unwritten laws. (*Decal.* 1)

[225] *How a Living Person Acts as a Law: The Case of Joseph*

The fact of "living unwritten laws" having been established, the question now is: how do they function in practice? Philo illustrates the answer by reference to Joseph:

> In the prison he displayed such a wealth of virtue that even the vilest of the inmates were astounded and overawed, and considered that they had found in him a consolation for misfortunes and a defence against future ills. (*Jos.* 80)[52]

One of those converted was the chief prison officer:

> (85) Who tamed by the nobility of the youth, not only allowed him some security from violence and hardship, but gave him the command of all the prisoners. . . . (86) Instead of the tortures and punishments which they used to endure . . . they were rebuked by his wise words and doctrines of philosophy, while the conduct of their teacher effected more than any words. (87) For by setting before them his life of temperance and every virtue, like an original picture of skilled workmanship, he converted even those who seemed to be quite incurable, who, as the long-standing distempers of their soul abated, reproached themselves for their past, and repented with such utterances as these: "Ah, where in old days was this great blessing we at first failed to find? See, when it shines on us we behold as in a mirror our misbehaviour and are ashamed." (*Jos.* 85–87)

---

[51] Text from Colson, *Philo*, vol. 6.

[52] All the texts from *Jos.* are from Colson, *Philo*, vol. 6.

Finally, Philo sums up the life of Joseph:

> He died in goodly old age, having lived 110 years, unsurpassed in comeliness, wisdom and power of language. His personal beauty is attested by the furious passion which a woman conceived for him; his good sense by the equable temper he showed amid the numberless inequalities of his life, a temper which created order in disorder and concord where all was naturally discordant; the power of his language by his interpretations of the dreams and the fluency of his addresses and the persuasiveness which accompanied them, which secured him the obedience, not forced but voluntary, of everyone of his subjects [τῶν ἀρχομένων ἀνάγκῃ μᾶλλον ἢ ἑκὼν ὑπήκουε]. (*Jos.* 269)

Obviously, for Philo, the salient point in the career of Joseph was that his personality, and the comportment flowing therefrom, were more important than his words and had far greater impact. Thus, without any compulsion, his subjects[53] fell in with his wishes. Their freedom, rather [226] than being compromised by his rule, was enhanced by it. The parallel with the case of Paul and Philemon (vv. 8 and 14) is most striking (see above).

Wider Issues of Unwritten Law

Even though Galatia belonged to the sphere of Hellenistic Judaism, there is no trace of any Jewish presence there. S. Mitchell has shown that, while Jewish communities existed on the western and southern fringes of Phrygia, there were none in North Galatia itself.[54] Thus, it cannot simply be assumed that the thought of Philo could have been known to the Galatians through local synagogues. Hence, we must inquire whether they could have known of "living laws" from other sources.

Given the wealth and prestige of Philo's family, it is extremely probable that its members involved themselves in public service.[55] Philo's bent was for philosophical contemplation, but he could not avoid his social

[53] Philo had previously written, "He [the Pharoah] then appointed him [Joseph] viceroy of the kingdom, or rather, if the truth be told, king, reserving indeed to himself the name of the office, but resigning to him the actual sovereignty" (*Jos.* 119).

[54] *Anatolia: Land, Men, and Gods in Asia Minor* (Oxford: Clarendon, 1993), 2:31–37.

[55] See Schürer, *History*, 3:815.

responsibilities. In *Spec. Leg.* 3.1–6 he pours out his heartfelt grief that his contemplative peace has been disturbed by "my pitiless masters, who are not only men, but also the great variety of practical affairs which are deluged upon me from without like a torrent." This may be an allusion to his leadership of the delegation that the Jews of Alexandria sent to the emperor Gaius in AD 39 and 40, but his choice for this responsible position suggests previous active involvement in the affairs of the community. In this capacity it would be extraordinary if he did not reflect on the way the Romans governed Egypt, in particular on their protection of the Jews, as Roman law demanded. Minorities tend to be nervous, being fully aware of their dependence on the goodwill of the state. To survive they needed good governance.

But how should Egypt be governed? E. R. Goodenough answers very simply that Philo believed that the ideal prefect should model himself on Joseph, whose virtues made him the perfect ruler in the golden age of Egypt.[56] Fascinating as the details of this achievement are, the important point for my purpose is that Philo drew on a much older and widespread Hellenistic view of kingship. Goodenough, for example, quotes Cicero, who says of the ideal ruler,

> [227] He embraces in himself all those qualities to which he incites and summons the citizens, and imposes no law on the people which he does not himself observe, rather he presents his life as law to the citizens [*suam vitam, ut legem, praefert suis civibus*]. (*De Republica* 1.52)

Goodenough then goes on to say, "in representing Joseph, the ideal *politicus*, as a reforming force in the personal lives of his subjects, Philo is again following conventional Hellenistic notions of the ideal king" as a living law.[57] As evidence for this we have,

> It is a king's duty to command what is right and forbid what is wrong. But to command what should be done and to forbid what should not be done is the peculiar function of law; so that it follows at once that the king is a living law, and the law a just king

---

[56] *The Politics of Philo Judaeus: Practice and Theory* (New Haven, CT: Yale, 1938), 42–63. See also his "The Political Philosophy of Hellenistic Kingship," *Yale Classical Studies* 1 (1928): 53–102.

[57] *The Politics of Philo*, 54.

[ὡς εὐθὺς εἶναι τὸν μὲν βασιλέα νόμον ἔμψυχον, τὸν δὲ νόμον βασιλέα δίκαιον]. (*Mos.* 2:4)[58]

The parallel with Cicero is striking. Later Goodenough says,

> Much of Philo's theory of the king has already appeared in connection with his discussions of Joseph. It has been seen that his thought of the king was determined by the current hellenistic notions best preserved in the Neo-Pythagorean fragments on kingship, and that in presenting the ideal prefect in an allegory of Joseph Philo used almost every aspect of the royal theory, even to calling the ruler *theos*, to show how Joseph was the true pattern for the ruler to follow.[59]

In other words, the idea of a person as a "living unwritten law" went far beyond the limits of Hellenistic Judaism. Thus, there is every possibility that the idea filtered down to the Galatians. It must have been part of the stock in trade of every wandering philosopher (e.g., Dio Chrysostom [228] between AD 82 and 96) who in preaching idealism could by innuendo safely criticize the Roman authorities.

---

[58] Text from Colson, *Philo*, vol. 6. In the course of his description of the ideal ruler, Xenophon (c. 430–c. 354 BC) says of Cyrus, "He could in no way more effectively inspire a desire for the beautiful and the good than by endeavouring, as their sovereign, to set before his subjects a perfect model of virtue in his own person" (*Cyropaedia* 8.1.21; text from W. Miller, *Xenophon*, vol. 6, LCL [Cambridge, MA: Harvard, 1914]).

[59] *The Politics of Philo*, 90. Similarly W. Richardson, "There could hardly be a closer resemblance between this [*Jos.* 80, 87] and the doctrines about the sovereign influence of the Sage-King to heal his subjects and associates as found described in Neo-Pythagorean and other Hellenistic sources, especially Diotogenes ap. *Stob.* IV. VII. 62 and Ecphantus ap. *Stob.* VII. 56. [quoted in Goodenough, *The Politics of Philo*, 98]. The Sage-King set in order and tuned the souls of his subjects and followers by his very presence, mien and nature, as also by his words of wisdom and his dooms. Being above men by his very nature, which was nearer to God's and more expressly formed in his image, he lifted other men also nearer to God and to a higher nature, according as those other men achieved through his influence that harmony of soul which was the characteristic of the Νόμος Ἔμψυχος. This is exactly that nature and influence of the patriarchal Νόμος Ἔμψυχος in Philo. Their innate and effortless goodness is divine [= superhuman] and has a sovereign efficacy with their associates" ("The Philonic Patriarchs as Νόμος Ἔμψυχος" in *Studia Patristica I*, TU 63, ed. K. Aland and F. L. Cross [Berlin: Akademie-Verlag, 1957], 515–25, here 520–21).

The Galatians and the Law of Christ

Keeping in mind the Philonic texts quoted above, we are now in a position to look more closely at Paul's vision of Christ as the "living unwritten law."

The stories of the Patriarchs show that it was not necessary for the Galatians to have personally encountered Christ. Paul had told them his story. In recent years Paul's knowledge of the historical Jesus has been increasingly acknowledged. His letters not only contain a number of clear allusions to the teaching of Jesus[60] but on several occasions evoke the comportment of Jesus.[61] The obvious assumption that Paul spoke of the historical Jesus when he founded new communities is transformed into a fact by 2 Corinthians 11:4: "If someone comes and preaches another Jesus than the one we preached."[62]

This conclusion is confirmed and enriched by Galatians 3:1, where Paul asserts that in his preaching "before their eyes Jesus was portrayed crucified" (οἷς ὀφθαλμοὺς Ἰησοῦς Χριστὸς προεγράφη ἐσταυρωμένος). This half-verse is packed with an extraordinary amount of concentrated meaning.

The verb here is προγράφω, which is literally "to write before." But "before" is ambiguous. It can be understood in both a temporal sense (e.g., "whatever was previously written" [Rom 15:4]) and in a locative sense "to set forth as a public notice" (LSJ, 1473b). This latter meaning has been adopted by some commentators, perhaps on the basis of Colossians 2:14.[63] Paul, however, is evidently thinking in terms of a word picture. Hence, recent translations and commentaries all rightly opt for the meaning "to portray" (*RSV*), or a synonym, "to exhibit" (*NRSV*), "to display" (*NAB*), "to (paint) a clear picture" (*JB*), even though this meaning for προγράφω is attested nowhere else. This unusual departure from the [**229**] two actually attested meanings is made all the more exceptional

---

[60] Drawn from the central portion of the Sermon on the Plain in Luke and the Missionary Discourse; see D. C. Allison, "The Pauline Epistles and the Synoptic Gospels: The Pattern of the Parallels," *NTS* 28 (1982): 1–32.

[61] Notably 2 Thess 3:5; Gal 2:16; 3:22-23; Phil 1:8; 3:9; 2 Cor 1:19; 10:1; Rom 3:22, 26;15:2-3.

[62] For details, see my "Another Jesus (2 Cor 11:4)," *RB* 97 (1990): 238–51 = chap. 12 in my *Keys to Second Corinthians* (Oxford: Oxford University Press, 2010).

[63] Burton, *Galatians*, 144–45; H. Schlier, *Der Brief an die Galater*, MeyerK (Göttingen: Vandenhoeck & Ruprecht, 1962), 119.

by the fact that translations and commentaries feel constrained by the context to introduce a reinforcing adverb that has no correspondent in the Greek text, e.g., "publicly" (*RSV, NRSV*), "openly,"[64] "so vividly,"[65] "clearly."[66] The paraphrase of J. B. Phillips perfectly articulates Paul's activity in terms of its impact on the Galatians: "O you dear idiots of Galatia, who saw Jesus the crucified so plainly."[67]

Paul provided a key clue to his meaning in Galatians 3:1 by mentioning "eyes." Aristotle says formally, "Things are set before the eyes by words that signify actuality" (λέγω δὴ πρὸ ὀμμάτων ταῦτα ποιεῖν, ὅσα ἐνεργοῦντα σημαίνει; *Art of Rhetoric*, 3.11.2). He then discusses the sort of vivid phrases he has in mind and concludes, "actuality means movement" (ἡ δ' ἐνέργεια κίνησις; 3.11.4). The words chosen by the orator are so graphic that the scene comes to life. The point is taken up in the *Rhetorica ad Herennium*: "It is oracular demonstration when an event is so described in words that the business seems to be enacted and the subject to pass vividly before our eyes" (*Demonstratio est cum ita verbis res exprimitur ut geri negotium et res ante oculos videatur*; 4.55/68).[68] With a reference to Cicero, Quintilian develops the theme more thoroughly:

> The person who will show the greatest power in the expression of emotions will be the person who has properly formed what the Greeks call φαντασίας (let us call them "visions"), by which the images of absent things are presented to the mind in such a way that we seem actually to see them without eyes and have them physically present to us. [When these are expressed in appropriate words] the result will be ἐνάργεια, what Cicero calls *illustratio*, and also *evidentia*, a quality which makes us seem not so much to be talking about something as exhibiting it [*non tam dicere videtur quam ostendere*]. Emotions will ensue just as if we were present at the event itself. (*Institutio Oratoria* 6.2.29–32)[69]

---

[64] Dunn, *Galatians*, 152.

[65] Betz, *Galatians*, 128.

[66] Longenecker, *Galatians*, 98.

[67] *Letters to Young Churches* (London: Fontana, 1955).

[68] Text from H. Caplan, *(Cicero) Ad C. Herennium*, LCL (Cambridge, MA: Harvard, 1989), 405. In the corresponding note he translates *demonstratio* as ἐνάργεια, which in rhetoric meant "vivid description" (LSJ 556a). See also Cicero, *De Oratore* 2.46.191–94.

[69] Text from D. A. Russell, *Quintilian, The Orator's Education*, books 6–8, LCL (Cambridge, MA: Harvard, 2001).

To transform hearers into spectators was the summit of the orator's art. When Paul's intense involvement with the life of Jesus was combined [230] with his great rhetorical skill, his portrait of Jesus left an indelible mark on the Galatians. It must not be thought, however, that Paul's oral preaching focused exclusively on the death of Jesus. The above quotation from the *Rhetorica ad Herennium* continues, "ocular demonstration . . . we can effect by including what has preceded, followed and accompanied the event itself" (4.55.68). Moreover, R. B. Hays has shown that "Christ crucified" was intended to evoke the whole kerygma, which must have had a narrative framework of the entire ministry of Jesus.[70] The Galatians, in consequence, would have no difficulty in understanding what Paul meant by "the law of Christ."

It must also be kept in mind that the Galatians did not have to rely on Paul's words about Christ. They had lived with him for the best part of two years. Paul thought of himself as another Christ, "always carrying in the body the dying of Jesus, so that the life of Jesus may also be manifested in our bodies" (2 Cor 4:10);[71] "we have the mind of Christ" (1 Cor 2:16; cf. Phil 2:5-7). In his very first letter Paul reminds the Thessalonians of what kind of men he and his companions proved to be among them and immediately continues, "You became imitators of us and of the Lord" (ὑμεῖς μιμηταὶ ἡμῶν ἐγενήθητε καὶ τοῦ κυρίου; 1 Thess 1:6). The order is significant. They had seen Paul, but they had only been induced to envision Jesus. Hence, explicitly, "Be imitators of me, as I am of Christ" (1 Cor 11:1). Earlier in Galatians Paul had exhorted his readers, "Become as I am, because I became as you" (4:12).[72] They were like him, in that as Gentiles in an area without a Jewish presence, they were outside the orbit of the law. Now they must become like him

---

[70] *The Faith of Jesus Christ: An Investigation of the Narrative Substructure of Gal 3:1–4:11*, SBLDS 56 (Chico, CA: Scholars Press, 1983), 143–49, 196–98. Nonetheless, Wilson is entirely correct in pointing out that the Christ of Galatians is above all the crucified Christ, e.g., 2:19-21; 3:1, 13; 5:11, 24; 6:12, 14, 17; cf. 1:4; 4:4-5 (*The Curse of the Law*, 114).

[71] "Life" here is the life of virtue; for the various senses of "life" and "death," see Philo, *Fug.* 55.

[72] Gal 6:1-10 is paralleled by Phil 4:8-9 in that both contain a series of admonitions that would be at home in any Hellenistic ethical tract (cf. Betz, *Galatians*, 292). The latter, however, contains a specific invitation to imitation: "do what you have learned and received and heard and *seen* in me."

in maintaining their freedom from the law. Paradoxically, Paul asks the Galatians to behave as if they (like him) were former Jews.[73] Their only law is now "the law of Christ."

Why Paul chose to use "law" in this context becomes clear once the situation of the Galatians is recalled. In keeping with his custom, he left them with a few vague guidelines (Gal 5:21). It was up to the Galatians to work out what being a Christian meant in practice; "work out your **[231]** salvation with fear and trembling" (Phil 2:12). They refused the challenge. They were frightened by freedom and paralyzed by prudence.[74] They could not be sure that their choices were correct. Only this profound sense of insecurity explains the welcome that the Galatians gave the Judaizers.[75] The 613 precepts of the law offered them precise guidance guaranteed by God himself. Now worry could give way to certitude. Paul was right not to underestimate the seduction of the law, but the only "law" that he could offer them was "the law which is Christ."[76]

---

[73] Martyn, *Galatians*, 420.

[74] So, rightly, Betz, "The Galatians had been given the 'Spirit' and 'freedom', but they were left to that Spirit and freedom. There was no law to tell them what was right or wrong. There were no more rituals to correct transgressions. Under these circumstances their daily life came to be a dance on a tightrope" (*Galatians*, 9).

[75] Wilson suggests that the intruders appealed to the curse of the Law to persuade the Galatians to accept circumcision (*The Curse of the Law*, 68–94). He suggests that this would have been a particularly effective tactic because the Galatians had a well-developed fear of divine vengance. Unfortunately, the inscriptions to which he appeals come from all over Asia Minor/Anatolia and date from one to several centuries after Paul. As emigrant Celts the Galatians no doubt had a distinctive religiosity that set them apart from their environment, and so its documentation must come from a very restricted area and be limited to the first century AD.

[76] In a later letter Paul will apply this concept to himself, "not being without the law of God but under the law of Christ" (μὴ ὢν ἄνομος θεοῦ ἀλλ᾿ ἔννομος Χριστοῦ; 1 Cor 9:21). The law of God is now articulated in the law which is Christ. P. Esler comments very appositely, "The 'law of Christ' represents Paul's most daring inversion of the position of the Israelite outgroup and the final nail hammered into his argument that the Mosaic law is quite irrelevant in the new dispensation" (*Galatians*, NT Readings [London: Routledge, 1998], 231–32).

10

The Origins of Paul's Christology
From Thessalonians to Galatians

The Christology of Galatians contrasts vividly with that of the Thessalonian correspondence.[1] The personal perspectives that dominate in Galatians and that have become distinctive features of Pauline thought are entirely missing in Thessalonians. Yet there are only three years between 1–2 Thessalonians and Galatians,[2] and in both cases the audience was made up of converted pagans.[3]

My purpose in this essay has been admirably articulated, *mutatis mutandis*, by Lord Robert Skidelsky in writing about his life of John Maynard Keynes: "A biography of Keynes has to be able to explain the logic of his thinking, but always keeping in mind the question of why Keynes thought the way he did, and said what he did at any particular time."[4]

As a biographer of Paul, these are precisely my interests. Thus, the historical questions that must be answered are: (1) How and why did

---

[1] Originally published in *Christian Origins: Worship, Belief and Society; The Milltown Institute and the Irish Biblical Association Millenium Conference*, JSOTSup 241, ed. K. O'Mahony (Sheffield: Sheffield Academic Press, 2003), 113–42, whose pagination appears in the text in **bold**.

[2] In my view 2 Thessalonians is authentic and was written not long after 1 Thessalonians in AD 50; see, in particular, Robert Jewett, *The Thessalonian Correspondence: Pauline Rhetoric and Millenarian Piety*, Foundations and Facets, New Testament (Philadelphia: Fortress, 1986). The next letter written by Paul was Galatians, probably in the spring of AD 53; see my *Paul: A Critical Life* (Oxford: Clarendon, 1996), 180–82.

[3] As regards the Thessalonians, see most recently Richard. S. Ascough, "The Thessalonian Christian Community as a Professional Voluntary Association," *JBL* 119 (2000): 311–28. The Gentile character of the Galatians is clear from Gal 4:8, on which see my *Paul: A Critical Life*, 200 note 62.

[4] *The Economist*, vol. 357, n. 8198 (Nov. 25–Dec. 1, 2000), 109.

Paul adopt the Christology that we find in Thessalonians? (2) How and why did he develop radical new insights in Galatians, when he had lived happily with his old Christology for the best part of twenty years?

In attempting to respond to these questions, I will begin with an outline of the Christology of Thessalonians. This directs us backward to Paul's initial contacts with Christianity, both as a persecutor and as a believer. Only then will we be in a position to confront Galatians, which directs us forward, in the sense that it contains the seeds, but only the seeds, of important furture developments.

I must emphasize that I am not concerned with the origins of Christology as such [114] but with the beginnings of Paul's personal Christology.[5] Even that is not strictly accurate because limitations of time and space restrict me to certain aspects revealed in Paul's three earliest letters. He developed new christological insights subsequently, but these are not my concern here. I hope to deal with them in a future publication.

The Thessalonian Correspondence

In 1 and 2 Thessalonians Jesus is named as Ἰησοῦς ("Jesus"; 2x), Χριστός ("Christ"; 4x), Χριστός Ἰησοῦς ("Christ Jesus"; 2x), κύριος ("Lord"; 22x), κύριος Ἰησοῦς ("Lord Jesus"; 10x), κύριος Ἰησοῦς Χριστός ("Lord Jesus Christ"; 14x), υἱὸς αὐτοῦ ("his son"; 1x).[6] Two designations found in other letters are entirely absent in the Thessalonian correspondence, namely, (a) unqualified Ἰησοῦς Χριστός ("Jesus Christ"), which appears for the first time in Galatians 1:1, and (b) the association of κυριός with Χριστὸς Ἰησοῦς ("Christ Jesus"), which is invariably found in the form Χριστὸς Ἰησοῦς ὁ κύριος μοῦ/ἡμῶν ("Christ Jesus my/our Lord"), whose earliest attestation is Philippians 3:8 or Colossians 2:6.

---

[5] This distinction is not kept in mind consistently by M. Hengel, "Christologie und neutestamentliche Chronologie," in *Neues Testament und Geschichte*, FS Cullmann, ed. H. Baltenweiler and B. Reicke (Zürich: Zwingli, 1972), 43–67; nor by M. Casey, "Chronology and Development of Pauline Christology," in *Paul and Paulinism*, FS Barrett, ed. M. D. Hooker and S. G. Wilson (London: SPCK, 1982), 124–34.

[6] See, in particular, B. Rigaux, *Saint Paul. Les épîtres aux Thessaloniciens*, EBib (Paris: Gabalda; Gembloux: Duculot, 1956), 171–76. In this listing I abstract from the use of the possessive pronoun either singular or plural.

The most striking fact to emerge from these statistics is the preponderance of κύριος, which occurs in forty-six out of fifty-five references to Jesus in the Thessalonian correspondence. These two letters together contain 2,304 words. Galatians contains a mere seventy-four words less (2,230), yet κύριος appears only four times! Nothing could illustrate more graphically the difference between the Christologies of Thessalonians and Galatians.[7] Galatians, in fact, uses κύριος 4.8 times *less* than the average of the other non-Thessalonian letters.

It is widely agreed that 1 Thessalonians 1:9b-10 represents a fragment of the kerygma of the early church:[8]

ἐπεστρέψατε πρὸς τὸν θεὸν ἀπὸ τῶν εἰδώλων
　δουλεύειν θεῷ ζῶντι καὶ ἀληθινῷ
　　καὶ ἀναμένειν τὸν υἱὸν αὐτοῦ ἐκ τῶν οὐρανῶν,
ὃν ἤγειρεν ἐκ [τῶν] νεκρῶν,
　Ἰησοῦν τὸν ῥυόμενον ἡμᾶς
　　ἐκ τῆς ὀργῆς τῆς ἐρχομένης.

You turned to God from idols
　to serve the living and true God
　　and to wait for his Son from heaven
Whom he raised from the dead
　Jesus who delivers us
　　from the approaching wrath

[115] The great majority of the references to Jesus in 1 and 2 Thessalonians can be classified according to the elements of this credal statement.

• "to wait for his Son from heaven":[9]

Here I group the twelve references to Jesus in an eschatological context, all of which contain the word κύριος:

---

[7] This important point completely escapes I. Howard Marshall, "Pauline Theology in the Thessalonian Correspondence," in Hooker and Wilson, *Paul and Paulinism*, 176.

[8] The arguments are cogently presented by Ernest Best, *A Commentary on the First and Second Epistles to the Thessalonians*, BNTC (London: Black, 1979), 81–87.

[9] On the messianic interpretation of "Son of God," see John J. Collins, *The Scepter and the Star: The Messiahs of the Dead Sea Scrolls and other Ancient Literature*, ABRL (New York: Doubleday, 1995), 163–69; also J. D. G. Dunn, *Christology in the Making: A New Testament Inquiry into the Origins of the Doctrine of the Incarnation* (London: SCM, 1980), 35.

1 Thessalonians 2:19; 3:13; 4:6, 15-17; 5:2; 5:24.
2 Thessalonians 1:7, 9 (= Isa 2:10, 19, 21); 2:1, 2, 8, 14.

• "Whom he raised from the dead":
   "We believe that Jesus died and rose again" (1 Thess 4:14); "our Lord Jesus Christ who died for us" (1 Thess 5:9). Both of these are primitive credal elements; cf. 1 Corinthians 15:3-5. Note the complete absence of any mention of the modality of Christ's death, namely, crucifixion.

• "Jesus who delivers us":
   The context specifies the eschaton, but the present participle clearly implies that deliverance is taking place here and now.[10] This is why on the Last Day purified believers will not be subject to the divine anger. Thus, I group here the sixteen references to the grace-giving activity of Jesus in the church:
   1 Thessalonians 1:1; 3:8, 11, 12; 5:9, 18, 28.
   2 Thessalonians 1:1, 2, 12; 2:13 (= Deut 33:12), 16; 3:3, 4, 5, 16, 18.

The Thessalonian correspondence contains one certain and one probable reference to *the example of Jesus*. "You became imitators of us and of the Lord" (1 Thess 1:6). Jesus' acceptance of his messianic vocation involved suffering, to the point where his whole existence became a "dying" (2 Cor 4:10).[11] "May the Lord direct your hearts to the love of God and the steadfastness of Christ" (2 Thess 3:5). Both genitives should be understood subjectively.[12] Christ is an example of perseverance. He never wavered in [116] his committment. As an inspiration, he becomes the source of this grace for believers (cf. Polycarp, *Phil* 8).

Next there are conventional references to *the gospel and its ministers*. "The word of the Lord" (1 Thess 1:8; 4:15; 2 Thess 3:1) is, of course, "the gospel of Christ" (1 Thess 3:2; 2 Thess 1:8), which when proclaimed by "apostles of Christ" (1 Thess 2:6) brings into being "the churches of God in Christ Jesus" (1 Thess 2:14). As emissaries of Christ, ministers are endowed with his power to exhort (1 Thess 4:1-2) and command (2 Thess 3:6, 12).

---

[10] So, rightly, Best, *1 and 2 Thessalonians*, 84.

[11] Since it is question of a process, νέκρωσις here should be translated as "dying" rather than as "death," which is appropriate only in Rom 4:19.

[12] So Rigaux, *Thessaloniciens*, 699–700; Best, *1 and 2 Thessalonians*, 329–30.

The remaining references are difficult to classify precisely, but in general they are circumlocutions made necessary by the failure of the early church to develop an adjective and an adverb based on "Christ."[13] Thus, "the dead in Christ" (1 Thess 4:16) are simply "deceased Christians." "Those caring for you in the Lord" (1 Thess 5:12) are "those who care for you in a Christian way."

This summary is sufficient to demonstrate that what Paul said about Jesus (cf. 2 Cor 11:4) during the first half of his missionary career could have been said by Peter or anyone else familiar with the preaching of the early church.[14] There is no hint of personal reflection. This forces us to ask: why did Paul find the traditional formulae so congenial?

Paul's Pre-Christian Knowledge of Jesus

When Paul came to Jerusalem after finishing his education in Tarsus, he joined the Pharisees (Phil 3:5; cf. Gal 1:14), whose messianic expectation is considered to be reflected in Psalms 17 and 18 of the *Psalms of Solomon*.[15]

These look forward to the advent of a king who will be the son of David (17:21), and the "Anointed Lord" (Χριστὸς κύριος; 17:32; cf. Lam 4:20; Luke 2:11) or the "Anointed of the Lord" (Χριστὸς κυρίου; 18:7 and the psalm title; cf. 18:5).[16] He will rid the nation of its enemies (17:22-25) and restore Jerusalem, "making it holy as of old" (17:30). Despite a certain militant dimension (17:24; 18:7), the Messiah is not altogether a military figure. "He shall not put his trust in horse and rider and bow, nor shall he multiply for himself gold and silver for war" (17:33). His weapon is "the word of his mouth" (17:24, 35, 36). As a righteous king, "taught by God" (17:32) and [117] "pure from sin" (17:36), he is judge (17:26-29, 43) and shepherd (17:40-41). By destroying sinners (17:23, 36) and driving out Gentiles (17:22, 28), "he will gather together

---

[13] See R. Bultmann, *Theology of the New Testament* (London: SCM, 1965), 1:329.

[14] For a complementary perspective, see Karl P. Donfried, "1 Thessalonians, Acts and the Early Paul," in *The Thessalonian Correspondence*, BETL 87, ed. Raymond F. Collins (Leuven: University Press/Peeters, 1990), 3–26.

[15] For a balanced *status quaestionis*, see Joseph L. Trafton, "Solomon, Psalms of," *ABD* 6:115–17.

[16] On this problem, see Robert R. Hann, "*Christos Kyrios* in *PsSol* 17. 32: 'The Lord's Anointed' Reconsidered," *NTS* 31 (1985): 620–27.

a holy people . . . and he shall not suffer unrighteousness to lodge any more in their midst . . . for all shall be holy" (17:26-27, 32; cf. 18:8). The messianic community will be sinless.

It was against this template, or something very similar, that Paul the Pharisee measured the messianic claim of the followers of Jesus and found it wanting. Altogether apart from what he considered its erroneous character, he found the very fact of the claim to be deeply disturbing. Perhaps more clearly than the vast majority of Jesus' disciples, he recognized the implications of the Christian position.[17]

Paul lived in a spiritual world in which present and future were clearly distinguished. The present was dominated by the Pharisaic version of "covenant nomism."[18] In order to retain God's favor displayed in election, the Pharisees were committed to obedience to the terms of the covenant, in particular to the scrupulous observance of all the food purity prescriptions.[19] The Messiah had no place in this world characterized by meticulous concern for the law. He was a figure of the future. The sequential nature of the relationship meant that there was no tension between law and Messiah. One day he would simply arrive in the community of salvation as defined and guaranteed by the law.

By proclaiming Jesus as the Messiah, Christians redefined the community of salvation in a way that Paul found completely unacceptable. By insisting on the necessity of belief in Jesus as Savior, they were effectively saying that the law could not guarantee salvation. By accepting "sinners" whom the law rejected, they were saying that the decisions of the law had been superseded.[20] The *coexistence* of the Messiah and the law made them deadly rivals.

---

[17] The importance of Paul's preconversion perception of the Christian message for the development of his Christology has been convincingly demonstrated by Terence L. Donaldson, "Zealot and Convert: The Origin of Paul's Christ-Torah Antithesis," *CBQ* 51 (1989): 655–82.

[18] On "covenant nomism," see E. P. Sanders, *Paul and Palestinian Judaism: A Comparison of Patterns of Religion* (London: SCM, 1977), 320.

[19] J. Neusner, *The Rabbinic Traditions Concerning the Pharisees before 70* (Leiden: Brill, 1971), 3:304, 318.

[20] Donaldson, "Zealot and Convert," 678–79. See also Ulrick Wilckens, "Die Bekehrung des Paulus als religionsgeschichtliche Problem," *ZTK* 59 (1959): 273–93 = *Rechtfertigung als Freiheit: Paulusstudien* (Neukirchen-Vluyn: Neukirchener Verlag, 1974), 11–32.

This should have made Paul and the followers of Jesus bitter enemies. If one was right, the other was wrong. There could not be two Saviors. In fact, the hostility was entirely one-sided. The majority of Jewish Christians were convinced that they could simply graft their belief in Jesus as the Messiah onto their law-controlled lifestyle (Acts 2:46). Paul was much more perceptive. He recognized the intrinsic contradiction between his [118] vision of Judaism and that of the Christians. The latter, of course, could not be right in proclaiming Jesus as the Messiah. Thus, they had to be corrected, a lesson that his victims, and Paul himself at a later stage (Gal 1:14), understood as persecution.

Paul's persecution of the church is unintelligible unless he knew that Jesus' followers believed him to be the Messiah. This was not all, however, because much later in his life Paul confessed that prior to his conversion he had thought about Jesus in a way of which he was now deeply ashamed (2 Cor 5:16).[21] What was he thinking of?

We may safely assume that Paul the Pharisee knew at least as much about Jesus as his contemporary Josephus, who claimed to have joined the Pharisees in AD 56 (*Life* 12) and who wrote a paragraph on Jesus in his *Antiquities of the Jews* (18.63-64).[22] This provides us with two pieces of factual data about Jesus: (1) he had been crucified by Pontius Pilate as the result of Jewish charges, and (2) his disciples thought of him as the Messiah. In addition, there is a negative assessment of his ministry, namely, that those who listened to Jesus had an appetite for novelties and ascribed works to him that were frankly unbelievable. In other words, Josephus hints, Jesus was a charlatan who preyed on the credulous. Thus, the action of the Jewish authorities was entirely justified, and the claim of Jesus' Messianist followers preposterous.

Conversion

These, then, were the ideas about Jesus that were running through Paul's mind when that extraordinary encounter with Jesus took place in the vicinity of Damascus. In terms of the primacy given to Jesus as κύριος in Thessalonians, which reflects almost twenty years of preaching,

---

[21] κατὰ σάρκα is an adverb, "in a fleshly way," qualifying ἐγνώκαμεν, "we knew."

[22] On this text, see my *Paul: A Critical Life* (Oxford: Clarendon Press, 1996), 73–75 and the references given there.

the most revelatory reference to the event is Philippians 3:12, κατελήμ-φθην ὑπὸ Χριστοῦ Ἰησοῦ ("I was apprehended by Christ Jesus.")

The use of the aorist founds the consensus that this is an allusion to Paul's conversion.[23] Given Paul's attitude toward Jesus at the time, the connotation of καταλαμβάνω here must be "to seize with hostile intent."[24] The idea of a sudden and ruthlessly effective action is well brought out by F. F. Bruce: "Paul recalls his conversion as the occasion on which a powerful hand was laid [119] on his shoulder, turning him right round in his tracks, and a voice that brooked no refusal spoke in his ear: 'You must come along with me.'"[25] Jacques Dupont agrees, "en se montrant à Paul le Christ s'est imposé à lui d'une manière *irrésistible*. . . . il a l'impression que le Christ s'est emparé de lui tout d'un coup, sans lui donner la possibilité de se dérober."[26] Similarly, Seyoon Kim, "[Jesus] arrested him with his overwhelming power (Phil 3:12)."[27]

It would be difficult, if not impossible, to find a more graphic illustration of what an act of lordship means. Paul's first conviction regarding the true identity of Jesus, therefore, must have been the acknowledgment that he was κύριος.[28] Subsequently, Paul makes clear his feeling that he was "compelled" to preach the gospel (1 Cor 9:16). He also claimed to live under pressure that confined and restricted (2 Cor 5:14).

The experience of those who had known Jesus during his lifetime was significantly different. They had already committed themselves to Jesus, and they had to go through a reconversion process, but it was

---

[23] Marvin R. Vincent, *A Critical and Exegetical Commentary on the Epistles to the Philippians and to Philemon*, ICC (Edinburgh: Clark, 1897), 108. Gordon D. Fee. *Paul's Letter to the Philippians*, NICNT (Grand Rapids, MI: Eerdmans, 1995), 346 note 32.

[24] BAGD 413, 1.b.

[25] *Philippians*, NIBC (Peabody: Hendrickson, 1989), 120; similarly Peter T. O'Brien, *The Epistle to the Philippians: A Commentary on the Greek Text*, NIGTC (Grand Rapids, MI: Eerdmans, 1991), 425.

[26] "La conversion de Paul et son influence sur sa conception du salut par la foi," in *Foi et salut selon s. Paul. Colloque oecumenique à l'Abbeye de S. Paul hors les murs, 16–21 Avril 1968*, AnBib 42 (Rome: PIB, 1970), 67–88, here 85.

[27] *The Origin of Paul's Gospel*, WUNT 2.4, 2nd ed. (Tübingen: Mohr, 1984), 108.

[28] According to Joseph A. Fitzmyer, "*Kyrios* was originally applied to the parousaic Christ and then gradually retrojected to other, earlier phases of Jesus' existence" ("Pauline Theology," *NJBC*, §54). On the contrary, the usage grew out of concrete experience, not a future hope.

nothing like as radical as Paul's encounter with the risen Jesus. The earliest recognition narrative records the way in which the risen Jesus is acknowledged. Mary Magdalen calls him "Rabboni" (John 20:16). This, and similar titles that had been accorded to Jesus in his lifetime, are more likely to reflect the actual expressions of faith in the first days after the resurrection. Their inadequacy to express who Jesus now was, however, must have led to their being abandoned rather quickly. This explains both the silence of other recognition narratives and the intentional contrast in John 20:19-20 between "Jesus" who appears and "the Lord" who is recognized. The confession of Thomas, "My Lord and my God" (John 20:28), represents the final stage in this development.

The experience of the change in their lives that Jesus was bringing about, particularly when viewed in the context of the power displayed in the conversion of those who had first heard of Jesus as a crucified criminal, must have brought "Lord" automatically to the lips of the Jerusalem community when they confessed Jesus. This certainly happened long [120] before Paul made his first visit to the Holy City (Gal 1:18) and had probably spread abroad. The tribulations of the early years are reflected in the longing of the Aramaic prayer for the return of Jesus, which Paul preserves in the form μαράνα θά ("Our Lord, come!"; 1 Cor 16:22; cf. Rev 22:20; *Didache* 10:6).[29]

Once Paul had experienced Jesus as κύριος he had to acknowledge him as Χριστός. Jesus was not just any "Lord" but the Jewish Messiah for whom he hoped.[30] Moreover, if Jesus was the Messiah, he was the "Son of God."[31] Thus, right from the very beginning of his existence as a Christian, "Jesus," "Christ," "Lord," and "Son" would have been intimately associated in Paul's mind, because they were rooted in his experience as interpreted in the light of his Pharisaic background. There was no need for him to borrow them from the Christian communities he knew in

---

[29] See Joseph A. Fitzmyer, "New Testament *Kyrios* and *Maranatha* and their Aramaic Background," in his *To Advance the Gospel* (New York: Crossroads, 1981), 223–29.

[30] Not surprisingly "Christ" is never confessed as "Lord" in the Pauline letters, whereas "Jesus is Lord" (1 Cor 12:3) and "Jesus Christ is Lord" (2 Cor 4:5) do appear; see Nils A. Dahl, "The Messiahship of Jesus in Paul," in his *Jesus the Christ: The Historical Origins of Christological Doctrine* (Minneapolis: Fortress, 1991), 15–25, here 16.

[31] "The notion that the messiah was Son of God in a special sense was rooted in Judaism" (Collins, *The Scepter and the Star*, 169).

Damascus and Jerusalem.[32] Rather, he felt at home in such communities because they also confessed the lordship of Jesus Christ, precisely as he did. He would have *recognized* the formula κύριος Ἰησοῦς (Rom 10:9; 1 Cor 12:3; Phil 2:11) and known precisely what it meant; he would not have had to learn it.

The Jesus Tradition

What Paul would have learnt (*pace* Gal 1:11-12) in Damascus, and particularly from Peter in Jerusalem, were the traditions about Jesus. Apart from references to the death and resurrection, the list of "facts" about the historical Jesus in the Pauline letters is short and well known. He was born into a Jewish family (Gal 4:4) of Davidic descent (Rom 1:3). He had several brothers (1 Cor 9:5), one of whom was called James (Gal 1:19). He was opposed to divorce (1 Cor 7:10-11) and taught that the gospel should provide a living for its ministers (1 Cor 9:14). On the night he was betrayed (1 Cor 11:23), he celebrated a meal of bread and wine with his followers and directed that it become a commemorative ritual (1 Cor 11:23-25).

[121] Do such sparse gleanings mean that Paul was uninterested in anything about Jesus except the passion and resurrection? A negative answer is recommended both by general principles and specific evidence.[33] Simple statements of the basic faith of the community (e.g., 1 Cor 15:3-5) are likely to have whetted the natural curiosity of Christians for further knowledge of him who was their hero, a quest that eventually resulted in the Synoptic Gospels, which are biographies in the way this (anachronistic) term was understood in the first century.[34]

---

[32] Those who insist that "Paul derived the use of 'Lord' for the risen Christ from the early Jewish-Christian community of Jerusalem itself" (Fitzmyer, "Pauline Theology," *NJBC*, §54) forget Paul's preconversion knowledge of Jesus and the fact that he had been a Christian for over three years before he went to Jerusalem (Gal 1:17-18).

[33] See most recently James D. G. Dunn, *The Theology of Paul the Apostle* (Grand Rapids, MI: Eerdmans, 1998), 185–95.

[34] See in particular David E. Aune, *The New Testament in Its Literary Environment*, Library of Early Christianity (Philadelphia: Westminster, 1987), 17–76; R. A. Burridge, *What Are the Gospels? A Comparison with Graeco-Roman Biography*, SNTSMS 70 (Cambridge: Cambridge University Press, 1992).

Moreover, the emerging Jesus movement needed a sacred tradition as the basis of its ongoing self-definition.[35] Those who were at the heart of that process had lived with Jesus from the time of his baptism by John (Acts 1:22; cf. John 1:35-51). Their memories of what Jesus had said and done[36] provided authoritative data for the resolution of theological and ethical problems and furnished reliable ammunition in apologetic or polemic exchanges with nonbelievers.[37] As such stories became disseminated within the Jesus movement, they constituted the shared knowledge that was a prime bonding factor. They underlay a common language inaccessible to outsiders. A word evoked a whole saying of Jesus; a phrase, an entire event. Those who did not catch an allusion revealed that they did not belong.

Thus, we should not expect to find in Paul's letters explicit, and attributed, quotations of the words of Jesus. In fact, as Dunn points out with great insight, "had he [Paul] cited Jesus' authority every time he referred to something Jesus said or did he would have *weakened* the force of the allusion as allusion. The allusion that has to be explained has lost its bonding effect."[38]

The existence of an allusion cannot be demonstrated. Its creation is an art, and its existence is "sensed" or "discerned." The issue is so delicate that it can only be approached intuitively. Nonetheless, lists of allusions to the sayings of Jesus are debated with an inappropriate rigor

[35] [See now J. D. G. Dunn, *Christianity in the Making*, vol. 1: *Jesus Remembered* (Grand Rapids, MI/Cambridge, UK: Eerdmans, 2003).]

[36] See Eusebius, *Church History*, 3.39.15, and the excellent, albeit unintentional, commentary by Victor Paul Furnish, *Jesus according to Paul*, Understanding Jesus Today (Cambridge: Cambridge University Press, 1993), 22–23.

[37] Heinz Schürmann, "Die vorösterlichen Anfänge der Logientradition. Versuch eines formgeschichtlichen Zugangs zum Leben Jesu," in *Der historische Jesus und der kerygmatische Christus. Beiträge zum Christusverständnis in Forschung und Verkündigung*, ed. H. Ristow and K. Matthiae (Berlin: Evangelische Verlagsanstalt, 1962), 342–70. [For an accurate estimate of the time span, see R. Bauckham, *Jesus and the Eyewitnesses: The Gospels as Eyewitness Testimony* (Grand Rapids, MI/Cambridge, UK: Eerdmans, 2006).]

[38] *Theology of Paul the Apostle*, 652; cf. 283. A. J. M. Wedderburn turns the situation on its head in writing that "the fact that they are almost all *allusions*, not explicit quotations, remains a problem" ("Paul and Jesus: The Problem of Continuity," *SJT* 38 [1985]: 189–203, here 190).

that irrestistibly evokes the dissection of a soufflé by means of a spade.[39] There is little [122] doubt, however, in the minds of the sensitive that "the persistent conviction that Paul knew next to nothing of the teaching of Jesus must be rejected. Jesus of Nazareth was not the faceless presupposition of Pauline theology. On the contrary, the tradition stemming from Jesus well served the apostle in his roles as pastor, theologian and missionary."[40]

The concentration on dominical sayings in the Jesus-Paul debate has led to neglect of an important aspect of Paul's appropriation of the Jesus tradition. This has been remedied by Dunn, who draws attention to a number of passages in Romans in which Paul appeals to the *example* of Jesus.[41] Τύπος διδαχῆς ("form of teaching"; Rom 6:17), Dunn argues, evokes Christ as the model of Christian conduct. The use of "Abba, Father" in Romans 8:15-16 is a conscious appropriation of the way Jesus prayed. "To put on Christ" (Rom 13:14) is given its full intelligibility only when understood as theatrical language for the effort to think oneself into another character, which here is Christ. "Implicit is the thought that the 'role model' is more than simply the single act of obedience to the death of the cross, but must include sufficient knowledge of how Jesus lived in relationships to serve as a model for living in Rome."[42] This conclusion is reinforced by the final example, "let each of us please his neighbour . . . for Christ did not please himself" (Rom 15:2-3), where Christ is the model of concern for the "weak" (cf. Rom 5:6). "Tenderness" or "compassion" (σπλάγχνα) is evoked as characteristic of the ministry

---

[39] A particularly good example of such heavy-handed treatment is to be found in Franz Neirynck, "Paul and the Sayings of Jesus," in *L'Apotre Paul. Personnalité, style et conception du ministère*, BETL 73, ed. A. Vanhoye (Leuven: University Press, 1986), 265–321. For those who did not catch the allusion, the English periodical *Punch* said that to criticize P. G. Wodehouse was "like taking a spade to a soufflé."

[40] Dale C. Allison Jr., "The Pauline Epistles and the Synoptic Gospels: The Pattern of the Parallels," *NTS* 28 (1982): 1–32, here 25.

[41] "Paul's Knowledge of the Jesus Tradition: The Evidence of Romans," in *Christus Bezeugen*, FS Trilling, ed. K. Kertelge, et al. (Leipzig: Benno-Verlag, 1989), 193–207, particularly 195–200.

[42] Dunn, "Paul's Knowledge," 198. See also M. Thompson, *Clothed with Christ: The Example and Teaching of Jesus in Romans 12.1–15.13*, JSNTSup 59 (Sheffield: Sheffield Academic Press, 1991).

of Jesus (Phil 1:8),[43] as are "meekness" and "gentleness" (πραΰτης καὶ ἐπιείκεια; 2 Cor 10:1). Thus, the references to the example of Jesus in Thessalonians (see above) were part of the normal pattern of Paul's thought.

If Paul's oldest and most insightful commentator is correct in recognizing that for the Apostle "Jesus" was the truth of "Christ" (Eph 4:21),[44] then his Christology cannot be divorced from his knowledge of the historical Jesus. The way Paul thought about Jesus as the Christ was profoundly influenced by the words and deeds attributed to him. Paul identified so closely with the historical Jesus (2 Cor 4:10-11) that he could claim ἡμεῖ δὲ νοῦν Χριστοῦ ἔχομεν ("we have the mind of Christ"; 1 Cor 2:16).

The Beginnings of a Personal Christology

[123] Paul wrote 1 Thessalonians in the late spring of AD 50 and 2 Thessalonians sometime during the summer of that year. He stayed on in Corinth for a further year and then went to Jerusalem for the dramatic meeting regarding the conditions under which Gentiles could be admitted as members of the church (Gal 2:1-10). The decision went in Paul's favor. Gentiles did not have to be circumcised. He returned to Antioch, his home base (Acts 13:1-3; 15:40), where he spent the winter of AD 51 to 52.

During that time, the famous "incident" involving Peter took place (Gal 2:11-14). James sent a delegation to Antioch to exhort Jewish converts to more stringent observance of the dietary laws. This effort to strengthen their Jewish identity was the counterpart of James' refusal to circumcise Gentile converts, which would have diluted and blurred Jewish identity.[45] The consequences for the church at Antioch were se-

---

[43] Dunn (*Theology*, 193 note 55) points out that the corresponding verb (σπλαγχ-νίζομαι) is used of Jesus' emotional response on several occasions during his ministry (Mark 1:41; 6:34; 8:2; 9:22; Matt 9:36; 20:34; Luke 7:13).

[44] See, in particular, I. de la Potterie, "Jésus et la vérité d'après Eph 4, 21," in *Studiorum Paulinorum Congressus Internationalis Catholicus 1961*, AnBib 18 (Rome: Pontifical Biblical Institute, 1963), 45–57.

[45] For the justification of this hypothesis, see my "Nationalism and Church Policy: Reflections on Gal 2:1-14," in *Communion et Réunion. Mélanges Jean-Marie Roger Tillard*, BETL 121, ed. G. R. Evans and M. Gourgues (Leuven: Peeters, 1995), 283–91 = chap. 5 above.

vere. In order to maintain table fellowship, which was the visible sign of unity, Gentile members of the community had to live like Jews. Antioch effectively became a law-observant church, which Paul could no longer represent.

As soon as snow cleared in the passes of the Taurus range in the spring of AD 52, Paul left Antioch forever. On his way to Ephesus he revisited the Galatians. The following spring he received a tremendous shock: a delegation from Antioch had arrived in Galatia and was endeavoring to persuade the Galatians to adopt the new law-observant ethos of Antioch, its mother church. Paul, it will be remembered, had been acting as an agent of Antioch (Acts 13:1-3) when he founded the churches of Galatia. In response, Paul wrote the letter to the Galatians.

This letter, written some three years after the Thessalonian correspondence, exhibits a completely different Christology. The severe drop in the frequency of κύριος ("Lord") has already been noted. This, however, is only a minor factor. Two other points are infinitely more significant.

The first is the number of references to the crucifixion: σταυρός, ("cross"; 5:11; 6:12, 14); σταυρόω ("to crucify"; 2:19; 3:1; 5:24; 6:14); κρεμάννυμι ἐπὶ ξύλον ("to hang on a tree"; 3:13). The closest any other epistle comes to these eight allusions is 1 Corinthians with six. Cross or crucifixion was not mentioned even once in 1–2 Thessalonians.

The second is a series of statements which emphasize the union of the believer with Christ and the union of believers among themselves [124]: Χριστῷ συνεσταύρωμαι ζῶ δὲ ουκέτι ἐγώ, ζῆ δὲ ἐν ἐμοὶ Χριστός ("I have been crucified with Christ. It is no longer I who live, but Christ in me"; 2:19-20); ὅσοι γὰρ εἰς Χριστὸν ἐβαπτίσθητε, Χριστὸν ἐνεδύσασθε . . . πάντες γὰρ ὑμεῖς εἷς ἐστε ἐν Χριστῷ Ἰησοῦ ("as many of you as were baptized into Christ have put on Christ . . . you are all one man in Christ Jesus"; 3:27-28); πάλιν ὠδίνω μέχρις οὗ μορφωθῇ Χριστὸς ἐν ὑμῖν ("I am again in travail until Christ is formed in you"; 4:19); κατηργήθητε ἀπὸ Χριστοῦ ("you were severed from Christ"; 5:4).

These extraordinary developments demand an explanation. We shall look first at crucifixion and then consider union with Christ.

A Crucified Messiah

Even though the first mention of the crucifixion of Jesus occurs in Galatians, Paul himself informs us that a crucified Messiah had been part of his oral preaching for a considerable time before that.̂ Ὦ ἀνόητοι Γαλάται, . . . οἷς κατ' ὀφθαλμοὺς Ἰησοῦς Χριστὸς προεγράφη ἐσταυρ-ωμένος ("O foolish Galatians . . . before whose eyes Jesus Christ was publicly portrayed as crucified"; Gal 3:1). The allusion is to his initial preaching in Galatia, which brings us back to the beginning of Paul's first independent missionary journey at the very least.[46] As I have said above, the density of meaning packed into these few words is incredible.[47]

Paul must have felt very deeply about the crucifixion of Jesus. It had made such an impact on him that he felt compelled to attempt to replicate it for others. Why?

One thing is certain. Paul did not inherit his stress on the crucifixion of Jesus from his contemporaries in the early church. None of the fragments of the primitive kerygma that Paul quotes (1 Thess 1:9-10; 4:14; 5:9; Gal 1:3-4; 1 Cor 15:3-5; Rom 1:3-4; 4:24-25; 10:9) mentions the crucifixion.[48] The eucharistic words (1 Cor 11:23-25) and two liturgical hymns (Phil 2:6-11; Col 1:15-20) are equally silent. Such reticence is entirely understandable. To preach a Messiah who had died without apparently achieving anything was difficult enough. To preach a crucified Messiah was virtually impossible. For Paul to make the crucifixion, of which he had been informed as a Pharisee (see above), the centerpiece of his ministry certainly demands explanation.

The Sinless Messiah

The most appropriate place to begin is with Paul's Pharisaic background, and in particular with the portrait of the Messiah drawn by *PsSol* 17 (see above). A unique feature of this presentation is that the expected Messiah will be καθαρός ("pure from sin"; 17:36), or, in other [**126**] words, οὐκ ἀσθήσει ("he will not stumble"; 17:38). Unusual as this may be,[49] in this psalm it harmonizes perfectly with the reiterated stress on the

---

[46] On that same journey Paul evangelized Corinth, where he also preached a crucified Christ (1 Cor 2:1-12).

[47] For the details, see pp. 140–41 in chap. 9 above.

[48] The standard list is given in Joseph A. Fitzmyer, *Paul and His Theology: A Brief Sketch*, 2nd ed. (Englewood Cliffs, NJ: Prentice Hall, 1989), 32.

[49] "There is no indisputable Jewish parallel for such a statement about the messiah" (Collins, *The Scepter and the Star*, 55).

holiness of the messianic people. The Messiah συνάξει λαὸν ἅγιον . . . καὶ κρινεῖ φυλὰς λαοῦ ἡγιασμένον ὑπὸ κυρίου αὐτοῦ ("shall gather together a holy people . . . and he shall judge the tribes of the people made holy by the Lord his God"; 17:26). Καὶ οὐκ ἔστιν ἀδικία ἐν ταῖς ἡμέραις αὐτοῦ ἐν μέσῳ αὐτῶν ὅτι πάντες ἅγιοι ("and in his days there shall be no wickedness in their midst, for all shall be holy"; 17:32); οἱ λόγοι αὐτοῦ ὡς λόγοι ἁγίων ἐν μέσῳ λαῶν ἡγιασμένων ("his words shall be as the words of the holy ones in the midst of peoples made holy"; 17:43).

In thus underlining the sanctity of the messianic people Psalm 17 reflects a mainstream Jewish vision of the eschaton. It is the teaching of the great prophets: ὁ λαός σου πᾶς δίκαιος ("all your people will be just"; Isa 60:21). Καθαρισθήσεσθε ἀπὸ πασῶν τῶν ἀκαθαρσιῶν ("you shall be clean from all your uncleannesses"; Ezek 36:25). Equally, it is found in wisdom texts: οἱ ἐργαζόμενοι ἐν ἐμοὶ οὐχ ἁμαρτήσουσυν ("those who work with me [wisdom] will not sin"; Sir 24:22). And in the intertestamental literature: "There shall be bestowed on the elect wisdom, and they shall all live and never again sin . . . and they shall not again transgress, nor shall they sin all the days of their life" (1 Enoch 5:8-9).

Common sense dictates that, as the leader of a holy people, the Messiah cannot be a sinner.[50] The silence of texts other than Psalm 17 must not be interpreted as denial of his sinlessness. On the contrary, the absolute righteousness of the Messiah is taken completely for granted.[51]

The Messiah Should Not Die

This has a consequence whose importance has not been recognized. It was widely believed that *the Messiah would not die*. The basis for this is complex. One element is a series of Jewish texts in which death is seen, not as integral to the structure of the human being, but as a penalty imposed for sin.

The oldest text is from Genesis: "but of the tree of knowledge of good and evil you are not to eat. On the day you eat of it, by death you shall

---

[50] So, rightly, Gene L. Davenport, "The 'Anointed of the Lord' in Psalms of Solomon 17," in *Ideal Figures in Ancient Judaism: Profiles and Paradigms*, SBLSCS 12, ed. John J. Collins and George Nickelsburg (Atlanta: Scholars Press, 1980), 67–92, here 80.

[51] See S. Mowinckel, *He That Cometh*, trans. G. W. Anderson (Oxford: Blackwell, 1959), 308–11.

die" (Gen 2:17). [127] In order to harmonize this verse with Genesis 3:19, commentators often understand it as an allusion to "spiritual" death, i.e., separation from God. It is much more likely, however, that Genesis 2:17 was intended, and was so understood, as an explanation of the origin of death. The formula used has a fixed juridical meaning, which implies that death is the consequence of a defined act. Physical death is held out as a threat to enforce obedience to the commandment. It cannot, in consequence, be considered integral to human existence. This relationship between sin and death is reiterated by the woman in Genesis 3:23. Death is a punishment inflicted from without.

This interpretation is confirmed by the Wisdom of Solomon: "God created humanity in a state of incorruptibility; in the image of his own eternity he made him, but through the devil's envy death entered the world as those who belong to him find to their cost" (Wis 2:23-24).

The reference is certainly to physical death, because it is a death which "entered the world." This excludes an allusion to a second death that takes place after physical death in another dimension of existence. Clearly, the fact of physical death has introduced a change into God's plan for humanity because God created humanity to live forever (cf. Wis 1:12-14). ἐπ᾽ ἀφθαρσίᾳ means "in" or "with" incorruptibility, not "for" incorruptibility. Even though Wisdom uses ἐπι with the dative twenty-two times, it never indicates finality. A state is clearly envisaged in Wisdom 1:13; 17:3, 7; 18:13.[52] The author of Wisdom knew that flesh of itself is φθαρτός ("subject to corruption"; Wis 9:15; cf. 19:21). That is why he chose the Epicurean term ἀφθαρσία to describe the original condition of humanity. The Epicureans believed that gods and humans were composed of atoms which tended to fly apart. Nonetheless, unlike humans, the gods lived for ever. The reason is that they were endowed with ἀφθαρσία.[53] The use of this term apropos of primitive humanity betrays the author's belief that ἀφθαρσία ("incorruptibility") was not a property of human nature. In opposition to Plato, the sage never predicates immortality of the human soul.[54] After humanity had sinned, the punishment that God inflicted was the removal of the gift of ἀφθαρσία

---

[52] Note also "the invention of idols was the corruption of life" (Wis 14:12).

[53] James Reese, *Hellenistic Influence on the Book of Wisdom and Its Consequences*, ABib 41 (Rome: PBI, 1970), 65–66.

[54] Reese, *Hellenistic Influence on the Book of Wisdom*, 62.

("incorruptibility"). This meant that human nature took its course. It was now θνητός ("liable to [128] death, mortal"; Wis 7:1; 9:14; 15:17). "Incorruptibility," however, could be recovered by the obedient possession of wisdom (Wis 9:18-19).[55]

A similar, but less developed, understanding of human nature is found in Ben Sira. "From a woman sin had its beginning, and because of her we all die" (Sir 25:24). This is not a spin-off from the profoundly mysoginist crititicism of women in Sirach 25:13-26.[56] It simply reflects the clear lesson of Genesis 2–3. If Eve through her sin is the cause of mortality, then death is not natural but an externally inflicted punishment.

The intimate relationship between sinful humanity (*not* humanity as such) and death is forcefully articulated in 1 Enoch: "Human beings were created to be like angels, permanently to maintain pure and righteous lives. Death, which destroys everything, would have not touched them, had it not been through through their knowledge by which they shall perish; death is now eating us by means of this power" (69:11; cf. 98:4). The reference to "knowledge" immediately points us, once again, toward Genesis 2–3. The original sin was eating the fruit of "the tree of knowledge" (Gen 2:17), and death is its consequence.[57]

In the case of the sinless Messiah, this right to live forever was reinforced by other factors, which have been well brought out by Mowinckel:

> It was only natural that in the specific, individual prediction or description of the Messianic kingdom, the kingly rule of the Messiah came as a glorious climax, beyond which neither thought nor imagination sought to reach.[58] . . . But, apart from the idea of an interim kingdom, the idea of the two aeons helped to make the the Messiah not only a specific individual, but an eternal being.[59]

---

[55] This, of course, introduces complications into the meaning of "death" in Wisdom, but simplistic harmonization is to be avoided; see Michael Kolarcik, *The Ambiguity of Death in the Book of Wisdom 1–6*, ABib 127 (Rome: PBI, 1991).

[56] So Egon Brandenberger, *Adam und Christus. Exegetisch-religionsgeschichtliche Untersuchung zu Röm. 5:12-21 (1 Kor. 15)*, WMANT 7 (Neukirchen: Neukirchener Verlag, 1962), 53.

[57] Many other texts could be cited to show the persistence of this belief in Judaism into the later rabbinic period, but my focus is on those which antedate Paul.

[58] This is confirmed by Davenport for *PsSol* 17 ("The Anointed of the Lord," 79).

[59] *He That Cometh*, 324. According to M. Hengel, to speak of the death of the Messiah was "an unprecedented novelty" which flew in the face of all popular expectation (*The*

The Gift of Self

[129] Yet the Messiah whom Paul recognized in his encounter on the road to Damascus had been put to death on the cross! Paul had to reconcile *a sinless Messiah who was also a dead Messiah*. It did not prove very difficult. If someone on whom death had no claim, in fact, died, only one explanation is possible. He *chose* to die. Once Paul had accepted this insight, the death of Jesus ceased to be a problem. Its modality then became the central issue: why did Jesus choose this horrible form of death? And Paul's answer is that Jesus willed it to demonstrate the extent of his love for us.

In order to justify this hypothesis, let us return to Galatians. In the opening greeting Jesus is identified as τοῦ δόντος ἑαυτὸν ὑπὲρ τῶν ἁμαρτιῶν ἡμῶν ("the [one] having given himself for our sins"; Gal 1:4). This formula is regularly treated as representative of the primitive kerygma.[60] This is highly improbable. While ὑπὲρ τῶν ἁμαρτιῶν ἡμῶν may reflect the influence of creeds such as 1 Corinthians 15:3-5 (cf. Rom 4:24), the same cannot be said of τοῦ δόντος ἑαυτόν ("the [one] having given himself"), as the list of allusions to Christ's self-sacrifice reveals:

- καὶ γὰρ ὁ υἱὸς τοῦ ἀνθρώπου οὐκ ἦλθεν διακονηθῆναι ἀλλὰ διακονῆσαι καὶ δοῦναι τὴν ψυχὴν αὐτοῦ λύτρον ἀντὶ πολλῶν ("The Son of Man came not to be served but to serve and to give his life as a ransom for many"; Mark 10:45 = Matt 20:28).

- τοῦ δόντος ἑαυτὸν ὑπὲρ τῶν ἁμαρτιῶν ἡμῶν ("The [one] having given himself for our sins"; Gal 1:4).

Atonement: The Origins of the Doctrine in the New Testament [Philadelphia: Fortress, 1981], 40). There is only one explicit reference to the death of the Messiah: "My Servant the Messiah shall be revealed, together with those who are with him, and shall rejoice the survivors four hundred years. And it shall be, after these years, that my servant the Messiah shall die, and all in whom there is human breath. Then shall the world be turned into the primeval silence seven days, like as at the first beginnings" (4 Ezra 7:28-30). The Hebrew original of this work must be dated in the early part of the second century AD; see Bruce Metzger in J. H. Charlesworth, *The Old Testament Pseudepigrapha* (New York: Doubleday, 1985), 1:520. It is now clear that the Messiah in 4Q285 "is the subject of the verb to kill, not its object" (Collins, *The Scepter and the Star*, 58–59).

[60] So, most formally, J. Louis Martyn, *Galatians*, AB (New York: Doubleday, 1997), 88; but also F. F. Bruce, *The Epistle to the Galatians*, NIGTC (Exeter: Paternoster, 1982), 75; J. D. G. Dunn, *The Epistle to the Galatians*, BNTC (Peabody, MA: Hendrickson, 1993), 35.

- πίστει ζῶ τῇ τοῦ υἱοῦ τοῦ θεοῦ τοῦ ἀγαπήσαντός με καὶ παραδόντος ἑαυτὸν ὑπὲρ ἐμοῦ ("I live by faith in the Son of God who loved me and gave himself for me"; Gal 2:20).

- ἑαυτὸν ἐκένωσεν ("He emptied himself"; Phil 2:7).

- ἐταπείνωσεν ἑαυτὸν γενόμενος ὑπήκοος μέχρι θανάτου, θανάτου δὲ σταυροῦ ("He humbled himself, becoming obedient unto death, even death on a cross"; Phil 2:8).

- ὁ Χριστὸς ἠγάπησεν ἡμᾶς καὶ παρέδωκεν ἑαυτὸν ὑπὲρ ἡμῶν ("Christ loved us and gave himself for us"; Eph 5:2) [130].

- ὁ Χριστὸς ἠγάπησεν τὴν ἐκκλησίαν καὶ ἑαυτὸν παρέδωκεν ὑπὲρ αὐτῆς ("Christ loved the church and gave himself for her"; Eph 5:25).

- ἄνθρωπος Χριστὸς Ἰησοῦ, ὁ δοὺς ἑαυτὸν ἀντίλυτρον ὑπὲρ πάντων ("The man Christ Jesus, who gave himself as a ransom for all"; 1 Tim 2:5-6).

- ὃ ἔδωκεν ἑαυτὸν ὑπὲρ ἡμῶν, ἵνα λυτρώσηται ἡμᾶς ("He who gave himself for us to redeem us"; Titus 2:14).

- πόσῳ μᾶλλον τὸ αἷμα τοῦ Χριστοῦ, ὃ διὰ πνεύματος αἰωνίου ἑαυτὸν προσήνεγκεν ἄμωμον τῷ θεῷ ("How much more shall the blood of Christ, who through the eternal Spirit offered himself without blemish to God"; Heb 9:14).

Chronologically, the two earliest references to Christ's self-sacrifice are to be found in Galatians, and there is no reason to think that Paul borrowed from anyone.[61] The next two allusions appear in a hymn (Phil 2:6-11) which is strongly influenced by Paul's preaching and which he adapted by explicitating the modality of Christ's self-giving, namely, "even death on a cross" (Phil 2:8).[62] An implicit evocation of self-giving appears in a parallel addition to the Colossian hymn εἰρηνοποιήσα διὰ

---

[61] So, rightly, Gabriella Berényi, "Gal 2,20: A Pre-Pauline or a Pauline Text?," *Biblica* 65 (1984): 490–537.

[62] One of the most formal references to Jesus Christ's choice of death is to be found in the opening verse of this hymn: οὐχ ἁρπαγμὸν ἡγήσατο τὸ εἶναι ἴσα θεῷ "he did not use to his own advantage his right to be treated as a god" (Phil 2:6); see my "Christological Anthropology in Philippians 2:6-11," *RB* 83 (1976): 37–40 and the references there given.

τοῦ αἵματος τοῦ σταυροῦ αὐτοῦ ("making peace by the blood of his cross"; Col 1:20).[63]

If the theme of Jesus' self-sacrifice is so firmly rooted in Paul's preaching, it would be very surprising were it not found in letters attributed to the "Pauline School." In fact, it surfaces in Ephesians, 1 Timothy, Titus, and Hebrews,[64] and nowhere else, with the exception of the dominical logion in Mark 10:45. Given Paul's rather detailed knowledge of the Jesus' tradition (see above), it is not at all impossible that he should have been [131] influenced by this gospel text,[65] provided, of course, that it is authentic, but this hypothesis is not at all necessary.

The evidence points unambiguously to the conclusion that Paul was the first to understand the death of Christ as a matter of choice. Jesus did not merely accept death, as do all other humans who are sinners; he decided to die. He opted for death. He made a decision that he did not have to make. Only now does it become possible to understand the tremendous importance that Paul gave the death of Jesus. It was the result of a decision that only he as the Sinless One (2 Cor 5:21) could make.[66] It became Paul's key to understanding what made Jesus Christ unique as a human being.

It goes without saying, of course, that Paul is working backward. Jesus did not have to die. But if he did die, and in a particular way, then he must have chosen that form of death. But what motive could justify the choice of the atrocious suffering of crucifixion?

Paul was given a clue by the kerygma he had inherited. According to the creed, "Christ died for our sins" (1 Cor 15:3). In 1 Thessalonians this became "our Lord Jesus Christ . . . died for us" (5:9). The implicit

[63] See my "Tradition and Redaction in Col 1:15-20," *RB* 102 (1995): 231–41.

[64] That Jesus chose death is perhaps also suggested by ἀφορῶντες εἰς τὸν τῆς πίστεως ἀρχηγὸν καὶ τελειωτὴν Ἰησοῦν, ὃ ἀντὶ τῆς προκειμένης αὐτῷ χαρᾶς ὑπέμεινεν σταυρὸν αἰσχύνης καταφρονήσας ("looking to Jesus the pioneer and perfecter of our faith, who instead of the joy that was set before him endured the cross, disregarding its shame"; Heb 12:2). The first and best attested meaning of ἀντί, "instead of, in place of" (BAGD, 73), with its connotation of choice, is usually set aside because exegetes are not aware of the relationship between sin and death outlined above; cf. C. Spicq, *L'épitre aux Hébreux*, EBib (Paris: Gabalda, 1953), 2:387.

[65] As Dunn has suggested rather tentatively (*Galatians*, 35).

[66] Paul, of course, is not the only one to note the sinlessness of Christ; see John 8:46; Heb 4:15; 7:26; 9:14; 1 Pet 1:19; 2:22.

concern of both these statements is with the benefits that resulted from the death of Christ. Humanity benefited from Christ's decision.

His vision of Christ as sacrificing himself led Paul to see this relationship from a slightly different angle. He was searching for a motive for Christ's choice. If, according to the traditional belief, the death of Christ resulted in benefits for humanity, then the simplest answer to Paul's problem was that Christ intended those benefits. His motive, therefore, in choosing to be crucified was to do good to others who were both unaware and uninterested.

Some reasoning such as this must underlie Paul's interpretation of Christ's decision as an act of love. In Galatians he speaks of "the Son of God who loved me and gave himself for me" (2:20). The "and" here is explanatory,[67] and the phrase should be translated "who loved me, that is, he gave himself for me." Self-sacrifice is the expression of Christ's love.[68]

It is now possible to understand why Paul, in opposition to his contemporaries, was led to put such emphasis on the modality of Christ's [132] death. It was the supreme manifestation of total self-giving, and thereby the model for Christian living.

In Union with a Faithful Christ

The second distinctive feature of the Christology of Galatians is a series of texts expressing the union of believers with Christ and among themselves. Nothing remotely similar is to be found in the kerygma that Paul inherited, nor in the Thessalonian letters. Moreover, in contrast to the crucifixion of Christ, there is no hint that Paul thought of Christ in this way prior to writing Galatians. In consequence, the factors that forced Paul to develop this insight are probably to be found in the situation that he had to confront in Galatia.

The Fidelity of Christ

One of the features of the approach of the intruders in Galatia was the importance they gave to the figure of Abraham.[69] They were law-observant

---

[67] BDF §442(9).

[68] So, rightly, Betz, *Galatians*, 125; Martyn, *Galatians*, 259.

[69] So, rightly, Longenecker, *Galatians*, xcvii; Dunn, *Galatians*, 11; and above all Martyn, *Galatians*, 125.

Christians from Antioch whose theology was that of Jerusalem. Their view of the relation between Jew and Gentile in terms of salvation was defined by God's promise to Abraham: "in you all the families of the earth shall be blessed" (Gen 12:3). To benefit by this blessing, however, the Gentiles had to accept the terms of the covenant, one of which was circumcision (Gen 17:12). Only in this way could they become "descendants of Abraham."[70]

In order to confront his opponents convincingly, Paul had to tackle them on their chosen ground. He had to find something in the figure of Abraham that would subvert the use that the intruders made of him. Paul's knowledge of the Scriptures enabled him to identify a crucial moment that ocurred *between* the promise of God to Abraham (Gen 12:3) and the covenant that God made with Abraham (Gen 17:1-22). "The word of the Lord came to Abram in a vision . . . and he believed the Lord, and the Lord reckoned it to him as righteousness" (Gen 15:1, 6 = Gal 3:6). The righteousness of Abraham, therefore, *antedated* the covenant of circumcision, and it was rooted in faith.

In consequence, it was not really circumcision but faith that made humans descendants of Abraham (Gal 3:7). The precision of Paul's knowledge of Genesis further enabled him to discern a debating point that would reduce his opponents to silence. The texts did not speak of many "descendants" but of a single "offspring" (Gen 13:15; 15:18; 17:18; 24:7). Ignoring the collective sense of the singular, Paul identified this offspring as Christ (Gal 3:16).

If the needs of the debate in Galatia led Paul to think of Christ as the offspring of Abraham, it would be extraordinary if the idea of "the faith of Christ" did not flit across his mind. If Abraham was made righteous by faith, then the same must be true of his offspring, namely, Christ. Once Paul thought of this, it must have seemed self-evident. Not only because the portrait of the Messiah in *PsSol* 17 strongly emphasizes his righteousness (vv. 23, 26, 29, 37, 40), but also because of what Paul knew of the ministry of the historical Jesus.

It is from this historical perspective that we must approach the much debated phrase πίστις Χριστοῦ ("faith of Christ"), which is found in three slightly different formulations in Galatians: διὰ πίστεως Χριστοῦ

---

[70] For a brilliant and convincing reconstruction of the speech of the intruders on Abraham and his importance for Christians, see Martyn, *Galatians*, 302–6.

("through [the] faith of Christ"; 2:16); ἐκ πίστεῶ Ἰησοῦ Χριστοῦ ("out of [the] faith of Christ"; Gal 2:16); ἐκ πίστεως Ἰησοῦ Χριστοῦ ("out of [the] faith of Jesus Christ"; Gal 3:22).[71] Problems arise from two sources.

First, πίστις can be understood as "faith," i.e., the act of belief, or as "fidelity." Usage justifies this distinction,[72] but it was irrelevant as far as Paul was concerned. In his view there was no saving "faith" without "fidelity." The initial act accepting Jesus as the risen Lord must be lived out in a highly specific lifestyle or it was meaningless; note the warning in 1 Thessalonians 4:6. Hence, it is best to translate πίστις by "fidelity" on the understanding that it is the externalization of a committment that Paul normally expresses by the cognate verb πιστεύω ("to believe"; Rom 10:9).

Second, the genitive Χριστοῦ can be interpreted subjectively ("the act of faith made by Christ" or "the fidelity shown by Christ") or objectively (Christ as the object of the act of faith; hence, "faith in Christ"). Two factors have bedeviled the choice between these theoretical possibilities:[73] (a) the controversy regarding justification by faith, which prioritized the act of believing and read Galatians from the perspective of later letters; (b) the assumption that Paul believed in the divinity of Christ, which [134] necessarily excluded the interpretation of the genitive as subjective, because God cannot believe in himself.

If we abstract from both of these extraneous and anachronistic considerations, the natural reading of πίστις Χριστοῦ is "the fidelity shown by Christ." No one has ever dreamed of treating the genitives in πίστις τοῦ θεοῦ ("the fidelity of God"; Rom 3:3)[74] or πίστις Αβραάμ ("the fidelity of Abraham"; Rom 4:16)[75] as objective genitives, i.e., "faith in God" or "faith in Abraham." And it should be the same when it is a question of Christ, particularly since Paul has already spoken of ὑπομονὴ τοῦ

---

[71] Other instances are to be found in Rom 3:22, 26, and Phil 3:9.

[72] LSJ 1408a.

[73] For documentation of the debate, see the bibliographies in Longenecker, *Galatians*, 87, and in Frank J. Matera, *Galatians*, Sacra Pagina 9 (Collegeville, MN: Liturgical Press, 1992), 104.

[74] "The faithfulness of God" (*RSV, NRSV*, Philipps); "God's faithfulness" (*NJB, NAB, NIV*); "la fidelité de Dieu" (BdeJ).

[75] "The faith of Abraham" (*RSV, NRSV, NJB*); "his faith" (*NAB*); "a faith like that of Abraham" (Philipps).

Χριστοῦ ("the steadfastness of Christ"; 2 Thess 3:5), which is a synonym of πίστις Χριστοῦ. The example of Christ is ever before Paul's mind.

Confirmation of the subjective reading of Χριστοῦ comes from a comparison of Galatians 2:16 and Galatians 2:21:[76]

Galatians 2:16	Galatians 2:21
οὐ δικαιοῦται ἄνθρωπος	εἰ γὰρ διὰ νόμου δικαιοσύνη
ἐξ ἔργων νόμου	
ἐὰν μὴ διὰ πίστεως Ἰησοῦ Χριστοῦ	ἄρα Χριστὸς δωρεὰν ἀπέθανεν
man is not justified	if justification were
by works of the law	by the law
but by the fidelity of Christ	then Christ died uselessly

The strict parallel between the negative first parts of these antinomies entitles us to assume that the second positive parts are saying the same thing in different ways. Thus, if Christ is the subject of the action ("dying") in 2:21, he is also the subject of the action ("faith/fidelity") in 2:16.[77]

A comparison of Galatians 2:16 and Galatians 3:22 is also highly instructive:[78]

Galatians 2:16	Galatians 3:22-23
οὐ δικαιοῦται ἄνθρωπος	
ἐξ ἔργων νόμου	
ἐὰν μὴ διὰ πίστεως Ἰησοῦ Χριστοῦ	ἵνα ἡ ἐπαγγελία ἐκ πίστεως Ἰησοῦ Χριστοῦ

[76] Martyn, *Galatians*, 271.

[77] A strictly grammatical point should also be kept in mind: "the objective genitive, strictly defined, demands not only a verbal ruling noun but also one whose cognate verb is transitive. The verb *pisteuô* is itself transitive only with the meaning 'to entrust' followed by two accusatives. In the case of *pistis Christou* one may be well advised, then, to speak of genitive of authorship or of origin" (Martyn, *Galatians*, 270 note 171).

[78] This is developed most effectively by Sam K. Williams, "Again *Pistis Christou*," *CBQ* 49 (1987): 431–47, especially 443–44.

καὶ ἡμεῖς εἰς Χριστὸν Ἰησοῦν ἐπιστεύσαμεν	δοθῇ τοῖς πιστεύουσιν . . .
	μέλλουσαν πίστιν ἀποκαλυφθῆναι.
man is not justified	
by works of the law	
but by fidelity of Christ	that the promise of fidelity of Christ
even we have believed in Christ	might be given to believers
	(Now before faith came, we were
	confined under the law . . .)
	until faith should be revealed

[135] In both cases, πίστις Χριστοῦ is associated with instrumental prepositions, διά and ἐκ ("through" and "from," respectively), which indicate that it is the means whereby salvation is achieved. In both cases, in addition to the reference to the "faith of Christ," the subjective faith of believers is explicitly evoked in the verbal form. When taken together, these observations strongly suggest (1) that Paul sees a distinction between "the fidelity of Christ" and "the faith of believers" and (2) that the two are nonetheless intimately related.

Before discussing how Paul envisaged this relationship, one further observation is important. In Galatians 3:23 πίστις "comes" and "is revealed." How and when? The personalized language is an obvious clue, which Paul proves to be correct in the very next verse. The control of the law ended when Christ came (Gal: 3:24). It is Christ, therefore, who reveals "fidelity" by exemplifing and actualizing it.[79] The conclusion flowing from the comparison of Galatians 2:16 and 2:21 is thereby confirmed.

The clear hint in Galatians 2:16 and 2:21 that the "fidelity of Christ" and the "faith" of believers were related as instrumental cause and effect, respectively, is developed in a surprising direction in Galatians 2:20, where Paul exploits the polyvalence of πιστίς in order to establish

---

[79] So, rightly, Williams, "Again *Pistis Christou*," 437–38, who very appositely refers to Heb 12:2, where Jesus is the great exemplar of faith.

a much closer link between Christ and believers than had hitherto been conceived.

A bond between believers and Christ could have been deduced from his vision of Christ as κύριος. If he is their Lord (Gal 1:3; 5:10; 6:12, 18), [136] then believers "belong to Christ"; ὑμεῖς Χριστοῦ (Gal 3:29; cf. 5:24), a formula that appears for the first time in Galatians.[80] This belonging, however, is much more than mere possession, as we discover in Galatians 2:20: Χριστῷ συνεσταύρωμαι· [20] ζῶ δὲ οὐκέτι ἐγώ, ζῇ δὲ ἐν ἐμοὶ Χριστός· ὃ δὲ νῦν ζῶ ἐν σαρκί, ἐν πίστει ζῶ τῇ τοῦ υἱοῦ τοῦ θεοῦ τοῦ ἀγαπήσαντός με καὶ παραδόντος ἑαυτὸν ὑπὲρ ἐμοῦ ("I have been crucified with Christ. It is no longer I who live, but Christ who lives in me. The life I now live in the flesh I live in fidelity, that of the Son of God who loved me and gave himself for me"). The number of insights condensed in this verse is extraordinary and betrays the ferment of Paul's mind once he began to think seriously about Christ as a person.

We have already considered the final words which highlight the fact that the supreme self-sacrifice of Christ was an act of love. Here we see that they are the most important part of an adjectival phrase introduced by the definite article, which defines Paul's "fidelity."[81] What does this tell us?

- "Fidelity" is manifested as "love" and "self-sacrifice."

- The standard against which Paul's "fidelity" is measured is that of Christ.

- Since Christ's "fidelity" went to the extreme limit of giving all for others, Paul's must do likewise. It is in this sense that he has been crucified with Christ. His "fidelity" is an ongoing, painful process.

- Paul's "fidelity," then, is nothing unless it imitates the "fidelity" of Christ so perfectly that the two can be identified. By the quality of his commitment concretized in his dedication to others, Paul in effect becomes Christ. This is why he says, "It is no longer I who live, but

---

[80] The other instances are 1 Cor 3:23; 15:23; 2 Cor 10:7; Rom 8:9; 14:8.

[81] Among the commentators, this is formally recognized by Matera, *Galatians*, 96, and Martyn, *Galatians*, 259. Similarly Williams, "Again *Pistis Christou*," 445. Those who insist that the genitive is objective are forced to ignore the crucial article (albeit with a certain hesitation, e.g., Dunn, *Galatians*, 146) and translate "I live by faith in the Son of God."

Christ who lives in me." It is in and through Paul that the risen Christ continues to live "in the flesh." Through Paul, Christ continues to be present in the world.

• Paul's "fidelity" was both the original goal and the achieved result of Christ's "fidelity." Paul's new "I" exists through grace, and as another Christ he is the channel of that grace to others.

Union with Christ

[**137**] If Paul could say "Christ lives in me" (cf. Phil 1:21) because of the conformity of his total dedication to that of Christ, then all committed believers could say likewise. Speaking together in the liturgical assembly, they would have to say "We are Christ." Thus, it was practically inevitable that Paul should write ὅσοι γὰρ εἰς Χριστὸν ἐβαπτίσθητε, Χπιστὸν ἐνεδύσασθε . . . 'πάντες γὰρ ὑμεῖς εἷς ἐστε ἐν Χριστῷ Ἰησοῦ ("as many of you as were baptized into Christ have put on Christ . . . you all are one man in Christ Jesus"; Gal 3:27). The grace of Christ given in baptism initiates the transformation of believers into Christ. They do not play at being Christ by adopting certain external characteristics. They become Christ, just as a great actor becomes the character he is playing.[82] Through an inspired effort of will, there is an actual transformation of the personality into a new entity from which flows words and deeds worthy of Christ. In opposition to an actor, however, who can shed his role, for the believer it must become a permanent way of being.

Paul's plaintive exclamation reveals another facet of this theme, τέκνα μου, οὓ πάλιν ὠδίνω μέχρις οὗ μορφωθῇ Χριστὸς ἐν ὑμῖν ("my children with whom I am again in travail until Christ is formed in you"; Gal 4:19). The imagery here is extraordinarily complex.[83] In essence, Paul has to repeat the painful process of giving birth to the Galatians. The newly born are to be collectively Christ; note the plural ἐν ὑμῖν ("in you") in contrast to the singular ἐν ἐμοί ("in me") of Galatians 2:20.[84]

---

[82] Burton, *Galatians*, 204; Dunn, *Galatians*, 204.

[83] See, in particular, B. R. Gaventa, "The Maternity of Paul: An Exegetical Study of Gal 4:19," in *The Conversation Continues*, FS Martyn, ed. R. T. Fortna and B. R. Gaventa (Nashville: Abingdon, 1990), 189–201.

[84] To bring out this point Martyn translates "in your congregations" (*Galatians*, 425).

As one with Christ, the believers are one with each other. "You though all are one man in Christ" (Gal 3:28). The way this insight is formulated is significant. The stress is on unity. It is expressed in the principal clause ("you are one"), whereas the multiplicity ("though all") is effectively a subordinate clause with the sense of "even though."[85] Paul will remain faithful to this structure in all future statements about unity and diversity.[86]

Conclusion

It is time to conclude. We have seen how both internal and external factors led Paul to develop his Christology in two directions unthought of by the traditional kerygma which he inherited: first, his stress on the modality of the death of Jesus and, second, his vision of a corporate Christ. In christological terms Galatians represents a quantum leap forward by comparison with 1 and 2 Thessalonians.

Nonetheless, Galatians is only a beginning. Ideas that will play a crucial explicit role in later letters, especially 1 Corinthians, appear there only in embryonic form, e.g., the believer is another Christ; believers in community are the Body of Christ. Other key aspects of Paul's distinctive Christology have not yet swum into his consciousness, notably its Adamic and Wisdom dimensions. These will appear for the first time in Philippians and 1 Corinthians, respectively. Paul's Christology is a coherent whole, which grew by incorporating radically different new ideas, whose unifying potential Paul first exploited.

Postscript

In this article I argued that it was the polemical situation in Galatia that stimulated Paul to develop his distinctive Christology. The arguments of his opponents, notably their stress on Abraham, forced him to focus on the person of Jesus in a way that he had not done before.

---

[85] See John A. T. Robinson, *The Body: A Study in Pauline Theology*, SBT 5 (London: SCM, 1952), 60.

[86] ἓν σῶμα οἱ πολλοί ἐσμεν ("we, who are many, are one body"; 1 Cor 10:17); πάντα δὲ τὰ μέλη τοῦ σώματος πολλὰ ὄντα ἕν ἐστιν σῶμα ("all the members of the body, being many, are one body"; 1 Cor 12:12); οἱ πολλοὶ ἕν σῶμα ἐσμεν ἐν Χριστῷ ("we, the many, are one body in Christ"; Rom 12:5).

Indirect support for my hypothesis comes from Philip Esler, who develops a parallel argument on the basis of a comparison of 1 Thessalonians with Galatians to show that "justification/righteousness" had not been an integral part of Paul's theology from the beginning, as many have thought, but was a subject thrust upon him by the situation that arose in Galatia.[87] For the first time, he had to confront Christian Jews, who maintained the enduring validity of the law while accepting Jesus as the Messiah.

The clarity of Esler's arguments make a summary easy. Words with a δικ-root, namely, δικαιόω, δίκαιος, δικαιοσύνη, δικαίωμά, and δικαίωσις, are not found in 1 Thessalonians, with the exception of δίκαιος in 2:10, where it is a question of Paul's comportment among the Thessalonians. Faith, the Spirit, and the significance of the death of Jesus are issues in both 1 Thessalonians and Galatians, but in the former they are never linked with "righteousness" as they are in the latter (cf. Gal 2:21; 3:1-14).

In 1 Thessalonians 1:3 Paul mentions the "work of faith, labour of love and endurance of hope" of the Thessalonians. The triad appears again toward the end of the letter in the form, "putting on the breastplate of faith and love and the hope of salvation for a helmet" (5:8), which was inspired by Isaiah 59:17 and/or Wisdom 5:18, both of which explicitly mention "righteousness": "He put on righteousness as a breastplate and placed the helmet of salvation on his head" (Isa); "he will put on righeousness as a breastplate, and he will don true judgment as a helmet" (Wis). Had "righteousness" been integral to Paul's vision of the Christian life when writing 1 Thessalonians, it would have been natural for him to have hewn much more closely to the OT original. As it stands, however, the only conclusion possible is that, at that point in his career, "righteousness" was irrelevant by comparison with "faith and love."

"Apart from the language of faith and love, the most important semantic field which Paul employs to designate the condition of the Thessalonians, in the present and in the future, is that of 'being made holy' (*hagios*) or 'sanctification.'"[88] Such language does not appear in Galatians, where its place is taken by "righteousness." The shift calls for explanation. The most natural one is that it was forced upon Paul by

---

[87] *Galatians*, NT Readings (London: Routledge, 1998), 153–59.
[88] Esler, *Galatians*, 157.

his opponents, who used it in the course of their argument that Gentiles should observe the law. Thus, Esler rightly concludes, "righteousness was not at the heart of Paul's thought. . . . It was subsidary teaching deployed only in certain situations, where there was an issue as to the manner in which Israelites and gentiles could coexist in the same community."[89]

I have recalled Esler's contribution in order to underline the critical role that the situation in Galatia played in Paul's development. Christology, however, was always at the heart of Paul's thought. In this sense, it is not parallel to righteousness. Structurally, however, the personal development of that Christology, which was stimulated by Paul's confrontation with the intruders in Galatia, is identical with his discovery of the utility of the concept of righteousness in dealing with the same opponents.

[89] Esler, *Galatians*, 159.

Bibliography

Adeyemi, F. *The New Covenant Torah in Jeremiah and the Law of Christ in Paul*. Studies in Biblical Literature 94. New York/Bern: Lang, 2006.

Allison, D. C. "The Pauline Epistles and the Synoptic Gospels: The Pattern of the Parallels." *NTS* 28 (1982): 1–32.

Ascough, R. S. "The Thessalonian Christian Community as a Professional Voluntary Association." *JBL* 119 (2000): 311–28.

Aune, D. E. *The New Testament in Its Literary Environment*. Library of Early Christianity. Philadelphia: Westminster, 1987.

Bachmann, M. "*Hierosolyma und Ierusalêm* im Galaterbrief." *ZNW* 91 (2000): 288–89.

Banks, R. *Paul's Idea of Community*. Exeter: Paternoster, 1980.

Barrett, C. K. *Freedom and Obligation: A Study of the Epistle to the Galatians*. London: SPCK, 1985.

———. *The New Testament Background: Selected Documents*. Rev. ed. New York: Harper & Row, 1987.

Baslez, M.-F. *Saint Paul*. Paris: Fayard, 1991.

Bauckham, R. *Jesus and the Eyewitnesses: The Gospels as Eyewitness Testimony*. Grand Rapids, MI/Cambridge, UK: Eerdmans, 2006.

Berényi, G. "Gal 2,20: A Pre-Pauline or a Pauline Text?" *Biblica* 65 (1984): 490–537.

Best, E. *A Commentary on the First and Second Epistles to the Thessalonians*. BNTC. London: Black, 1979.

Betz, H. D. "The Literary Composition and Function of Paul's Letter to the Galatians." *NTS* 21 (1975): 353–79.

———. *Galatians: A Commentary on Paul's Letter to the Churches in Galatia*. Hermeneia. Philadelphia: Fortress, 1979.

Bietenhard, H. "Die syrische Dekapolis von Pompeius bis Trajan." *ANRW* II/8 (1977): 220–61.

Bonnard, P. *L'épitre de saint Paul aux Galates*. CNT 9. 2e éd. Neuchatel: Delachaux & Niestle, 1972.

Booth, W. C. *A Rhetoric of Irony*. Chicago: University of Chicago, 1974.

Brandenberger, E. *Adam und Christus. Exegetisch-religionsgeschichtliche Untersuchung zu Röm. 5:12-21 (1 Kor. 15)*. WMANT 7. Neukirchen: Neukirchener Verlag, 1962.

Bruce, F. F. *Paul: Apostle of the Free Spirit*. Exeter: Paternoster, 1977.

———. *The Epistle of Paul to the Galatians*. NIGTC. Exeter: Paternoster, 1982.

———. *Philippians*. NIBC. Peabody: Hendrickson, 1989.

Bultmann, R. *Theology of the New Testament*. London: SCM, 1965.

Burfeind, C. "Paulus in Arabien." *ZNW* 95 (2004): 129–30.

Burridge, R. A. *What Are the Gospels? A Comparison with Graeco-Roman Biography*. SNTSMS 70. Cambridge: Cambridge University Press, 1992.

Burton, E. de Witt. *A Critical and Exegetical Commentary on the Epistle to the Galatians*. ICC. Edinburgh: Clark, 1921.

Byrne, B. *"Sons of God"—"Seed of Abraham": A Study of the Idea of the Sonship of God of All Christians in Paul against the Jewish Background*. ABib 83. Rome: Biblical Institute Press, 1979.

Cai, R., ed. *S. Thomae Aquinatis Doctoris Angelici super epistolas S. Pauli lectura*. Romae/Taurini: Marietti, 1953.

Calder, W. M., and G. E. Bean. *A Classical Map of Asia Minor*. Ankara: British School of Archaeology, 1958.

Casey, M. "Chronology and Development of Pauline Christology." In *Paul and Paulinism: Essays in Honor of C. K. Barrett*, 124–34. Edited by M. D. Hooker and S. G. Wilson. London: SPCK, 1982.

Charlesworth, J. H. *The Old Testament Pseudepigrapha*. New York: Doubleday, 1985.

Charlesworth, M. P. "Tiberius." In *CAH* 10:648–52.

Cho, G.-H. *Die Vorstellung und Bedeutung von "Jerusalem" bei Paulus*. Neutestamentliche Entwürfe zur Theologie 7. Tübingen: Francke, 2004.

Collins, J. J. *The Scepter and the Star: The Messiahs of the Dead Sea Scrolls and Other Ancient Literature*. ABRL. New York: Doubleday, 1995.

———. "A Symbol of Otherness: Circumcision and Salvation in the First Century." In *"To See Ourselves as Others See Us": Christians, Jews and "Others" in Late Antiquity*, 163–86. Edited by J. Neusner and E. Frerichs. Chico, CA: Scholars Press, 1985.

Coppins, W. *The Interpretation of Freedom in the Letters of Paul with Special Reference to the "German" Tradition*. WUNT 2.261. Tübingen: Mohr Siebeck, 2009.

Cosgrove, C. H. "Arguing Like a Mere Human Being. Galatians 3.15-18 in Rhetorical Perspective." *NTS* 34 (1988): 536–49.

Dahl, N. A. *Jesus the Christ: The Historical Origins of Christological Doctrine*. Minneapolis: Fortress, 1991.

Danby, H. *The Mishnah*. Oxford: Oxford University Press, 1933.

Das, A. A. "Another Look at ἐὰν μὴ in Galatians 2:16." *JBL* 119 (2000): 529–39.

Davenport, G. L. "The 'Anointed of the Lord' in Psalms of Solomon 17." In *Ideal Figures in Ancient Judaism: Profiles and Paradigms*. Edited by J. J. Collins and G. Nickelsburg. SBLSCS 12. Chico, CA: Scholars Press, 1980.

Donaldson, T. L. "Zealot and Convert: The Origin of Paul's Christ-Torah Antithesis." *CBQ* 51 (1989): 655–82.

Donfried, K. P. "1 Thessalonians, Acts and the Early Paul." In *The Thessalonian Correspondence*. Edited by Raymond F. Collins. BETL 87. Leuven: University Press/Peeters, 1990, 3–26.

Duncan, G. S. *The Epistle of Paul to the Galatians*. MNTC. London: Hodder & Staughton, 1934.

Dunn, J. D. G. *Christology in the Making: A New Testament Inquiry into the Origins of the Doctrine of the Incarnation*. London: SCM, 1980.

————. *Romans*. WBC 38. Dallas: Word Books, 1988.

————. *The Epistle to the Galatians*. BNTC. London: Black, 1993.

————. *Jesus, Paul, and Galatians*. Louisville: Westminster/Knox, 1998.

————. *The Theology of Paul the Apostle*. Grand Rapids, MI: Eerdmans, 1998.

————. *Christianity in the Making*. Vol. 1: *Jesus Remembered*. Grand Rapids, MI/Cambridge, UK: Eerdmans, 2003.

————. *The New Perspective on Paul: Collected Essays*. WUNT 185. Tübingen: Mohr Siebeck, 2007.

————. "The Relationship between Paul and Jerusalem according to Galatians 1 and 2." *NTS* 28 (1982): 461–78.

————. "The Incident at Antioch (Gal 2:11-18)." *JSNT* 18 (1983): 3–57.

————. "The New Perspective on Paul." *BJRL* 65 (1983): 95–122.

————. "Paul's Knowledge of the Jesus Tradition: The Evidence of Romans." In *Christus Bezeugen*, 193–207. Edited by K. Kertelge, et al. FS Trilling. Leipzig: Benno-Verlag, 1989.

————. "Jesus, Table-fellowship and Qumran." In *Jesus and the Dead Sea Scrolls*, 254–72. Edited by J. H. Charlesworth. ABRL. New York: Doubleday, 1992.

Dupont, J. "La conversion de Paul et son influence sur sa conception du salut par la foi." In *Foi et salut selon s. Paul. Colloque oecumenique à l'Abbeye de S. Paul hors les murs, 16–21 Avril 1968*, 67–88. AnBib 42. Rome: Pontifical Biblical Institute, 1970.

Esler, P. F. *Galatians*. NT Readings. London: Routledge, 1998.

Evans, G. R., and M. Gourgues. *Communion et Réunion. Mélanges Jean-Marie Roger Tillard*. BETL 121. Leuven: Peeters, 1995.

Fee, G. D. *The First Epistle to the Corinthians*. NICNT. Grand Rapids, MI: Eerdmans, 1987.

————. *Paul's Letter to the Philippians*. NICNT. Grand Rapids, MI: Eerdmans, 1995.

————. *Galatians: Pentacostal Commentary*. Blandford Forum: Deo, 2007.

Fitzmyer, J. A. *To Advance the Gospel*. New York: Crossroads, 1981.

————. *Paul and His Theology: A Brief Sketch*. 2nd ed. Englewood Cliffs, NJ: Prentice Hall, 1989.

Freeze, J. H. *Aristotle: The Art of Rhetoric*. LCL. Cambridge, MA: Harvard, 1926.

Fung, R. Y. K. *The Epistle to the Galatians*. NICNT. Grand Rapids, MI: Eerdman, 1998.

Furnish, V. P. *II Corinthians*. AB. New York: Doubleday, 1984.

————. *Jesus according to Paul*. Understanding Jesus Today. Cambridge: Cambridge University Press, 1993.

Gaventa, B. R. "The Maternity of Paul: An Exegetical Study of Gal 4:19." In *The Conversation Continues*, 189–201. Edited by R. T. Fortna and B. R. Gaventa. FS Martyn. Nashville: Abingdon, 1990.

Gernet, L. "La création du testament." *REG* 33 (1920): 123–68.

Gide, P., and E. Caillemer. "Adoptio." In *Dictionnaire des antiquités grecques et romaines*. Edited by C. Daremberg and E. Saglio. Paris: Hachette, 1912.

Goodenough, E. R. *By Light, Light: The Mystic Gospel of Hellenistic Judaism*. New Haven, CT: Yale, 1935.

————. *The Politics of Philo Judaeus: Practice and Theory*. New Haven, CT: Yale, 1938.

————. "The Political Philosophy of Hellenistic Kingship." *Yale Classical Studies* 1 (1928): 53–102.

Goodfriend, E. A. "Adultery." *ABD* 1:80–86.

Haenchen, E. *The Acts of the Apostles*. Oxford: Blackwell, 1971.

Hahn, S. W. "Covenant, Oath, and the Aqedah: Διαθήκη in Galatians 3:15-18." *CBQ* 67 (2005): 79–100.

Hall, R. G. "Epispasm and the Dating of Ancient Jewish Writings." *JSP* 2 (1988): 71–86.

Hann, R. R. "Christos Kyrios in PsSol 17. 32: 'The Lord's Annointed' Reconsidered." *NTS* 31 (1985): 620–27.

Hays, R. B. *The Faith of Jesus Christ: An Investigation of the Narrative Substructure of Gal 3:1–4:11*. SBLDS 56. Chico, CA: Scholars Press, 1983.

Heinemann, I. "Die Lehre vom ungeschriebenen Gesetz im jüdischen Schrifttum." *HUCA* 4 (1927): 149–71.

Hengel, M. "Christologie und neutestamentliche Chronologie." In *Neues Testament und Geschichte*, 43–67. Edited by H. Baltenweiler and B. Reicke. FS Cullmann. Zürich: Zwingli, 1972.

————. *Der Sohn Gottes, Die Entstehung der Christologie und die jüdisch-hellenistische Religionsgeschichte*. 2nd ed. Tübingen: Mohr, 1977.

————. *The Atonement: The Origins of the Doctrine in the New Testament.* Philadelphia: Fortress, 1981.

————, and Anna Maria Schwemer. *Paul between Damascus and Antioch: The Unknown Years.* Louisville: Westminster Knox, 1997.

————. *Paulus zwischen Damaskus und Antiochien. Die Unbekannten Jahre des Apostles.* WUNT 108. Tübingen: Mohr Siebeck, 1998.

Hennecke, E., and W. Schneemelcher. *New Testament Apocrypha* II. London: Lutterworth, 1965.

Hietanen, M. *Paul's Argumentation in Galatians: A Pragma-Dialectical Analysis.* Library of NT Studies 344. London: Clark, 2007.

Hirzel, R. Q. Ἄγαφος νόμος.*" Abhandlung der philologisch-historischen Classe der Königlich Sachsischen Gesellschaft der Wissenschaften* 20, no. 1 (1900): 16–18.

Hoehner, H. *Herod Antipas.* SNTSMS 17. Cambridge: Cambridge University Press, 1972.

Holzmeister, U. "Genetivus Epexegeticus in NT." *VD* 25 (1947): 112–17.

Horsley, R. A. "Wisdom of Word and Words of Wisdom in Corinth." *CBQ* 39 (1977): 224–39.

Hurd, J. *The Origin of 1 Corinthians.* London: SPCK, 1965.

Jaubert, A. *La notion d'alliance dans le Judaïsme aux abords de l'ère chrétienne.* Patristica Sorbonensia 6. Paris: Seuil, 1963.

Jeremias, J. "IEROUSALHM/IEROUSOLUMA." *ZNW* 65 (1974): 273–76.

Jewett, R. *A Chronology of Paul's Life.* Philadelphia: Fortress, 1979 = *Dating Paul's Life.* London: SCM, 1979.

————. *The Thessalonian Correspondence: Pauline Rhetoric and Millenarian Piety.* Foundations & Facets, New Testament. Philadelphia: Fortress, 1986.

————. "The Agitators and the Galatian Congregation." *NTS* 17 (1970–71): 196–212.

Kim, S. *The Origin of Paul's Gospel.* WUNT 2.4. 2nd ed. Tübingen: Mohr, 1984.

Klauck, H.-J. *2 Korintherbrief.* Neu Echter Bibel 8. Würzburg: Echter, 1986.

Knox, J. *Chapters in a Life of Paul.* New York: Abingdon, 1950.

Kolarcik, M. *The Ambiguity of Death in the Book of Wisdom 1–6.* ABib 127. Rome: Pontifical Biblical Institute Press, 1991.

Lagrange, M.-J. *Saint Paul. Épitre aux Romains.* EBib. Paris: Gabalda, 1922.

————. *Saint Paul. Epitre aux Galates.* EBib. Paris: Gabalda, 1925.

Lausberg, H. *Handbuch der literarischen Rhetorik. Eine Grundlegung der Literaturwissenschaft.* 3rd ed. Stuttgart: Steiner, 1990.

Légasse, S. *Paul apôtre. Essai de biographique critique.* Paris: Cerf/Fides, 1991.

————. *L'épître de Paul aux Galates.* LD Commentaires 9. Paris: Cerf, 2000.

Lémonon, J.-P. *L'épitre aux Galates.* CBNT 9. Paris: Cerf, 2008.

Lewis, N., Y. Yadin, J. C. Greenfield. *The Documents from the Bar Kokhba Period in the Cave of Letters: Greek Papyri, Aramaic and Nabatean Signatures and Subscriptions*. Judean Desert Studies 2. Jerusalem: Israel Exploration Society, 1989.

Lightfoot, J. B. *Saint Paul's Epistles to the Colossians and to Philemon*. London: Macmillan, 1904.

————. *Saint Paul's Epistle to the Galatians*. London: Macmillan, 1910.

Lim, T. *Holy Scripture in the Qumran Commentaries and Pauline Letters*. Oxford: Clarendon, 1997.

————. "The Legal Nature of Papyrus Yadin 19 and Galatians 3:15." In *When Judaism and Christianity Began: Essays in Memory of Anthony J. Saldarini*, 361–76. Edited by A. Avery-Peck et al. JSJSup 85. Leiden/Boston: Brill, 2004.

Llewelyn, S. R., ed. *New Documents Illustrating Early Christianity: A Review of the Greek Inscriptions and Papyri Published in 1980–81*. Vol. 6. Macquarie University: Ancient History Documentary Research Centre, 1992.

Longenecker, R. N. *Galatians*. WBC 41. Dallas: Word Books, 1990.

Lüdemann, G. *Paulus, der Heidenapostel*. Band 1. *Studien zur Chronologie*. Göttingen: Vandenhoeck & Ruprecht, 1980 = *Paul Apostle to the Gentiles: Studies in Chronology*. London: SCM, 1984.

Malherbe, A. J. "The Beasts at Ephesus." *JBL* 87 (1968): 71–80.

Marshall, I. H. "Pauline Theology in the Thessalonian Correspondence." In Hooker and Wilson, *Paul and Paulinism*, 173–83.

Martin, R. P. *2 Corinthians*. WBC 40. Waco, TX: Word Books, 1986.

Martyn, J. L. *Galatians*. AB. New York: Doubleday, 1997.

Matera, F. J. *Galatians*. Sacra Pagina 9. Collegeville, MN: Liturgical Press, 1992.

McEleney, N. "Conversion, Circumcision and the Law." *NTS* 20 (1973–74): 319–41.

Meier, J. P. *A Marginal Jew: Rethinking the Historical Jesus*. Vol. 4: *Law and Love*. AYBRL. New Haven, CT: Yale, 2009.

Mielcarek, K. *Ierousalêm. Hierosolyma. Starotestamentowe i hellenistyczne korzenie Łukaszoweo obrazu świętego miasta w świetle onomastyki greckiej*. Studia Biblica Lublinensia 11. Lublin: Wydawnictwo KUL, 2008.

Mitchell, S. *Anatolia: Land, Men, and Gods in Asia Minor*. Oxford: Clarendon, 1995.

Mofatt, J. *An Introduction to the Literature of the New Testament*. 3rd ed. New York: Scribner's, 1918.

Mosès, A. *De specialibus legibus III et IV*. Œuvres de Philon d'Alexandrie 25. Paris: Cerf, 1970.

Mowinckel, S. *He That Cometh*. Translated by G. W. Anderson. Oxford: Blackwell, 1959.

Murphy-O'Connor, J. *L'existence chrétienne selon saint Paul*. LD 80. Paris: Cerf, 1974.

———. *Paul the Letter-Writer*. GNS 41. Collegeville, MN: Liturgical Press, 1995.

———. *Paul: A Critical Life*. Oxford: Clarendon, 1996.

———. *Saint Paul's Corinth: Texts and Archaeology*. 3rd ed. Collegeville, MN: Liturgical Press, 2002.

———. *Paul: His Story*. Oxford: Oxford University Press, 2004.

———. "Christological Anthropology in Philippians 2:6-11." *RB* 83 (1976): 25–50.

———. "Freedom or the Ghetto (1 Cor., viii, 1-13; x, 23-xi, 1)." *RB* 85 (1978): 543–74 = chap. 8 in *Keys to First Corinthians*. Oxford: Oxford University Press, 2009.

———. "Another Jesus (2 Cor 11:4)." *RB* 97 (1990): 238–51 = chap. 12 in *Keys to Second Corinthians*. Oxford: Oxford University Press, 2010.

———. "A First-Century Jewish Mission to Gentiles." *Pacifica* 5 (1992): 32–42.

———. "Paul and Gallio." *JBL* 112 (1993): 315–17.

———. "Tradition and Redaction in Col 1:15-20." *RB* 102 (1995): 231–41.

Müssner, F. *Der Galaterbrief*. HTKNT 9. Freiburg: Herder, 1974.

Nanos, M. D. *The Irony of Galatians: Paul's Letter in First-Century Context*. Minneapolis: Fortress, 2002.

Negev, A. "The Nabataeans and the Provincia Arabia." *ANRW* 2, no. 8 (1977): 549–635.

Neirynck, F. "Paul and the Sayings of Jesus." In *L'Apotre Paul. Personnalité, style et conception du ministère*, 265–321. Edited by A. Vanhoye. BETL 73. Leuven: University Press, 1986.

Neusner, J. *The Rabbinic Traditions about the Pharisees before 70, III*. Leiden: Brill, 1971.

Nolland, J. "Uncircumcised Proselytes?" *JSJ* 12 (1981): 173–94.

O'Mahony, K. ed. *Christian Origins: Worship, Belief and Society; The Milltown Institute and the Irish Biblical Association Millenium Conference*. JSOTSup 241. Sheffield: Sheffield Academic Press, 2003.

O'Brien, P. T. *The Epistle to the Philippians: A Commentary on the Greek Text*. NIGTC. Grand Rapids, MI: Eerdmans, 1991.

Phillips, J. B. *Letters to Young Churches: A Translation of the New Testament Epistles*. Fontana Books. London: Collins, 1955.

Pigeon, C. "La Loi du Christ en Galates 6:2." *Studies in Religion/Sciences Religeuses* 29 (2000): 425–38.

Plank, K. A. *Paul and the Irony of Affliction*. SBL Semeia Studies. Atlanta: Scholars Press, 1987.

Potterie, I. de la. "Jésus et la vérité d'après Eph 4, 21." In *Studiorum Paulinorum Congressus Internationalis Catholicus 1961*, 45–57. AnBib 18. Rome: Pontifical Biblical Institute, 1963.

————. "Les deux noms de Jérusalem dans l'évangile de Luc." *RSR* 69 (1981): 57–70.

————. "Les deux noms de Jérusalem dans les Actes des Apotres." *Biblica* 62 (1982): 153–87.

Räisänen, H. "Galatians 2.16 and Paul's Break with Judaism." *NTS* 31 (1985): 543–53.

Ramsay, W. M. *A Historical Commentary on St. Paul's Epistle to the Galatians.* 2nd ed. London: Hodder & Stoughton, 1900.

Rastoin, M. *Tarse et Jérusalem. La double culture de l'apôtre Paul en Galates 3:6-4:7.* ABib 152. Rome: Pontifical Biblical Institute, 2003.

Reese, J. *Hellenistic Influence on the Book of Wisdom and Its Consequences.* ABib 41. Rome: PBI, 1970.

Richardson, W. "The Philonic Patriarchs as Νόμος Ἔμψυχος." In *Studie Patristica I*, 515–25. Edited by K. Aland and F. L. Cross. TU 63. Berlin: Akademie-Verlag, 1957.

Riesner, R. *Die Frühzeit des Apostles Paulus. Studien zur Chronologie, Missionsstrategie und Theologie.* WUNT 71. Tübingen: Mohr Siebeck, 1994.

Rigaux, B. *Saint Paul. Les épitres aux Thessaloniciens.* EBib. Paris: Gabalda; Gembloux: Duculot, 1956.

Robertson, A. T. *A Grammar of the Greek New Testament in the Light of Historical Research.* Nashville, TN: Broadman Press, 1934.

Robertson, A., and A. Plummer. *A Critical and Exegetical Commentary on the First Epistle of St Paul to the Corinthians.* ICC. Edinburgh: Clark, 1911.

Saldarini, A. J. *The Fathers according to Rabbi Nathan.* Leiden: Brill, 1975.

Sanday, W., and A. C. Headlam. *A Critical and Exegetical Commentary on the Epistle to the Romans.* ICC. Edinburgh: Clark, 1902.

Sanders, E. P. *Paul and Palestinian Judaism: A Comparison of Patterns of Religion.* London: SCM, 1977.

————. *Paul, the Law, and the Jewish People.* Philadelphia: Fortress, 1983.

————. "Jewish Association with Gentiles and Galatians 2:11-14." In *The Conversation Continues: Studies in Paul and John in Honor of J. Louis Martyn*, 170–88. Edited by R. T. Fortna and B. R. Gaventa. Nashville: Abingdon, 1990.

Saulnier, C. "Lois romaines sur les Juifs selon Flavius Josèphe." *RB* 88 (1981): 161–98.

————. "Hérode Antipas et Jean le Baptiste. Quelques remarques sure les confusions chronologiques de Flavius Josèphe." *RB* 91 (1984): 362–76.

Schäfer, R. *Paulus bis zum Apostelkonzil. Ein Beitrag zur Einleitung in den Galaterbrief, zur Geschichte der Jesusbewegung und zur Pauluschronologie.* WUNT 2.179. Tübingen: Mohr Siebeck, 2004.

Schewe, S. *Die Galater zurüchgewinnen. Paulinische Strategien in Galater 5 und 6*. FRLANT 208. Göttingen: Vandenhoeck & Ruprecht, 2005.

Schlier, H. *Der Brief an die Galater*. MeyerK. Göttingen: Vandenhoeck & Ruprecht, 1962.

Schmidt, A. "Das *Missionsdekret* in Galater 2:7-8 als Vereinbarung vom ersten Besuch Pauli in Jerusalem." *NTS* 39 (1992): 149–52.

Schmithals, W. "Die Thessalonicherbriefe als Briefcompositionen." In *Zeit und Geschichte. Dankesgabe an Rudolf Bultmann zum 80. Geburtstag, im Auftrag der Alten Marburger und in Zusammenarbeit mit Hartwig Thyen*, 295–315. Edited by E. Dinkler. Tübingen: Mohr Siebeck, 1964.

Schramm, G. "Meal Customs (Jewish Dietary Laws)." *ABD* 4:648–50.

Schreiner, T. R. *Galatians*. Zondervan Exegetical Commentary on the NT. Grand Rapids, MI: Zondervan, 2010.

Schürer, E. *The History of the Jewish People in the Age of Jesus Christ (175 B.C.–A.D. 135)*. Rev. ed. G. Vermes and F. Millar. Edinburgh: Clark, 1973.

Schürmann, H. *Der Einsetzungsbericht, Lk 22,19-20. II Teil. Eine quellenkritischen Untersuchung des lukanischen Abendmahlberichtes, Lk 22, 7-38*. NTA 20/4. Münster: Aschendorf, 1955.

———. "Die vorösterlichen Anfänge der Logientradition. Versuch eines formgeschichtlichen Zugangs zum Leben Jesu." In *Der historische Jesus und der kerygmatische Christus. Beiträge zum Christusverständnis in Forschung und Verkündigung*, 342–70. Edited by H. Ristow and K. Matthiae. Berlin: Evangelische Verlagsanstalt, 1962.

Schwartz, D. R. *Agrippa I: The Last King of Judaea*. TSAJ 23. Tübingen: Mohr, 1990.

Scott, I. W. "Common Ground? The Role of Galatians 2:16 in Paul's Argument." *NTS* 53 (2007): 425–35.

Scott, J. M. *Adoption as Sons of God: An Exegetical Investigation into the Background of UIOQESIA in the Pauline Corpus*. WUNT 2.48. Tübingen: Mohr, 1992.

Scullard, H. H. *From the Gracchi to Nero: A History of Rome from 133 B.C. to A.D.68*. 5th ed. London/New York: Methuen, 1982.

Slingerland, D. "Acts 18:1-18, the Gallio Inscription and Absolute Pauline Chronology." *JBL* 110 (1991): 439–49.

Smallwood, E. M. *Philonis Alexandrini Legatio ad Gaium*. Leiden: Brill, 1961.

———. *The Jews under Roman Rule from Pompey to Diocletian: A Study in Political Relations*. SJLA 20. Leiden: Brill, 1981.

Smith, D. E. "Table Fellowship." *ABD* 6:302–4.

Spicq, C. *L'épitre aux Hébreux*. EBib. Paris: Gabalda, 1953.

———. *Agapè dans le Nouveau Testament. Analyse des textes*. EBib. Paris: Gabalda, 1955.

————. *Notes de lexicographie néo-testamentaire*. OBO 22/2. Fribourg: Éditions universitaires; Göttingen: Vandenhoeck & Ruprecht, 1978.

Stanton, G. "The Law of Moses and the Law of Christ: Galatians 3:1–6:2." In *Paul and the Mosaic Law: The Third Durham-Tübingen Research Symposium on Earliest Christianity and Judaism*, 99–166. Edited by J. D. G. Dunn. WUNT 89. Tübingen: Mohr Siebeck 1996.

Starcky, J. "Pétra et la Nabatène." *DBSup* 7 (1966): 886–1017.

Strack, H. L. *Einleitung in Talmud und Midrash*. München: Beck, 1982.

Stendahl, K. "The Apostle Paul and the Introspective Conscience of the West." *HTR* 56 (1963): 199–215.

Suhl, A. *Paulus und seine Briefe. Ein Beitrag zur paulinischen Chronologie*. Gütersloh: Mohn, 1975.

Sylva, D. D. "*Ierusalêm* and *Hierosolyma* in Luke-Acts." *ZNW* 74 (1983): 207–21.

Taylor, J. "The Ethnarch of King Aretas at Damascus." *RB* 99 (1992): 719–28.

Thompson, M. *Clothed with Christ: The Example and Teaching of Jesus in Romans 12.1–15.13*. JSNTSup 59. Sheffield: Sheffield Academic Press, 1991.

Trafton, J. F. "Solomon, Psalms of." *ABD* 6:115–17.

Yonge, C. D. *The Works of Philo Complete and Unabridged*. Peabody, MA: Hendrickson, 1993.

Vincent, M. R. *A Critical and Exegetical Commentary on the Epistles to the Philippians and to Philemon*. ICC. Edinburgh: Clark, 1897.

Vouga, F. *An die Galater*. HNT. Tübingen: Mohr Siebeck, 1998.

Walker, W. O. "Translation and Interpretation of ἐὰν μὴ in Gal 2:16." *JBL* 116 (1997): 515–20.

————. "Does the 'We' in Gal 2:15-17 Include Paul's Opponents?" *NTS* 49 (2003): 560–65.

Wedderburn, A. J. M. "Paul and Jesus: The Problem of Continuity." *SJT* 38 [1985]: 189–203.

Westerholm, S. *Israel's Law and the Church's Faith: Paul and His Recent Interpreters*. Grand Rapids, MI: Eerdmans, 1988.

Wilckens, U. "Die Bekehrung des Paulus als religionsgeschichtliche Problem." *ZTK* 59 (1959): 273–93 = *Rechtfertigung als Freiheit: Paulusstudien*, 11–32. Neukirchen-Vluyn: Neukirchener Verlag, 1974.

Williams, S. K. "Again *Pistis Christou*." *CBQ* 49 (1987): 431–47.

Wilson, T. A. *The Curse of the Law and the Crisis in Galatia: Reassessing the Purpose of Galatians*. WUNT 2.225. Tübingen: Mohr Siebeck, 2007.

Windisch, H. *Der zweite Korintherbrief*. MeyerK. Göttingen: Vandenhoeck & Ruprecht, 1924.

Winger, W. "The Law of Christ." *NTS* 46 (2000): 537–46.

Witherington III, B. *Grace in Galatia: A Commentary on Paul's Letter to the Galatians.* Grand Rapids, MI: Eerdmans, 1998.

Wolfson, H. A. *Philo: Foundations of Religious Philosophy in Judaism, Christianity, and Islam.* Cambridge, MA: Harvard, 1948.

Zahn, T. *Der Brief des Paulus an die Galater.* KNT. Helsingfors: A. Deichert'sche Verlagsbuchhandlung Nachf, 1907.

Zerwick, M. *Graecitas Biblica.* SPIB. 3rd ed. Rome: PIB, 1955.

New Testament Index

Pagination in **bold** indicates detailed treatment.

Index of Nonbiblical Authors

Index of Subjects